In His Own Voice

THE DRAMATIC

AND OTHER

UNCOLLECTED

WORKS OF

PAUL LAURENCE

DUNBAR

In His Own Voice

Edited by Herbert Woodward Martin & Ronald Primeau

with a foreword by Henry Louis Gates, Jr.

OHIO UNIVERSITY PRESS   *Athens*

Paul Laurence Dunbar's full-length play entitled *Herrick,* housed in the Carter G. Woodson Papers, Library of Congress, is the property of The Association for the Study of African-American Life and History, Inc., and appears here with their permission.

Herrick, "Ole Conju'in Joe," "To a Golden Girl," "Happy, Happy, Happy," "John Hay," "A Lament," "A Letter," "The Lonely Hunter," "The Making Up," "Ode," "Our Hopes and Home," "Tim," "To Miss Mamie Emerson," "Kitty," "Rocking in the Old Canoe," "A Girl," "New York," and "The Drowsy God" appear courtesy of Ms. Mildred M. Norman, Ms. Gwendolyn Burton Raise, and Sergeant F. C. William H. Smith, U.S. Army, retired.

"Ole Conju'in Joe" was transcribed from a typewritten carbon copy held by the University of Dayton Library. Its provenance is not known.

The photographs of Paul Laurence Dunbar appear courtesy of the Dayton and Montgomery County Public Library, Paul Laurence Dunbar Collection. Cover: Paul Laurence Dunbar, ca. 1896 (age 24). Frontispiece: A youthful Dunbar, 1890 (age 18).

Ohio University Press, Athens, Ohio 45701
© 2002 by Ohio University Press
Printed in the United States of America
All rights reserved

Ohio University Press books are printed on acid-free paper ⊗ ™

Library of Congress Cataloging-in-Publication Data

Dunbar, Paul Laurence, 1872-1906.
    In his own voice : the dramatic and other uncollected works of Paul Laurence Dunbar / [edited by] Herbert Woodward Martin, Ronald Primeau.
        p. cm.
    Includes bibliographical references and indexes.
    ISBN 0-8214-1421-6 (acid-free paper) — ISBN 0-8214-1422-4 (pbk. : acid-free paper)
        1. African Americans—Literary collections. I. Martin, Herbert Woodward. II. Primeau, Ronald. III. Title.

PS1556 .A4 2002
811'.4—dc21

2001044793

For

Margaret Walker Alexander
who unraveled the veil over our eyes and taught us
how to sight-read Dunbar's infinite music.

Contents

From *Clorindy, or the Origin of the Cakewalk*

Foreword

I FIRST HEARD Paul Laurence Dunbar's poetry as a child. My father, born in 1913 and blessed with a photographic memory, was fond of reciting long passages of poetry, to my brother and me, as we sat around the television in our living room, or at my bedside as I struggled to go to sleep. While my father's repertoire was quite broad—he loved poems such as Kipling's "If," Longfellow's "Psalm of Life," and Longfellow's "The Bare-footed Boy"—his absolute favorite poem, without a doubt, was Paul Laurence Dunbar's "In the Morning," with his "The Party" a close second. In other words, I was raised on Dunbar's lyrics, especially this one:

> Lias! Lias! Bless de Lawd!
> Don' you know de day's erbroad?
> Ef you don' git up, you scamp,
> Dey'll be trouble in dis camp.

Recently, I asked the statesman Vernon Jordan (born in 1935) what his favorite poem was. Without missing a beat, he began to recite "In the Morning," his eyes aglow just as my father's were. And when I had children, born in 1980 and 1982, whenever I had to wake them up for school, I found myself reciting "In the Morning" to them, just as my father had done for me.

The tradition of black people memorizing poetry written by black writers is strong, indeed, and merits a study of its own. And of these poets, with the possible exception of Langston Hughes, no poet is more canonical than Paul Laurence Dunbar; "The Party," "When Malindy Sings," "An Ante-Bellum Sermon," "When De Co'n Pone's Hot," "A Negro Love Song," and "Sympathy" —these are among Dunbar's most accomplished poems, and his most frequently anthologized—"anthologized" by memorization, by word of mouth, by speakers.

Dunbar's reputation suffered from what we might think of as a "poetics of respectability," an embarrassment with, and a shying away from, dialect poetry, which was a fundamental tenet of Harlem Renaissance aesthetics at least since James Weldon Johnson argued in 1922 that dialect had but "two stops, pathos and humor." What's more, its centrality to the racist stage genres of minstrelsy and vaudeville had corrupted its poetic potential hopelessly, or so the argument went. Even the quickest glance backwards from 1922 would have led directly to the towering figure of Dunbar, whose dominance in the history of the tradition—especially in the period immediately preceding the Renaissance—had to be transcended, undermined, or circumvented if Renaissance poetry was to find its voice. No, Dunbar as a poetic model just would not do. And despite the publication of several biographies and editions of his work, Dunbar has never regained the dominant position within the tradition that he held at the turn of the century. Nevertheless, no poet in the tradition was more crucial in the shaping of a distinct African American poetic diction or voice than he.

PUT SIMPLY, Paul Laurence Dunbar during his lifetime was the most famous black writer in the world. This fact is all the more astonishing given his extremely humble origins, and given his short career as a writer, a professional career that spanned barely fourteen years. Perhaps because of the brevity of his career, few scholars have realized how prolific Dunbar was, and how prolific he was in such a wide range of genres. Herbert Martin and Ronald Primeau's splendid edition of Dunbar's uncollected works will go far toward enabling a complete revaluation of Dunbar's place in the canon of American and African American literature.

Dunbar was a high school graduate, and it was in high school that he began to publish verse, publishing in Orville Wright's *West Side News* and for a time editing *The Tattler*, a black newspaper also owned and printed by Wright, of Wright Brothers fame. As would Langston Hughes three decades later, Dunbar became an elevator operator upon graduating from high school in 1891.

A year later, Dunbar became a member of the Western Association of Writers, voted in on the basis of the opening address he delivered at its annual meeting that year in Dayton, an appearance arranged by one of Dunbar's high school teachers. James Newton Matthews, a poet in attendance at the meeting, soon published an article about Dunbar, which launched his career, leading to commissions from newspapers and within a year to the publication in 1893 of his first volume of poetry. Dunbar was a local celebrity, a regional poet in the truest sense, and a black one at that. Then again, blackness was a metaphorical "region" within the republic of letters and Dunbar was its head.

That local notoriety led to a writing assignment at the Columbian Exposition in Chicago in 1893, where he met, and briefly worked for, Frederick Douglass, just two years before Douglass's death. Following Douglass's address, Dunbar read his poem "Colored Soldiers," on Negro American Day. One can scarcely imagine a more brilliant manner through which to launch a national career.

Over the next few years, Dunbar's rise was nothing short of meteoric. He published his second volume of poetry, *Majors and Minors,* in 1895; a year later, William Dean Howells published an essay on Dunbar in *Harper's Weekly* that made Dunbar the veritable father of a "pure" or an "authentic" black literary tradition, a tradition that Howells, remarkably, defined by the absence of miscegenation in the author's ancestry, as if the writings of mulattos such as Frederick Douglass or Harriet Jacobs had not really counted. Howells's review made Dunbar a star in the nation's literary firmament, in the very same year in which the Supreme Court decided the infamous Plessy v. Ferguson "separate-but-equal" case. At the height of the legal institutionalization of Jim Crow segregation, then, black America saw the rise of its first national poet, a poet—as Howells would put it in his introduction to Dunbar's *Lyrics of Lowly Life* (1896)—who was "the only man of pure African blood and of African civilization to feel the Negro life aesthetically and express it lyrically."

Dunbar was astonishingly prolific over the next few years. In 1898 alone, following a lecture tour in England, he published a novel (*The Uncalled)* and a short story collection *(Folks From Dixie),* and wrote, with Will Marion Cook, the Broadway musical *Clorindy.* One of his biographers, Charles W. Carey, Jr., describes his next five years in the following way:

> In 1899 Dunbar published two collections of poems, *Lyrics of the Hearthside* and *Poems of Cabin and Field,* and embarked on a third reading tour. However, his health deteriorated so rapidly that the tour was cut short. The official diagnosis was pneumonia, but his doctor suspected that Dunbar was in the early stages of tuberculosis. To help ease the pain in his lungs, he turned to strong drink, which did little more than make him a near-alcoholic. He gave up his much-beloved speaking tours but continued to write at the same

breakneck pace. While convalescing in Denver, Colorado, he wrote a western novel, *The Love of Landry* (1900), and published *The Strength of Gideon and Others Stories* (1900), another collection of short stories. He also wrote two plays, neither of which was ever published, as well as some lyrics and sketches. In the last five years of his life, he published two novels, *The Fanatics* (1901) and *The Sport of the Gods* (1901, in *Lippincott's;* 1902, in book form); two short story collections, *In Old Plantation Days* (1903) and *The Heart of Happy Hollow* (1904); eight collections of poetry, *Candle-Lightin' Time* (1901), *Lyrics of Love and Laughter* (1903), *When Malindy Sings* (1903), *Li'l Gal* (1904), *Chris'mus Is A-comin' and Other Poems* (1905), *Howdy, Honey, Howdy* (1905), *Lyrics of Sunshine and Shadow* (1905), and *Joggin' Erlong* (1906); and collaborated with Cook on another musical, *In Dahomey* (1902). *(American National Biography Online)*

Dunbar's extraordinarily promising career was cut short by tuberculosis, to which he succumbed in 1906.

THROUGH THIS collection of Dunbar's dramatic pieces, essays, short stories, and poems—all heretofore uncollected—Herbert Martin, along with co-editor Ronald Primeau, has enabled us for the first time to consider the full range and sweep of Dunbar's talents as a writer. This collection adds no less than seventy-five uncollected works in six genres, including an unpublished short story, an unpublished play, and six songs. Taken together, they attest both to Dunbar's enormous energy and talent but also, sadly, to the promise of a career still in its adolescence, cut short by illness. Had Dunbar lived even half as long as Du Bois (born four years earlier than Dunbar, in 1868, but died in 1963), we can only imagine how different would have been the shape of the Harlem Renaissance and indeed the shape of African American literature itself. Martin and Primeau's edition of Dunbar's uncollected works allows us to experience an undiscovered Dunbar, a writer of great range, wit, subtlety, and irony. It will also lead to renewed academic and critical analysis, and an even deeper appreciation of Dunbar's status as the greatest African American poet before the Harlem Renaissance. The debt of the tradition to Herbert Martin and Ronald Primeau will be difficult to repay. Few publications alter literary history fundamentally, but that is the great accomplishment of this one.

Henry Louis Gates, Jr.

Preface

THIS VOLUME IS the product of a thirty-year partnership between Dunbar and his principal interpreter in our time, co-editor Herbert Woodward Martin. Identified with Dunbar almost from birth, Martin had avoided the association throughout his early life. As a young boy in Alabama, he was told he looked like Dunbar and asked to recite poems in school. He grew annoyed with the comparison and feared being blamed by his friends for additional assignments in poetry. He avoided Dunbar's poems for decades even though he remembers hearing his mother read the poems and learning about Dunbar and the Harlem Renaissance poets when he was in college in Toledo. The earlier annoyances as well as skepticism in the sixties over dialect poetry and "plantation" writers kept the two poets at more than arm's length.

When he accepted a position as poet in residence at the University of Dayton in 1970 in the city where Dunbar had lived and worked, Martin began to read, teach, perform, and research the poems and songs of the long-deceased author who became his "mentor." When Martin moved to Dayton, he visited Dunbar's house and grave site and began to meet people who had lived the history and knew the impact Dunbar had made in the city. Still, their coming together would be slow and deliberate. The year after Martin moved to Dayton, Addison Gayle published his ground-breaking *Oak and Ivy: A Biography of Paul Laurence Dunbar* (1971). Perhaps even more influential was the flourishing of Broadside Press in Detroit under the direction of Dudley Randall who also published *The Black Poets* (1971), an insightful look at—among many things—Dunbar's role as an important "forerunner" to both the Harlem Renaissance of the 1920s and the second Renaissance of black poets in the 1960s. To make a long story somewhat shorter, Martin soon discovered that the 100th anniversary of Dunbar's birth was approaching and that he was the one to organize a centennial celebration in Dayton in October, 1972. A distinguished group of poets and scholars, including Alvin Aubert, Nikki Giovanni, Margaret Walker, Michael S. Harper, Etheridge Knight, Sonia Sanchez, Saunders Redding, and Alice Walker, among others, participated in tributes to Dunbar. A revival of interest in Dunbar was on.

Two centennial celebrations of Dunbar's birth—one in Dayton, Ohio and the other in Irvine, California—started as commemorations, almost in the way of birthday parties as the invitations went out. But the events produced many surprises. In Dayton, major poets read their way through the entire Dunbar poetry canon. Margaret Walker reminded many in the audience that they had heard Dunbar while they were growing up and that they did know how to read him if they would only let go. Scholars addressed the fiction, and many of those gathered started to think again about how many letters and essays and stories Dunbar had written in less than two decades. Poets composed poems of tribute. Jay Martin edited a volume of articles based on the Irvine conference (Martin 1975), and throughout the decade Dunbar's stature grew as writers and critics alike noted the accuracy of his ear as well as his ability to create realistic characters.

AFTER PERFORMING Dunbar's poetry for over two decades, Martin became curious about the lost plays purported to have circulated shortly after 1900. A series of unrelated events led to several important discoveries. In his Research and Bibliography class at the University of Dayton, Martin would review the bibliographical puzzles and gaps in Dunbar's canon and send graduate students on searches for missing facts. Then, in the summer of 1993, while preparing for a seminar, the professor got a dose of his own medicine. First, a librarian working with rare manuscripts at the University of Dayton unearthed a copy of "Ole Conju'in Joe," a short story unknown to that point. This discovery sent Martin looking in earnest for the plays known to have been lost. He eventually found *Herrick* in the Carter G. Woodson Papers at the Library of Congress, and the idea of publishing a collection was born.

Acknowledgments

THIS PROJECT COULD not have been brought to its culmination without the assistance of Paul J. Morman, Dean of Arts and Sciences at the University of Dayton. We are also in eternal debt to Ms. Carolyn Ludwig at the University of Dayton and Ms. Carole Pasch at Central Michigan University, who made an electronic copy of this manuscript—with its tedious corrections —in record time. Their expertise and good cheer are treasures. University of Dayton English department secretaries have been of abiding assistance every step of the way: Diane Boomershine, Mona Guerrier, Laura Kolaczkowski, Jackie Love, Janine Scott, and Karen Updyke.

Ms. Mary Woofskill in Manuscript Collections at the Library of Congress and Mr. Raymond Nartker in the Rare Books Collection of the University of Dayton led the way to, respectively, *Herrick* and "Ole Conju'in Joe." Our deepest gratitude to Gene Jarrett of Brown University who directed our attention to two essays included in this volume: "England As Seen By A Black Man," and "Our New Madness." Thanks also to the Kent State University Library, which gladly loaned its Carter G. Woodson microfilm twice; to the Library of Congress for a copy of *Uncle Eph's Christmas;* to Ms. Joellen P. El-Bashir, senior manuscript librarian at Howard University's Moorland-Spingarn Research Center, for copies of *Jes' Lak White Fo'ks, In Dahomey,* and *Clorindy, or the Origin of the Cakewalk;* to University of Dayton librarians— particularly David Buckley, Edward Garten, Heidi Good, Jack O'Gorman, and Robin Reed—who extended courtesies beyond the call of duty; to the Paul Laurence Dunbar Library on the campus of Wright State University for their aid and assistance; to the Dayton and Montgomery County Public Library for making available copies of the *Dayton Tattler* (and especially to Ms. Nancy Horlacher, who not only located the photographs for us but made the Library's entire collection available to us); to the National Cash Register Company for a copy of "Ode" from their archives; and to Sarah J. Primeau who offered wise advice on drafts of the introductions. We are also most grateful to Sharon Rose of Ohio University Press for her many extremely helpful editorial suggestions.

We are grateful to the Ohio Historical Society for its microfilm of the Paul Laurence Dunbar Collection. We are also grateful to Mrs. LaVerne Sci, site manager of the Paul Laurence Dunbar House, who gave us the addresses of the poet's surviving relatives.

Nothing is ever accomplished without the assistance of our family members. Elizabeth Martin, Julia Martin, Sarah Robinson, and Katherine Primeau were always willing to take phone messages and perform other unexpected tasks.

Our deepest thanks to all.

General Introduction

FOR OVER ONE HUNDRED years Paul Laurence Dunbar's reputation in American literature has been solid. In 1896, William Dean Howells's review of *Majors and Minors* assured Dunbar recognition, situated his works in a variety of complex traditions, and generated more controversies than anyone at the time could have imagined. Howells praised Dunbar's dialect poems— a judgment that not only triggered notoriety but also obligated poet and readers alike to debate the merits of his standard-English works while privileging what Dunbar himself would refer to with melancholy as "a jingle in a broken tongue" ("The Poet"). Dunbar's reputation rose quickly following Howells's commentary, but he then painfully and with mixed success attempted to avoid the typecasting such repute can create.

Dunbar was born in Dayton, Ohio in 1872—less than a decade after the Emancipation Proclamation in 1863—and very much into the conflicts and uncertainty surrounding Reconstruction. His parents had both been slaves, though his father had escaped and fought in the Union army. Though much of his work captures and celebrates the joys and sorrows of African Americans during and after life on the plantations, his was a voice of protest against injustice rather than accommodationist acceptance of slavery and its aftermath. While he often created humor and parody in his poems as well as for the stage, he avoided the trap of minstrelsy which mocked "Negro" life through the song and dance of white actors in blackface. In poems, essays, and fiction, as well as dramatic works, Dunbar wrote about the difficult questions of progress after emancipation, the adjustments of reconstruction, the perils and the promise of migration to Northern cities, and the paradoxes of portraying "Negro" life authentically while a residue of stereotypes remained strong in society on the whole. Dunbar took on the challenges of being forceful when audiences often wanted him to be more subservient. He experimented with— and mastered—numerous literary forms when many had hoped he would specialize in dialect (preferably with large doses of humor). These controversies are now well known through the many studies of Dunbar's life and works. In the end, he would never shy away from the dangers he was forced to confront. The previously uncollected works in this volume will contribute to our understanding of how he was able to negotiate his way through these and other considerable challenges of his times.

IN HIS OWN time and in every subsequent period of American literature, Dunbar has been a figure to be reckoned with, though not without debate. Foremost among the ways his poems have been preserved and transmitted throughout the generations has been in live performance: through his own readings, through mothers and grandmothers reciting his poems and singing his songs for younger generations, and in numerous public performances by, among many, Maya Angelou, Margaret Walker, James Patterson, and Herbert Woodward Martin. Many recordings have preserved the conventions of the oral tradition found in his work. Through shifting literary tastes, several wars, the Great Depression, and many debates about what is valued most in literature, Dunbar's works have lived in the storytelling, song, and homes of African American families.

Over time, scholars have debated Dunbar's literary achievements. From the beginning, commentators disagreed about the authenticity of the peculiarly Ohioan brand of Southern dialect in his poems. There has been debate about his mastery of standard English, literary conventions, and genres. Some have found his standard English forms to be uninspired, though most commentators see his wide-ranging achievement in so many genres as both admirable and part of his plan to create ironic commentaries on politics and social issues (Gayle 1971; Bender 1975; Williams 1975; Blount 1990). Added to all this was considerable praise that he produced a great deal of work in a very short career which, in its span of about fifteen years, has been compared to the short life of English poet John Keats.

Dunbar has been known primarily as a poet. "We Wear The Mask," "Sympathy," and "An Ante-Bellum Sermon" established his credentials as a master of dialect and an ironist of considerable import. His short stories have been considered for the most part to be rather ordinary. He was a prolific essayist and letter writer, though his work in those genres has never been known widely. As a dramatist he has been neglected for two reasons. Manuscripts of what are suspected to be his best plays have been lost, and the lyrics he wrote for some musical comedies were either considered to be humiliatingly minstrellike or were misread in ways that overlooked his ironic humor and effective parody. Lack of access to his dramatic texts has also distorted how we have evaluated his mastery of dialogue—in both standard English and dialect. Without the plays, we have overlooked how he subverted minstrel and plantation conventions even as he successfully worked his way through the conventions of British comedy.

Dunbar's lyrics for the musicals *In Dahomey* and *Clorindy* embarrassed him during his lifetime and often rendered critical commentators silent in later years. Even when he was striving for the authenticity of actual speech or crafting irony, the pervasive degradation synonymous with the minstrel tradition mired his efforts in at best self consciousness and at worst humiliation. After viewing a performance of *Clorindy*, he is purported to have promised he had created his last "coon song" (Gayle 1971, p. 88). When he followed two years later with songs for *Uncle Eph's Christmas* and *Jes Lak White Fo'ks* (1900), he was resolved to work against the conventions of the minstrel show and the character of the coon. In her insightful introduction to *The Collected Poetry of Paul Laurence Dunbar* (1993), Joanne M. Braxton identifies Dunbar's tendency to "signify" by inverting conventional demeaning images. Braxton quotes Audre Lorde's suggestion that Dunbar often intended to "dismantle the master's house using the masters' tools" (in *Sister Outsider*, as paraphrased by Braxton, p. xxx.) The selections in this volume provide further evidence of that dismantling not only in the one-act plays but also in *Herrick*.

Debates about Dunbar's goals and achievements are sometimes as much a reflection of the values and concerns of reviewers as they are a measure of his own accomplishments. Dialect poetry, for example, has gone in and out of favor depending on whether or not folk literature and the oral tradition are being celebrated. Accordingly, Dunbar's works have been compared to Mark Twain or relegated to the status of lesser art forms. Capturing the authentic speech of plantation life would be laudable to those who want to reconstruct the daily lives of a people but embarrassing or annoying to anyone who might deem such output to be inappropriately accommodationist. Standard English works are sought after when critics see them as part of Dunbar's artistry in mastering a variety of forms; they are overlooked when the times are sure that dialect, humor, or even pathos are the appropriate province for a writer of Dunbar's race and background. How much irony commentators find in his work often depends on the ability of an age to understand the constraints imposed as well as the opportunities afforded by dominant conventions.

ALL THESE DEBATES have swirled around in the attention paid to Dunbar over the decades. No matter how heated the controversies became, attention never swayed from his works, and beginning in the 1920s and continuing to the present moment his influence has grown steadily. We need only recall some of the influences of his work on the natural language and rhythms of Langston Hughes or Zora Neale Hurston or the tributes paid to him by James Weldon Johnson as early as 1922 and by Dudley Randall a half-century and a whole world later (Randall 1971). Decade by decade, artists and scholars paid attention to Dunbar, and many expressed that greatest form of flattery: imitation or adaptation of his work to a different medium. Often these tributes have been taken for granted.

Consider some of Dunbar's other legacies. The well-known line from "Sympathy" ("I know why the caged bird sings") inspired the title of an autobiographical work by Maya Angelou and provided major thematic ingredients in Ralph Ellison's *Invisible Man*. His poems also shaped works by Paule Marshall and Jim Cummins and energized Gwendolyn Brooks's capturing of life on the south side of Chicago. Dunbar's poetry has been set to music by a wide range of composers, from Samuel Coleridge Taylor in the nineteenth century to William Grant Still, Will Marion Cook, Howard Swanson, Phillip Magnusson and Aldophus Hailstork throughout the twentieth century. His dialect poems have encouraged generations of African American writers trying to capture the language of daily life. His standard English works have shown the way to writers trying to break out of preconceived expectations and restrictions. Over time, his essays and letters have underscored his concerns with political issues. His fiction has inspired Richard Wright, Ralph Ellison, James Baldwin, Toni Morrison, and Alice Walker.

Nonetheless, controversies have been longstanding. We acknowledge that Dunbar was caught between the agrarian and plantation traditions. Debates about dialect continue. The desirability of his using dialect was questioned by some members of the black middle class who wanted nothing to do with its suggestions of ignorance and naïveté. James Weldon Johnson was aware of Dunbar's obligations to deal with a double audience of white and black readers with different expectations and values (Johnson, 1928). Like many writers throughout history, Dunbar was also trapped between attempts to express his culture and to be mainstream. Langston Hughes's 1926 proclamation that writers must strike out on their own and write what they need to and want to write came too late for Dunbar, but in many ways his accumulated wealth of dialect and standard English poems, essays, stories, and dramatic works proves that he went his own way in spite of all the pressures he faced.

Dunbar lived a short life, and his prolific output in so brief a time has been both fortuitous and problematic for scholars piecing together his career. He had written a great deal by the time he graduated from high school in 1891. Over the next seven years he published two major books of poems and was courted by notables on a tour of England. Then, between 1898 and 1902, he wrote short stories, novels, plays, and essays with some success and bittersweet reception. Because his career was abbreviated by tuberculosis and an early death (in 1906), speculation is likely to continue about his intentions and what he could have achieved. The materials in this volume will add a significant chapter to our understanding of his goals and accomplishments—especially as a dramatist.

Dunbar's methods of composition have made it difficult for scholars to collect and comment on his works. For example, he experimented with several genres simultaneously and drafted material while in school, while operating an elevator in Dayton, and while traveling. He read widely and often responded to his reading or took stands on political issues in letters and essays. He wanted to capture the authentic language of the everyday, so he often wrote about people he knew. He never had a chance to collect his writings into a Complete Works where he could select and arrange his widely varying efforts into a conscious pattern.

There have been many editions of Dunbar's works over time. Much of his poetry and fiction was published during his lifetime. A *Complete Poems* was issued later by Dodd, Mead in 1913. Posthumously, his poetry has received the most attention, his drama the least (Brawley 1936, Cunningham 1947, Martin 1975, Pawley 1975). The pattern has been to add to his canon over time as widely scattered individual pieces are gathered together or lost manuscripts are found. For example, Jay Martin and Gossie Hudson made available for the first time as late as 1975 many previously uncollected or unpublished works by Dunbar in their *Paul Laurence Dunbar Reader*. Dunbar's poems have been included in important collections, such as Hayden, Burrows, and Lapides 1971; Randall 1971; and Redding and Davis 1971. Although the available collections of Dunbar's work have established his reputation and exposed a wide audience to his genius, gaps have developed when texts were unpublished or lost.

This volume continues where the *Paul Laurence Dunbar Reader* (Martin and Hudson 1975) and *The Collected Poetry of Paul Laurence Dunbar* (Braxton 1993) leave off. Featured most prominently is Dunbar's dramatic voice in the unpublished play *Herrick* and in the two one-acts, *Uncle Eph's Christmas* and *Jes Lak White Fo'ks,* published separately in 1900 and then largely ignored for a century. Added to these selections are forty-one poems, fifteen essays, seven short stories and six songs which have yet to be collected and so have not received the attention they deserve. This generous expansion of the available canon also includes a short story published for the first time: "Ole Conju' in Joe," found in the rare manuscript collection in the University of Dayton Library. These seventy-five new and previously uncollected works in six genres add modestly to the body of poems, fill in gaps in the essays and short stories, and add to his reputation as a dramatist.

By making these works available in one place, this collection will contribute to long-standing debates, enlarge the Dunbar canon, and provide fresh evidence that he mastered certain genres and literary conventions in order to comment ironically on them. The works will establish more solidly Dunbar's reputation as a dramatist and give us better tools for assessing his accomplishments as a short-story writer and essayist. The poems, brought together here for the first time, will demonstrate his technical virtuosity and special ability to master several genres in record time. Whatever debates continue about the pressures he faced in his own times, about how he was either trapped in or liberated by his ironic use of restrictive genres and conventions, and about his mastery of or failings in both dialect and standard English, the works in this volume show how he broke ground for many writers to come. His bold experiments, his daring ventures into styles and schools of thought loaded with land mines, the freshness of his dialogue, and his often bitterly ironic commentaries—all made it possible for those he influenced to find their way, to make fewer errors, and maybe even to lift some of the barriers that so plagued his efforts.

THIS VOLUME IS divided into four parts by genre. First, a chronology places Dunbar's writing in the context of his life. Then the plays lead off because they are our most important contribution and addition to the canon. The sections that follow present essays, short stories, and poems—most previously published but now available for the first time in book form. The selections in each genre are treated in greater detail in a series of introductions to each part. The volume concludes with a bibliography of primary and scholarly works to guide the reader who wishes to pursue further research.

A Brief Dunbar Chronology

1872   Paul Laurence Dunbar is born on June 27 in Dayton, Ohio, where he spends his childhood and adolescent years.

1873   Dunbar's parents, Joshua and Matilda, separate. They later divorce.

1878   Dunbar writes his first poem, "An Easter Ode."

1884   Recites "An Easter Ode" at the Eaker Street A. M. E. Church in Dayton.

1885   Joshua Dunbar dies and is buried in Dayton's National Cemetery.

1888   "Our Martyred Soldiers," his first published poem, appears June 8 in the Dayton Ohio *Herald*.

1889   The poet contributes poems and sketches to boyhood friends Orville and Wilbur Wright's *Westside News*.

1890   Dunbar edits the *Dayton Tattler* with the Wright brothers. He edits and contributes to the *High School Times* at Central High School where he is also president of the Philomathean Literary Society.

1891   Dunbar writes the class song and graduates from high school with Orville Wright.

1891–1893   Dunbar works as an elevator operator at the Callahan Building in Dayton.

1893   Dunbar publishes *Oak and Ivy* with the financial assistance of William Blocher.

        Frederick Douglass employs Dunbar as a clerk in the Haytien Building of the World's Columbian Exposition in Chicago, Illinois.

1895   The poet publishes his second volume, *Majors and Minors*. William Dean Howells writes a glowing review of the book for *Harpers Weekly*.

1897   Dunbar becomes engaged to Alice Ruth Moore and then departs for London, England. He is abandoned by his agent but is graciously assisted by John Hay, the U.S. Ambassador to Great Britain. He returns to the U.S. and works as an assistant in the Reading Room of the Library of Congress. He collaborates with the African British composer Samuel Coleridge Taylor on *African Romances.*

1898   Dunbar marries Alice Ruth Moore. He resigns his job at the Library of Congress to work full time on his own writing. He collaborates with Will Marion Cook on *Clorindy, or the Origin of the Cakewalk.* He again collaborates with Samuel Coleridge Taylor, this time on his only opera, *Dream Lovers.* A book of short stories, *Folks From Dixie,* and Dunbar's first novel, *The Uncalled,* also appear.

1899   Excellent medical advice sends him to Colorado to recuperate from tuberculosis. He publishes *Lyrics of The Hearthside* and *Poems of Cabin Field.*

1900   Dunbar publishes his second volume of short stories, *The Strength of Gideon and Other Stories.* His second novel, *The Love of Landry,* is published.

1901   He participates in the inaugural parade of President Theodore Roosevelt. *Candle Lightin' Time* is published as well as his third novel, *The Fanatics.*

1902   He and Alice separate by mutual consent. *In Dahomey,* a musical and second collaboration with Will Marion Cook, is written. He publishes his final novel, *The Sport of the Gods.*

1903   Dunbar publishes *Lyrics of Love and Laughter; When Malindy Sings;* and his third book of short stories, *In Old Plantation Days.*

1904   *Li'l' Gal* (a book of poems); *Lyrics of Sunshine and Shadow* (a book of poems); and his last book of short stories, *The Heart of Happy Hollow,* are published.

1905   Dunbar participates in Roosevelt's second inaugural parade and publishes *Howdy, Honey, Howdy* (a book of poems).

1906   He publishes *Joggin' Erlong,* his last book of poems, and succumbs to tuberculosis in Dayton, Ohio, on February 9.

PART ONE

Dramatic Pieces

INTRODUCTION TO
THE DRAMATIC PIECES

THOUGH DUNBAR'S REPUTATION rests primarily on his poetry, the dramatic selections presented in this volume attest to his abilities as a playwright and song lyricist. The centerpiece of his output for the stage in standard English is *Herrick*, a comedy of manners published here for the first time. At least one additional full-length play (*Winter Roses*) remains lost—though Benjamin Brawley has related accounts of its plot which he no doubt heard from Richard B. Harrison (Brawley 1936, p. 71). As sources of major controversy in his canon, the dialogue and song lyrics in Dunbar's one-acts (*Uncle Eph's Christmas* and *Jes Lak White Fo'ks*) deserve reexamination for the way they successfully undermine many conventions of the minstrel tradition. Two fragments (*The Gambler's Wife* and *The Island of Tanawana*) showcase some of Dunbar's earliest efforts for the stage and prefigure several of his later subjects and themes. The libretto for *Dream Lovers* and the songs from *In Dahomey* and *Clorindy* are included here to make them accessible now that *The Paul Laurence Dunbar Reader* (Martin and Hudson 1975) is out of print. Taken together, this considerable body of dramatic pieces contributes much to our appreciation of various voices Dunbar created. The dramatic works also underscore his exceptionally fine ear for irony and nuance—ingredients that are increasingly apparent as well in performances of his poetry.

Plays

Herrick was written near the end of Dunbar's career. A copy was sent to Richard B. Harrison, the actor who played De Lawd in Marc Connolly's *Green Pastures*. Harrison was a distinguished actor who had more theatrical connections than did Dunbar. There is mention in *The Paul Laurence Dunbar Reader* that "Cornelius Otis Skinner and others" had some interest in

3

getting this play produced but ultimately ended up rejecting it (p. 266). No reasons were given. The script remained in Harrison's possession until two years after Dunbar's death when he signed his copy and returned it to the poet's widow in 1908. She in turn gave the manuscript to Carter G. Woodson, father of Negro History Week and the founder of the *Journal of Negro History*. That is where it remained until Herbert W. Martin located it in the summer of 1993. A copy was subsequently located in the Paul Laurence Dunbar Papers in the Ohio Historical Society Library, Columbus, Ohio.

Paul Laurence Dunbar and Bob Herrick

Herrick, An Imaginative Comedy in Three Acts is written in the form and style of an eighteenth-century English comedy of manners. Based loosely on the life of poet Robert Herrick, Dunbar's plot follows the efforts of Bob Herrick to woo the lady Cynthia. Complications arise with the appearance of several other suitors and the objections to Herrick advanced by Cynthia's father, Sir Peter Temple. Father and suitors conspire against Herrick who wins nonetheless due to his charm, wit, and gift of gab. Herrick talks his way out of several traps and into the heart of Cynthia with lines like these: "A heart as soft, a heart as kind / A heart as sound and free / As in the whole world there can't find / That heart I'll give to Thee." And again: "Thou art my life, my love, my heart / The very eye of me / And has command of every part / To live and die for thee." Here is Herrick in soliloquy: "How smilingly the sun looks on the earth, / Me thinks, he's glad that Cynthia lives; / Glad with the gladness I feel, when here alone / I do unbare my brow and know the joy / That she doth breathe this same perfumed air / Which loves my brow with its caressing touch. / Ah, Cynthia, 'tis thy breath perfumes the air / Me thought it was a rose. Ah, no 'tis not, / No rose as sweet as thou ere sucked its life / And took its glory from the common earth." The language and imagery here are a long way from Dunbar's plantation scenes, the Lucy poems, or the angry protest poems.

Consistent with Dunbar's goals, he no doubt wrote *Herrick* at least in part to show he could master the language and the nuance of British comedy and to round out his achievements as a composer of richly complex and diverse dialogue. But Dunbar may have had other goals in mind as well. He no doubt wrote the play while he was in England and was therefore within months of marrying Alice Moore. Her family was among the social elite in New Orleans and may have looked down on the self-made Dunbar, who had worked as an elevator operator in a Dayton office building. The real Robert Herrick was not "to the manor born" either, and achievement through hard work was for Dunbar a kind of personal theme. While he wrote *Herrick* to make an attempt at the conventions of this very English genre, he took considerable pleasure as well in the exploits of his underdog hero. Then, too, Dunbar was always at some pains to show his range at a time when black writers were expected to write only about black subjects and black people.

Herrick is a pivotal work in Dunbar's career path. There are no black characters in the play, and Dunbar uses none of the dialect often found in his works. Instead, he reproduces authentic speech patterns of English drama and has some fun mastering and modifying several conventions of plot, character, and theme in the genre. *Herrick* is one of Dunbar's most ambitious attempts to be judged on his own talents with no efforts to fit any preconceived critical judgments—no matter how well intended. With all the stereotypical patterns and predictable literary goals set aside, Dunbar's ear is accurate, his characters well-developed and interesting, his insights into human nature unwavering. Beyond those caveats and the correctives *Herrick* brings to our understanding of Dunbar, there are parallels in the lives of these two poets whose aspirations were beaten down in similar ways by the forces of class and race prejudice. Dunbar explored the parallels he created to underscore his ever-abiding themes of class segregation, determination, endurance, and aspiration. Just as Freddie is a stand-in for Dunbar in the novel *The Uncalled,* so also Bob Herrick's dilemmas mirror many of Dunbar's own struggles.

The similarities between Dunbar and Herrick underscore the anguish of two aspiring poets confronting obstacles. For example, Sir Peter plots to keep Herrick away from his daughter: "I tell you my good fellows, he's a damned presumptuous dog. Are the times so poor, so damnably poor that every barking upstart of a poetaster may aspire to the hand of the leading lady in the country?" Sir Peter throughout plans to trap Herrick, to make him look foolish, and to load the odds against any achievements to which he might aspire. After his supporter, aptly named Will Playfair, speaks on Herrick's behalf, Sir Peter explains what they have planned:

> You gentlemen, have I asked to meet her here, and with you asked that rhyming, dangling boy, Bob Herrick. A woman's mind is a light thing and

Cynthia in her younger days did lean toward him, and in your hands tonight I leave the chance to break this fancy's chain, to make a boor of him; before she comes to make him drunk, and when she's here to make him so behave before her face that she will as soon hear of the devil and his hellish chants as Bob Herrick and his ladies' songs.

While Mr. Harlowe Wetheridge, Sir Harry Hastings, and Sir Godfrey Gailspring move forward to seal Sir Peter's plot, Cynthia has been hiding in the house and warns Herrick of the impending mischief ("I will warn him so to arm that he will turn aside the shafts of all their foul intentions"). Together they preempt the events planned to ruin Herrick, and Dunbar gives the poet several triumphant retorts as he wins the day:

> I know not if it be you yourself, Sir Peter, who has set these cowards on to taunt me and in this unmanly manner to put me to the test, but this I know: Robert Herrick doth defy you all and tells you right now here in your own house that poets know not only how to twang the lute and make song, but how to wield a soldier's arm as well. And if these gentlemen singly come to put affront upon, name your own weapons, and you shall find me deft as well with steel as with quill.

The triumph of Herrick over his mockers enacts the vindication Dunbar looked for in his own career.

Herrick wins decisively. With Cynthia's help he is able to take the bait, drink a little, dissemble a lot, and rout all his adversaries. He even foils a second plot involving fake robbers and, when the accomplices retreat from the plan, Herrick conquers the real highwaymen who arrive and in the process saves Cynthia and her father as well as the other women. In the end even Sir Peter has to recognize the genuine courage and valor and triumph of Dunbar's standby, the poet Bob Herrick. Dunbar gives his hero not only unquestionable vindication but scores of great lines. "You scorn me that I make my lines and love the sound of the absorbing lute," he proclaims to his detractors. "But let me tell thee, Robert Herrick's name shall live as good Chris Marlowe's doth when thou and all thou hast art mould." The poet responds to recurring accusations: "Thou sayest I am drunk. Drunk with the wild winds and breath of life. Drunk with the sweet wine of thy daughter's eyes. Drunk with the love of life and with mine own art."

Dunbar no doubt created Bob Herrick's challenges to match some of his own—and his hero's magnanimous triumphs project his hopes for his own art. Consider further the Dunbar-Herrick linkage in more of the lines given to the hero. When everyone accuses Herrick of being drunk with regularity, he shakes off the help of his friend Will Playfair, pretends to sleep when a servant enters, and then arises to have his say when the stage is his:

> This is the province of the poet, to wake when others sleep, to sleep perchance, when others wake, who knows? To be the jest of others and himself to jest. To love and be despised of his lessers. Ah, me, the world has fallen on evil days, when no one doth respect the poet's song and give him ear. 'Tis strange, 'tis passing strange, with good Will Shakespeare yet so shortly dead, and rare Ben Jonson singing still. Will had his Lucy and his stolen deer, and I my Temple and my stolen love. Ha, ha, we go a merry gait who ride that fleet steed Pegasus, and feed on Fancy's bread.

Herrick is an effective play. The plot, characters, and dialogue move along successfully, and Dunbar shows he is proficient with the conventions of the genre as well as the subtleties of creating something new with the format.

Herrick is not only a valuable lost play but also an opportunity for Dunbar to embody in his hero a way of getting back at the frustrations and roadblocks confronting poets of the last four hundred years. "I'd rather be a singer chasing the fleeting rhyme and prisoning thoughts in pearls to grace another's wine than all the Lucy's and the Temple's that burden England's soil" Herrick confides: "For they, with minds as heavy as their wallets are, eat, drink, breathe, die, while we with souls as light as Fancy's self live on and on and on. Ha, ha." Not only do Herrick-Dunbar get the last laugh, but they get to enjoy some very fine love lyrics which Bob Herrick composes about Cynthia:

> And now a kiss to sun and day and air,
> For they are glad with me that she is there;
> Yes, 'tis the very essence of alloy
> That mortals leap too soon unto their joy;
> So, I will bide me here a little while,
> Enjoy the morning and the morning's smile
> And while I walk thy golden paths along
> Weave to thee, Cynthia, my wooing song.

It is perhaps all the more ironic that *Herrick* had been lost for so long, because the play mounts some of Dunbar's best defenses against the indifference and impertinence which greeted much of his work. *Herrick* showed that he could handle theme, venue, and place without being singled out as an African American author with one idea and one theme. As a bonus, in bold and witty speeches Herrick is able to voice many of Dunbar's views about the nature and impact of poetry. Views often overlooked in poems like "The Poet," "Sympathy," "The Mask," or "Equipment" get a new hearing in Bob Herrick's saucy victories. Routing all real and fake robbers and taking the hand of Cynthia, Bob Herrick has his way at the curtain: "Go on, good Hastings, tempt my ire no more, I've had enough, our comp'ny waits, go thou before."

WITH THE DISCOVERY of *Herrick,* co-editor Herbert Woodward Martin was nudged into the role of Dunbar scholar. He had created—and performed for over ten years—a Paul Laurence Dunbar one-man show, and now he accepted the challenge of textual research as well. Among the Herbert W. Martin Papers at the University of Toledo is a fragment that contributes to our understanding of how a contemporary interpreter might perform Dunbar. At the conclusion of his program notes ("Making a Libretto") for the opening of the opera *Paul Laurence Dunbar: Common Ground* (1995), Martin assumes Dunbar's persona and comes back from the dead to praise with "ecstasy" the achievements of composer Adolphus Hailstork's "Soulful Song." In that same spirit in this prose fragment "Dunbar" begins by defending himself against the charges that he had sometimes been too accommodationist. "I am neither upset nor angry," the isolated ghostlike presence observes. "I simply wonder who among us has not had to submit to compromise at one time or another."

As Dunbar's canon expands and we learn more about the complexity of his efforts—some failures, many successes—we are entrusted in scholarship and performance to set the record straight. "Even as I speak to you now I have had to pay a certain young poet for the use of his body and voice," he adds tongue-in-cheek. "And since I am dead, there is no reason to feel jealousy. So I shall give him time after the defense of my position to read to you these poems." Every generation finds its own time difficult, the "Dunbar" of this fragment continues: "My lifetime was no exception, but I wrote as best

I could under and despite the circumstances. I do not ask for praise or acceptance, only for the next few moments that you listen to my words of protest, love, pain, humor, and joy. I hope they will renew your confidence and speak . . . " and the fragment breaks off. Perhaps Martin thought "Dunbar" had said enough, and it was up to us to finally listen.

Musicals

Until now Dunbar's contributions to musical theater have been linked most often with *Clorindy,* his own displeasure with "coon songs," and the suspicion that at times he took on such projects merely for profit. But in *Jes Lak White Fo'ks* and *Uncle Eph's Christmas* he reproduced the conventions of the genre in order to undermine many of its assumptions. In these musicals, Dunbar chose to include tropes of the minstrel show tradition—some even offensive—in part because he was then able to attract an audience who would see and hear his modification, mockery, and other critiques of that stereotyping. His use of certain conventions became enabling conditions for advancing his satire in several directions, as both a mockery of stereotypical roles and a probing insight into the behavior and motivation of white folks. Consider the chorus of the song "Emancipation Day" from *Clorindy:* "On Emancipation Day / All you white folks clear de way / . . . Coons dressed up lak masqueraders / Porters armed lak rude invaders / When dey hear dem ragtime tunes / White folks try to pass fo' coons on Emancipation Day." Not only does this display the double ironies of role playing and whites wanting to release themselves through black culture, it also represents Dunbar's incorporation of elements of the minstrel tradition into his own satire. As John Fiske has shown us (1989a, 1989b), that is how popular culture works in a democratic society: the public expresses its own values through what it makes popular, all the while selectively espousing or undermining the dominant values of the culture as a whole. Similarly, Dunbar conformed to conventions of various genres in order to become popular enough to create an ironic commentary on many of the values of his time. Gary D. Engle underscores the problems faced by Dunbar and his musical collaborator Will Marion Cook: "For better or worse, the characteristic art of a democracy is shaped by the will of the audience, not by the artist. Popularity becomes one measure of artistic value"(1978, p. xiii). Perhaps the "for better" of this proposition for Dunbar and Cook was that the artist is able to use popularity to undermine and critique the values he or she seems to espouse.

Because clowning minstrelsy was a staple of the stage at the time and Dunbar wanted a forum, the issue is not that he used those conventions but how he moved them in new directions that would give his art an authenticity as well as some distance from the actions and attitudes he was mocking. In *Jes Lak White Fo'ks* and *Uncle Eph's Christmas,* Dunbar makes space for his own artistry within the often suffocating confines of the genres he was expected to follow. *Uncle Eph's Christmas* emphasizes pure entertainment—even fluff—rather than plot and is loaded with malapropisms and other elements of slapstick common in the kind of drama he was writing. The minstrel-style dialect and malapropisms might be construed by some as "Amos and Andy" degradation, but the presence of these deliberate distortions of language in the script shows that Dunbar is fully aware of the mechanics and traditions of eighteenth-century dramas. Further, ironies are tucked into corners everywhere and even burst forth on occasion as in Darky Dan's song:

> You white folks don't 'lect no man
> Less he's of yo' nation.
> What you want to do's to keep
> Black folks in dey station.
> But dese black folks boun' to have
> Some one go a starrin'
> So in Dixie Land, I spend
> All my time a Czarin.'

This is hardly the usual fare of the minstrel tradition's self-degrading humor. In contrast, the attacks are directed at the white folks and their political manuevering. Dunbar also consistently emphasizes the value of an education. Beyond the conventional trappings of character—often offensive—and the irony Dunbar creates through indirection—these dramatic entertainments revel in the sheer play of language.

Jes Lak White Fo'ks is a comedy of manners that uses the theme of social aspirations to satirize the values of white society. The theme of the play is summed up in an early speech given by Mr. Pompous Johnsing. After digging up a treasure chest of gold, Pompous decides that you can't "advertise dah gold all ovah town" because "de white fo'ks / grab it up for themselves / Some folks ain't got no mo'sense 'n ter walk up to trouble an' ask fu' an introduction . . . / we won't tell white folks, jes' de colo'ed folks." After a chorus of "Spread de news, spread de news / Mistah Johnsing's found de gold / Found de gold dat once was hid," Pompous pushes everyone away and states impressively Dunbar's major concerns in the play: "I want yo all to und'stand I got a plan in regard to dis gold. I got social aspirations. You know when white men gets rich dem don' stay hyeah wha ezybody knows 'em en knows dey ain' much. Dey go to Europe, and by 'n by you readin' de papers en you say: 'Huh! Heah Mr. Wilham Vanderbilt Sunflower's daughter married a duke.'" But Pompous Johnsing declares that he doesn't want any "bargain counter duke" for his daughter. While she doesn't have "a diploma from Vassar," he has been engaged in diplomatic relations with an African King for her to marry a prince. "I ain' ready yit. I goin' get Mandy a family tree. Dey er so cheap in Europe dey use 'em fer kindlin' wood. Mandy she'll have a family tree. Jes' lak white folks."

Of course Pompous' declarations are send-ups, and the rest of this short play piles on the kind of satire reflected in the song "The Colored Girl from Vassar." "Have you heard the latest that is 'startling all the nation?'" asks Mandy about the "school that was so very rare / that a poor dusky maid couldn't breathe its very air." The chorus assures all that you can't go there unless you are a millionaire. Mandy becomes that "first dark belle who ever went to Vassar" and the chorus fills in, "She played her part so well she came from Madagascar." She didn't tell them about her "dark papa," and when she was admitted "the papers howled and said it was a shame." While they agreed that she definitely "was to blame" and that "she had played an awful little game," yet "they had to own that [she] got there just the same." The send-up continues in the song "Evah Niggah Is a King," sung by Pompous with every assurance that while the white folks "ain' got all de title" they need, "When a darky starts to huntin' / He is sho' to prove a king." The chorus re-iterates: "Evah Niggah is a king / Royalty is jes de ting / Ef yo' social life's a bungle / Jes you go back to yo' jungle / An remember dat yo daddy was a king." Just in case Dunbar's audience misses the satire and inserts his play back into the plantation-school pigeonhole, he turns Pompous loose one more time with rhyme and style and panache:

To get in high society
I've always had ambition
And since I've got the dough now
We are sure to have position
A royal prince my little girl shall wed
For since the day of Lords and dukes has sped
It takes a prince to place you at the head
of the best society.

Now Mandy knows her father and tells him that he's got to be kidding. Of course the tone, the rhymes, the music suggest that her conclusions are dead on: "Father you're only mocking / Such levity is only shocking." At this point Mandy and the chorus burst into numerous choruses of song about not caring for fools because "love dignifies the soul it rules." New money, old money, aristocrats, and moving to Europe—none of it matters because "The humble cot becomes a throne / Whose dwelling place love makes her own." The called-for prince arrives only to be rejected by both Mandy and Pompous who, the stage directions tell us, "decides after all that an honest American Negro is a man who will look after his daughter and make a living for her his best." In the end, the satire comes full circle and Pompous' resolve wins out: "And anyhow he is happier as an ordinary darkey therefore he decides to quit acting just lak white folks."

In many ways the satire of Pompous Johnsing's views on the world epitomizes the contributions of this volume. It is easy here to see why Dunbar was so frustrated when people missed his irony, so dismayed when readers confused his subtle lyrics with plantation stereotypes, so trapped when critics demanded a narrow range of work from a writer who mastered so many forms and techniques. These previously uncollected works will help to correct some of the misconceptions that have persisted from Dunbar's times up to our own.

Musical Lyrics and Fragments

In order to gain acceptance and develop his own voice, Dunbar ventured into the dangerous waters of plantation life and minstrels on the musical stage. Two of his less-than-successful ventures remain *Clorindy, or the Origin of the Cakewalk* and *In Dahomey,* after which performers would be called back to perform encores of songs like "The Hottest Coon in Dixie."

Perhaps more damage was done by the titles of these songs than by the meaning of their lyrics. Still, both titles and song lyrics must have caused some discomfort if not outright offense. Observe where Dunbar writes in "Who Dat Say Chicken in dis Crowd":

There were speakers from Georgia and some from Tennessee
Who were makin' feathers fly
When a roostah in a bahn ya'd flew up to whah those people could see
Then those darkies all did cry:

Chorus:
Who dat say chicken in dis crowd?
Speak de word agin' and speak it loud
Blame de lan' let white folks rule it
I'se a lookin' for a pullet
Who dat say chicken in dis crowd?

The song is peppered with the use of derogatory words like "darky," "dark-ies," and "coon" and such imagistic phrases as: "Darkies standin' on tip-toe makin' goo-goos at de show"; "Darkies eyes look jes' lak moons"; and "Coons dressed up lak masqueraders." But there is another reading to be advanced for these lyrics, which were popular in their day. There is a subtle quietness, a positiveness offered beneath the lyrics' immediate surface. What could Dunbar have meant by these lyrics from "Evah Darkey Is a King?"

Scriptures say dat Ham was de first black man
Ham's de father of our nation
All de black fo'ks to dis very day belongs
Right in de Ham creation

Ham he was a king in ancient days
An' he reigned in all his glory
Den ef we is all de sons of Ham
Nchelly dat tells de story. So!
White fo'ks what's got darkey servants
An' doan nevah speak insulting
Fer dat coon may be a king

This song also suggests that African Americans are descended from royalty and that some whites realized that innate presence and were disposed to treat them well. Observe also how "On Emancipation Day" invites the listener in and then shuts the door in the last two lines:

On Emancipation Day
All you white folks clear de way
Brass ban' playin' several tunes
Darkies eyes look jes' lak moons
Marshall of de day struttin'
Word he is so gay
Coons dressed up lak masqueraders
Porters armed lak rude invaders
When dey hear dem ragtime tunes
White folks try to pass fo' coons.

Are we to assume that the blacks are having a good deal more fun than the white people are, and that this leads the whites to envy? There is little doubt that blacks dancing and singing in a production of *In Dahomey* or *Clorindy* created a powerful sense of excitement and delight on Broadway and even on the London stage. In these two plays, Dunbar seems to have been less successful in achieving irony than he was in *Uncle Eph's Christmas* or in *Jes Lak White Fo'ks*.

The Gambler's Wife concerns a family whose ups and downs depend upon chance. The husband is a gambler and the wife has grown tired of the extremes with which she must contend. When we first encounter Madge, she is remarking: "I am tired of this life, and what sensible woman would not be? I am in a continual state of doubt and anxiety. Miserable wretch that I am, that most accursed thing—a gambler's wife—continually vacillating from sudden wealth to more sudden poverty. One day greeted by a husband's smile; the next, spurned by a demon's curses."

The ups and down of good fortune are not the only worries on Madge's mind. Because her husband is no longer her lover, she has taken a lover herself. But her husband returns home unexpectedly while she is awaiting a visit from her lover. A letter announcing his early return arrived that day, but her forgetful servant failed to give it to her. Immediately we note the difference in the use of language when Ceasar, the servant, speaks:

Ceasar: Miss Da'll, da wuz a note come fo' you dis mo'nin', but fo' de Lawd, I fo'got to delier it.

Madge: You forgot, Ceasar?

Ceasar: Yes, I fo'got. You don't spose my memory's disfallible, case I's a servant, does you? (Aside) I'o white folks is awful to wuk fo'.

Ralph Darrell, the husband, is a scoundrel and an opportunist. When he realizes that his wife has been unfaithful and is going to elope with a millionaire, he is quick to seize the moment as one which will bring him quick resources and perhaps a sexual encounter with his not-yet-divorced wife. He plots a sinister design as follows:

> Darrell: . . . do you think that I am going to let this chance to handle that cool thirty thousand which St. Clair settles on you, slip by? Oh, no I'm going to finger Arthur St. Clair's money.
>
> Madge: What do you mean?
>
> Darrell: You are not well enough known here for your sudden departure to cause any excitement so play out your little game of eloping with Arthur St. Clair, and when you are married and receive your settlement of thirty thousand I shall ask you to give me ten and to fill whatever subsequent demands I may make.

There is a touch of Ibsen in such a plot. The only apparent release from one scene to another is humor. The father, George St. Clair, sees this new wife in an unfavorable light and his son, Arthur, as a fool taken advantage of. He is no doubt more observant than his son, but he thinks himself a judge of superior character when he remarks: "My knowledge of human character tells me, that though women are at best a bad lot, Madge St. Clair, my son's wife, is the worst of her sex. Why she's got a bad eye. Any man with common sense could see that she is wicked. Her very voice betrays her. They say that love is blind and I am half inclined to believe that it is deaf and dumb also; poor son my poor son."

It is a pity the other acts are lost. It would have been interesting to see how Dunbar resolved the problems his characters faced, for educational and social aspirations are there in each of his dramas. When these themes are cast in many of his plays with dark skin they are perceived to be *old*. Yet a play like *Herrick*, with white characters employing British English, might not be ignored or dismissed. As Dunbar's career progressed, he might have seen the stage as the one place he could be taken seriously, the one place where he could be assured of being remembered as more than a dialect poet. Success on stage could also afford a way to infuse new life into his neglected standard English poems so that he would not be accused of writing on "the same old Negro themes."

The fragment of *The Island of Tanawana* is mentioned in Virginia

Cunningham's *Paul Laurence Dunbar and His Song* (1947) and discussed at considerable length by Thomas D. Pawley in "Dunbar as Playwright" (1975, pp. 71–73). Pawley speculates that *Tanawana* is one of the works rejected and called "hopeless" by the publisher Lippincott in 1901. The first act is complete in this controversial musical comedy laden with slapstick vaudeville and farcical humor. The plot deals with themes of great wealth, interracial romance, elopement, and unresolved conflict. In this excerpt, which includes all we have of the second act, there are flashes of brilliant word play and a foreshadowing of the Theatre of the Absurd. The fragment is included here to show Dunbar experimenting with intrigue and a variety of characters and gags. No additional portions of this work have been found.

PLAYS

Herrick

An Imaginative Comedy in Three Acts

Act I

Scene i: [setting] The hall of Sir Peter Temple's house in Devonshire. The table is equipped with jugs and tankards, pipes also lying about as for a meeting of gentlemen roisterers. As curtain rises, Sir Peter in advance of three young men, Mr. Will Playfair, Mr. Harlowe Wetheridge and Sir Harry Hastings.

Sir Peter:
I tell you my good fellows, he's a damned presumptuous dog. Are times so poor, so damnably poor that every barking upstart of a poetaster may dare aspire to the hand of the leading lady in the country?

Sir Hastings:
Mr. Wetheridge:
(together)
Right, Sir Peter. *(Will Playfair silent)*

Sir Peter:
What say you to it Playfair? You are the son of one of our good squires. What say you to the presumption of this man Herrick?

Mr. Playfair:
I scarce know what to say, Sir Peter. I' fact, I scarce have right to speak in this, our cause. First off, Bob Herrick is my friend, I, a rival, too aspire for your

fair daughter's hand with these two other gentlemen, and therefore, must some enmity feel 'gainst him who is the peer himself of any here who speaks him ill.

Sir Hastings:
Come, come, a gentle speech, that, good Will.

Mr. Wetheridge:
'Tis seldom Will says aught 'gainst any man.

Sir Peter:
And yet, I find him all too gentle now. Why, 'tis a thing should rouse the blood of any gentleman, and make it mount first to his fear, then drop to his heart, where it should shoot fair forth into his hand and make *him* turn his sword 'gainst the parading churl.

Mr. Playfair:
Your pardon, good Sir Peter, if I say that Bob comes of no new family, and no base; tho' far it be from me to plead my rival's cause. But I am here with you and these by you enjoined, to work what is your will in any honest way to check his suit. Then, for the later fight, there will be three, and happy he who wins fair Cynthia's hand. The thought doth rouse my heart. Go on.

Sir Peter:
Well spoke. Now to our plot. Know ye to-night my daughter comes with her good Aunt Lucinda from the country where she has taken retreat from numerous suitors and her own unrest. Now, I have brought her hitherward that she may look on those whom most I favor; take some account of these and their family, manners and wealth that she may think on marriage with one of them. You gentlemen, have I asked to meet her here, and with you asked that rhyming, dangling boy, Bob Herrick. A woman's mind is a light thing and Cynthia in her younger days did lean toward him, and in your hands to-night I leave the chance to break this fancy's chain, to make a boor of him; before she comes to make him drunk, and when she's here to make him so behave before her face that she will as soon hear of the devil and his hellish chants as Bob Herrick and his ladies' songs.

Mr. Wetheridge:
Sir Hastings:
(together)
Ha, ha, a good plot, Sir Peter, and worthy of you.

Mr. Playfair:
(Slowly) But is it fair?

Sir Peter:
Fair?

Mr. Wetheridge:
Fair?

Sir Hastings:
On, fair be damned. What's this that speaks of fairness in the game of love? Who would be fair with poets who but sing and pour the insidious poison of their verse into a lady's ear and make her drunk then poison all her maiden life.

Mr. Wetheridge:
Ha, fairness, Will in time of war and unto him who wears his sword beside his hips, but in the hour of love and unto him who only sings and tinkles softly on his gentle lute, all things from men who wear the sword are fair.

Sir Peter:
Good Harlowe, thou hast spoken well, and Will objects no more.

Mr. Playfair:
Sir Peter, I have done.

Sir Peter:
And now, to further what I have said, when Lady Cynthia comes, you, my gentlemen, are to put this Sir Poet to the test before her face, to taunt him with his verse. Make him the butt of your own keenest jests. Laugh at his airs, his gait, his form.

Mr. Playfair:

(Slowly) Laugh at his gait, so you laugh not upon the halting of his verse, I doubt me if he will care.

Sir Peter:

Then taunt him on the halting of his verse. Say how he halts and stumbles over the lovesick lines. Quote some of it to him and laugh you loud and long at it.

Mr. Wetheridge:

We'll do it, by the rood.

Sir Hastings:

Aye, we'll laugh, ha, ha.

Mr. Wetheridge:

I will mock him how he walks when entering a room with lovesick looks cast on each lady's face. Ha, ha.

Sir Hastings:

And I will sing him some sweet song as he is wont to sing it to his lute, ha, ha.

Mr. Playfair:

I prithee, gentlemen, not too fast. Know you the temper of the man whom you would taunt?

Sir Peter:

Temper!

Sir Hastings:

Temper!

Mr. Wetheridge:

Temper, ha, ha! I will mock him to his very face, and he will answer with an epigram.

Sir Peter:
But gentlemen, good gentlemen, I prithee first remember thy friendship to our guest and ere thou bringest him to the test later do thou make him drunk, drunk as the swine who reel in Circe's wood.

Mr. Wetheridge:
We'll make him drunk, ha, ha.

Sir Hastings:
We'll make him rolling drunk, ha, ha.

Mr. Playfair:
(Calmly) Aye, we'll make him drunk, though we be drunk ourselves.

Sir Peter:
Ho, to the plot. Good gentlemen, a cup with me in my most private room before you come to clip the feathers of the cock who sings but never crows. *(Exeunt laughing. As they pass out, the arras at the back of the stage is pulled to one side, and the roguish face of Cynthia peeps out. She laughs and comes down center looking after the departing gentlemen.)*

Cynthia:
(Mocking them) We'll make him drunk, ha, ha. We'll make him rolling drunk, ha, ha. Good Will Playfair, thou has spoke truly. Thou will make him drunk though thou be drunk thyselves. I warrant that thou will be drunk yourselves ere you made good Bob Herrick drunk when Cynthia has warned him of thy plot. Oh, father, father, thou art keen, but now I know where comes some of that wit that meets your wisdom point to point. Ha, ha, ha, I wonder where my Aunt Lucinda is? *(Going to door and looking out)* I left her on the road and hither flew because scented something of a noisome plot. Oh, man, oh man, you may compel a woman's hand; you may command a woman's mind, but ah, you cannot force a woman's heart nor stifle yet a woman's will. Oh, Herrick, Bob. I wonder where my Aunt Lucinda is. If she comes not ere Bob comes, I will warn him so to arm that he will turn aside the shafts of all their foul intentions. *(At door)* Who's there? *(Enter Robert Bob Herrick.)*

Cynthia:

Oh!

Mr. Herrick:

The sun rises on my day at last.

Cynthia:

Oh, Master Herrick.

Mr. Herrick:

What? Master Herrick? So long a day since I was Bob and thou wert Cynthia. Nay, nay not Master Herrick, but thy Bob, thy darling singing Bob whom thou didst love, thou saidst. *(Cynthia raises her hand deprecatingly)* How now, has thy love grown cold? Dost thou not remember how long years ago we stood beneath that oak that spreads its branches by thy father's brook and I did take thy hand as I do now and kiss it with the selfsame throbbing heart and ask thee wouldst thou love me evermore? Hast thou forgot what answer thou didst make?

Cynthia:

(Bending her head) Nay, Robert, oh,—I—I—I—am older now.

Mr. Herrick:

Ah, Cynthia, love is like good wine, and mellower, richer grows with age. Dost love me now?

Cynthia:

I cannot tell.

Mr. Herrick:

(Bending towards her) I say, does love me now?

Cynthia:

I may not say.

Mr. Herrick:
And I repeat, dost love me now, Cynthia? The tell-tale blush comes up thy cheek as dawn comes up the sky. Fie, fie upon thee. Tell me, dost thou love me?

Cynthia:
'Tis most unmaidenly of me, Bob, but oh—I love thee, yes, thy Cynthia loves thee. *(They embrace.)* And how much thou shalt know and quickly. They have made a plot. They will get thee drunk. I will be brought before thee; they will disgrace thee in my presence. Remember, drink thou not deeply Bob. *(A burst of laughter from without.)* They are coming.

Mr. Herrick:
I thank thee dear, I thank thee, but they may spare their pains, I am already drunk with love of thee. *(Holding her by the hand.)*

Cynthia:
I must fly.

Mr. Herrick:
One kiss give me here, and then farewell until the trial hour. *(Exit Cynthia. Opposite door enter the men who give a burst of laughter at sight of Herrick who has seated himself at the table. They burst into acclamations of welcome.)*

Mr. Wetheridge:
How art thou, Bob?

Sir Hastings:
Why, my old friend.

Sir Peter:
I am glad to see thee Herrick:

Mr. Playfair:
(Slapping him on the shoulder) Ah, good old pal, how sits thy head upon thy shoulders?

Mr. Herrick:
I thank you gentlemen. I thank you. Am I not late?

Sir Hastings:
Not late according to the hour, but always do you come too late for those who love you, Bob.

Mr. Herrick:
I thank you Harry Hastings. Thou hast a tongue as nimble as thy sword.

Sir Peter:
Come, gentlemen, let's not dally paying compliments as men who 'tempt to storm a lady's heart with words, but to the wind. Am I too old to join you?

All:
No, no, come on, Sir Peter. The wine, the wine. *(They draw around the table. Will Playfair passes at back of Herrick saying in an aside as he goes "Drink thou not deep good Bob, remember this." They seat themselves at the tables.)*

Sir Peter:
Now Hastings, a song, a song to make the wine go down as smooth as melody itself.

Sir Hastings:
Nay, call you not on me. We have a singer here. *(Bows to Herrick.)*

Mr. Herrick:
Nay, look thou not at me good Hastings. My songs are as the crude and tumbling brook that ripples down to meet the stormy sea, coloured with earth and filled with leaves it finds beside the way; while thine is like the clear and trickling rill that purls o'er pebbles white, clear trained by the hand of man.

Mr. Wetheridge:
Hear, hear, how the poet talks in verse.

Mr. Playfair:
I prithee come to the wine.

Mr. Herrick:

Aye, to the wine. *(Looking strangely at Playfair)* And may it do the most good to the honestest man. *(They fill their mugs drinking.)*

Sir Peter:

And now, sing Sir Harry.

Sir Hastings:

(Sings)

> Come fill with me your drinking cup,
> And fill it to the brim,
> And he who will not drink it up
> A murrain, then, on him.

> *Chorus:*
> Come fill, good friends, and drink with me
> The juice that sparkles bright,
> We'll give us o'er to jollity
> And speed the hours to-night.
> Good wine it warmeth chilly blood,
> No chilly blood have we,
> Still we will drink the ruby flood,
> Lest cold we come to be.

All:

Bravo, bravo, good, good!

Sir Peter:

Fill, fill gentlemen.

Mr. Wetheridge:

Pipes, no, pipes! *(They lift their pipes and Will Playfair leans toward Herrick, whispering "I prithee drink not deep.")*

Mr. Herrick:

I thank thee Will.

Sir Peter:

I pray thee, fill, good Bob. The wine is light, and sure thy head is strong.

Mr. Herrick:

Nay, poets have not hearts nor heads too strong, and yet, because thou askest, I will fill. *(He fills his cup.)*

Sir Hastings:

No good without return. Herrick, let us hear something of thy sweet verse, something late, something with which thou hast charmed some maiden's willing ear.

Mr. Wetheridge:

Nay, nay, thou art rude. He sings not to charm the ears of ribald men.

Sir Peter:

(His spleen breaking out.) Ah, no, he tunes his notes to softer hearers' hearts, bah!

Mr. Herrick:

Nay, nay, Sir Peter, think me not an idle dangler at the ladies' heels. I pay my court to one, it is true, to whom no man who sits about this board dare say he doth not do likewise, and here, with all due respect before her father's face, list to me luteless give the "Song to Cynthia." *(As he rises, they fill his cup again. Wetheridge nods at Will Playfair. Playfair smokes in silence. Herrick rises a bit unsteadily. Hastings nods at Wetheridge, Wetheridge nods in turn.)*

Mr. Herrick:

(Looking off) What's that? *(They turn their heads. He quickly pours his wine upon the floor.)*

Sir Peter:

I saw naught.

Mr. Wetheridge:

Nor I.

Mr. Playfair:
Nor I.

Sir Hastings:
'Twas but some fantasy of thine own brain.

Mr. Herrick:
(Laughs unsteadily) The ghost, perhaps, of wasted yesterdays. *(He raises his cup)* Gazooks, but I be dry. *(Apparently drains it to the bottom. Quick glances flash around the table.)*

Sir Peter:
Fill it again, good Bob, ere thou dost speak, to mellow up thy voice. *(Herrick fills his cup unhandily, spilling the wine. Then he rises, and speaking thoughtfully, gives the poem "To Cynthia.")*

Mr. Herrick:

To Cynthia

Bid me to live and I will live
    Thy protestant to be;
Or bid me love and I will give
    A loving heart to thee.

A heart as soft, a heart as kind
    A heart as sound and free
As in the whole world thou canst find
    That heart I'll give to thee.

Bid that heart stay and it will stay,
    To honour thy decree;
Or bid it languish quite away
    And't shall do so for thee.

Bid me to weep and I will weep
    While I have eyes to see;
And having none, yet I will keep
    A heart to weep for thee.

Bid me despair, and I'll despair
  Under that cypress tree;
Or bid me die, and I will dare
  E'en Death to die for thee.

Thou art my life, my love, my heart,
  The very eyes of me,
And has command of every part
  To live and die for thee.

(All applaud, he lurches forward, spilling the wine from his cup.)

Sir Peter:
How now, man, hold thyself together. Art drunk so early?

Mr. Herrick:
Nay, nay, I am not drunk. I—I—am busy. I *(rising from the table and staggering forward)* I—I have a quatrain in my head. I fain would work it out. *(The others drink as he walks around.)* It's—it's—it's a story of the good Samaritan who fell among thieves. *(Burst of laughter from the table.)*

Mr. Playfair:
What, Bob, thou hast thy Scripture wrong. Why, thou must spend thy Sabbaths elsewhere than sitting 'neath the parson's voice.

Mr. Herrick:
(Looks at him drowsily) I spend my Sabbaths where God's preachers are, beneath the woodland trees, by running brooks, outside the breath of men's deceit. I say of men's deceit.

Sir Peter:
Come, come, it must not be thus gentlemen. Another bumper. Thou wilt not be drunk good Bob for thou must know the Lady Cynthia has returned and 'tis my will that she should come to us to-night to take your greetings.

Mr. Herrick:
Nay, nay, I will not be drunk. *(Staggering)* Aye, call Cynthia, but let me rest

here on this couch, and compose my quatrain. *(Drops on couch. The others rise stealthily, but go out staggeringly. Playfair lingers as he passes Herrick.)*

Mr. Playfair:
I told thee that thou shouldst tipple light.

Mr. Herrick
(In same low tone) Good Will, go on, I am safe. *(Exeunt. Herrick sits up on the couch. A servant comes in to remove the things, he lies down and snores ostensibly. When the servant has gone he rises.)*

Mr. Herrick:
This is the province of the poet, to wake when others sleep, to sleep perchance, when others wake, who knows? To be the jest of others and himself to jest. To love and be despised of his lessers. Ah, me, the world has fallen on evil days, when no one doth respect the poet's song and give him ear. 'Tis strange, 'tis passing strange, with good Will Shakespeare yet so shortly dead, and rare Ben Jonson singing still. Will had his Lucy and his stolen deer, and I my Temple and my stolen love, ha, ha, we go a merry gait who ride that fleet steed Pegasus, and feed on Fancy's bread. And yet, I'd rather be a singer chasing the fleeting rhyme and prisoning thoughts in pearls to grace another's wine than all the Lucy's and the Temple's that burden England's soil. For they, with minds as heavy as their wallets are, eat, drink, breathe, die, while we with souls as light as Fancy's self live on and on and on. Ha, ha.

> So come Sir Peter, with your minions, come
> You'll find your poet more than usual at home.

(Lies down. Re-enter Sir Peter leading Cynthia who is followed by her Aunt Lucinda. The gentlemen walk behind rather unsteadily. They point to Herrick, laughing.)

Cynthia:
And is this he whom you have brought me here to meet asleep?

Sir Hastings:
I will prod him for you lady. *(Touches Herrick with his sword. Herrick straightens up and looks about him drowsily. Gets up, half stumbling.)*

Sir Peter:
I have brought the Lady Cynthia to you, Master Robert Herrick. *(She gives him her hand and he takes it without a word.)*

Mr. Wetheridge:
Master Herrick has been giving us some of his verses, my lady to yourself. I doubt not but he hath more upon him.

Sir Hastings:
Aye, tax him for them.

Sir Peter:
My sister, Mistress Temple, thou knowest. *(Herrick bows to Miss Lucinda without a word.)*

Sir Hastings:
I prithee, lady, tax him for his lines. He cannot be niggardly when 'tis his sole wealth which he spends so lavishly.

Mr. Wetheridge:
(Laughing) Even with that he is poor. *(Herrick for the first time raises his head squarely flashing a glance at Wetheridge.)*

Cynthia:
I prithee, Master Herrick, do thou give us some few lines of thine own making.

Lucinda:
(Simpering) Aye, Master Herrick, something sentimental.

Mr. Wetheridge:
Yes, with youth and flowers and birds and loves and doves, ha, ha.

Cynthia:
(Coldly) Pray, Master Wetheridge, has thou not asked that I and my dear aunt prefer this fair request?

Mr. Wetheridge:
Your pardon, Lady Cynthia.

Cynthia:
Thou will, wilt thou not, good Master Herrick, as I say?

Mr. Herrick:
(Looks at her dazedly) Nay, nay.

Lucinda:
(Goes near him) Then try for me good Master Herrick. 'Tis long since I have heard thy lines.

Mr. Herrick:
Nay, nay, nay.

Mr. Wetheridge:
Our song bird now grows silent.

Mr. Playfair:
Perhaps our man is not i' the mood. Poets have moods, you know.

Cynthia:
Thou are well named Will Playfair.

Sir Hastings:
(Stung by Cynthia's manner) Ah, well, the ladies shall not be disappointed. If our poet will not sing his lines, I will sing myself.

Cynthia:
I did not know you wrote verses, Sir Harry.

Sir Hastings:
'Tis only a quatrain on a poet. Wilt hear it?

All:

Gladly.

Sir Hastings:

Well, say the poet is our Master Herrick. *(Herrick raises his head and looks at him. Hastings laughs.)*

> The hero of our idle hours,
> Who twangs his lute in ladies' bowers;
> His only pride is to be strong,
> His only strength lies in a song.

Mr. Wetheridge:
Sir Peter:
(together)

(Laughing) Good, good, ha, ha.

Mr. Herrick:

(Clapping his hand to his side) Gad! *(Playfair standing to one side and Cynthia turning away.)*

Cynthia:

Thou art too bad, Sir Harry.

Lucinda:

Indeed it has none of sentiment.

Mr. Herrick:

Have I served as the subject of that poem, Sir Harry? *(His hand to his side.)*

Sir Hastings:

(Laughing) As thou wilt, sit Poet. Why holdest thou thy hand to thy side, hast thou a pain? I see no other reason. Thou wearest no sword as I do.

Mr. Herrick:

(Dropping all affectation of drunkenness) No, Sir Harry, I wear my sword as thou dost thy wits, happily on occasion. It may be that thou shalt find it by

my side when next we meet. Then let us hope that I will use my sword less clumsily than thou usest thy wit. *(Hastings puts his hand to his sword.)*

Mr. Playfair:
Come, gentlemen, come.

Sir Peter:
Master Herrick, thou dost forget thyself.

Mr. Herrick:
I do not forget myself. I only now remember. I know not if it be you yourself, Sir Peter, who has set these cowards on to taunt me in this unmanly manner to put me to the test, but this I know, Robert Herrick doth defy you all and tells you now right here in your own house that poets know not only how to twang the lute and make a song, but how to wield a soldier's arm as well. And if these gentlemen singly come to put affront upon me, name your own weapons, and you shall find me deft as well with steel as with quill.

Sir Hastings:
A lusty braggart.

Mr. Wetheridge:
I will put that to the test, good Bob, some day.

Mr. Herrick:
Aye, make your some day not too long.

Cynthia:
Brave spoken gentlemen. I thank you for those words.

Sir Peter:
Cynthia!

Mr. Herrick:
I thank you lady for that small grace.

Sir Peter:

What, Cynthia! Thou takest sides with him, a drunkard and a brawler? *(To Herrick)* Out, sir, upon thee, out upon thee for a graceless scamp. Why thou art drunk.

Mr. Herrick:

Look not on me, Sir Peter, but on those others whom you have set on to make me drunk, who stand the steadier, they or I? Look on Sir Harry Hastings and on Wetheridge. I stand as straight in my boots as did my sires when they faced death upon a foreign field, and they, they waver as their fathers did when quailing at a foeman's shaft. You scorn me, aye, my verses and my art? You scorn me that I make my lines and love the sound of the absorbing lute, but let me tell thee, Robert Herrick's name shall live as good Chris Marlowe's doth when thou and all thou has art mould. Thou sayest I am drunk. Drunk with the wild winds and the breath of life. Drunk with the sweet wine of thy daughter's eyes. Drunk with the love of life and with mine own art. But with the poison that thou pourest in my cup, I tell thee, if thou sayest I am drunk, thou liest in thy throat, and these are Herrick's words. Look at thy minions how they droop. *(The two others are lying on couches in different attitudes of intoxication.)* Behold the fowlers caught within their own snare. When they awake, Sir Peter, then another plot. Good Mistress Cynthia, Madam dear, most humbly yours. *(Sir Peter fuming about, Cynthia delighted, Lucinda simpering.)*

Sir Peter:

A murrain on him, a murrain on him.

Mr. Herrick:

> You proved me sir, to your own sorrow
> Farewell, we'll meet again to-morrow.

(Exits jauntily, laughing.)

Curtain

Act II

Scene i: A garden path. Enter Cynthia and Lucinda, right.

Cynthia:
Ah, what a morning for a stroll.

Lucinda:
Aye, niece, it is most fair, nigh everyone's abroad.

Cynthia:
Methinks no soul remains within the house on a day like this unless it be those dullards who last night assayed to make Bob Herrick drunk, ha, ha, but I was like to kill myself with laughing. How they did stagger when he stood most straight, ha ha!

Lucinda:
Ah, Master Herrick's head is as strong as his heart.

Cynthia:
(Effusively) Well said, good Aunt Lucinda. Truly thou has a most discerning eye. This, this, is such a day as Bob would love.

Lucinda:
He would make a poem of it.

Cynthia:
It was my thought. He would make a song of it, and liken all the sunshine to some lady's hair.

Lucinda:
(Simpering) Ah, yes, I know.

Cynthia:
He would say that the glint upon the dew wet leaves was like the light within her eyes.

Lucinda:
(Enthusiastically) Would he not?

Cynthia:
That the perfume of the roses was her breath.

Lucinda:
Yes, yes.

Both:
(Hugging themselves) Oh, Bob!

Cynthia:
How well you love him, Aunt Lucinda.

Lucinda:
(Hiding her face) False one, and hast thou probed our secret so soon? Well, love we are a tell-tale face.

Cynthia:
Your secret? Tell-tale face? Ah—what—?

Lucinda:
Fie, thou dost dissemble now. But thine eyes were keen, ah, I for very joy of it could not hide myself from them. Long since I did mistrust that Herrick cast the eyes of love on me.

Cynthia:
(Restraining her mirth) I cannot doubt thee.

Lucinda:
But never were my eyes so fully oped until thy father spoke last night. Said he, "Lucinda, hast thou not seen?" "Not I" said I. "Bob Herrick loves thee," he pursued. "Loves me?" "Aye" quoth he, "loves thee, he is mad about thee. Aye, he hath worn a black cloak for love of thee, but poor timid bashful boy, fearing to approach and sue thee for thy maiden charms, he pays his court to Cynthia where full numbers gives him courage," and then I saw.

Cynthia:

Oh, then you saw.

Lucinda:

But thy keen eyes did fathom the whole plot, and thou hast found us out. So I'll be straight with Bob from this day forth and do your father's bidding, encourage him, keep him apart, hold him in conversation when that others surround you.

Cynthia:

(Giving way to mirth) Oh, good Aunt Lucinda, do. Keep him from all the other brawlers, for though I doubt not his bravery there be a many of them and he might come to harm, now since my suitors singly come to woo me this morning. Come away to your task good Aunt Lucinda. *(Laughing and running off)* Come away!

Lucinda:

(Ambling off) Oh, if Bob should see me running like this, a very hoyden. *(Stops, arranges her skirt, and walks sedately off. An interval passes and then a groan is heard from without. Enter Sir Harlowe Wetheridge slowly from the left.)*

Mr. Wetheridge:

Oh, my head, my head, it seems as if ten thousand furies warred together within, and would burst it asunder. Ah, one of the forces is in retreat now and is coming out on this side. Oh, let me rest awhile. *(Stands in center holding his head. Groan heard on the other side. Enter Sir Harry Hastings, backing in right.)*

Sir Hastings:

Ugh, the next time I try to make Bob Herrick drunk, a plague on him! My head, my head! If no one were looking I'd rest me here awhile. *(Walks into Wetheridge, they each start guiltily and take their hands from their head.)* Well met, Harlowe, I was—ah—admiring the beauty of the morning. *(Aside)* My head!

Mr. Wetheridge:
And I was but saying to myself that it was more than passing fair. *(Aside)* Oh, me!

Sir Hastings:
I must e'en have my walk after breakfast, or I'm broken for the day.

Mr. Wetheridge:
And I—I love the air.

Sir Hastings:
How bright and clear the sunlight is. *(Aside)* It's burning my brain.

Mr. Wetheridge:
And listen to that bird singing, how sweet! *(Aside)* Oh, if 'twould stop!

Sir Hastings:
I see thou lovest nature too.

Mr. Wetheridge:
Yes, 'tis that which brought me out. Nature compelled me.

Sir Hastings:
How sits thy head upon thy shoulders after last night's bout?

Mr. Wetheridge:
As lightly and joyously as ever, and how thine own?

Sir Hastings:
*(Aside)*Liar—Ah, mine is clear as is this morning's sky.

Mr. Wetheridge:
(Aside) Liar—A worthy simile.

Sir Hastings:
Wilt come and walk with me? *(Aside)* Heaven forbid. Forfend.

Mr. Wetheridge:
Aye gladly. *(Aside)* Oh, damn!

Sir Hastings:
Then come, thy arm, good Harlowe. *(Aside)* I need it.

Mr. Wetheridge:
Take both good Harry. *(Aside)* Wouldst thou couldst take my head as well.

Sir Hastings:
Now for the sunshine and the breeze *(aside)* and misery.

Mr. Wetheridge:
Now for a stroll *(aside)* and death. *(Exeunt both with forced jauntiness. Laugh heard from the left. Enter Will Playfair from left.)*

Mr. Playfair:
There they go, the two blundering fools lying to each other I'll warrant, about their easy heads. Herrick's worth two of them and yet because I rival him for Cynthia's hand, I seem as one of their ilk. Bah, I'm tired of it. It is sweet to get away for a while from the dust and stench of such an unworthy chase. 'Tis too much for me. After this, I'll hunt alone and never more join such a crowd. They stifle with all their planning and their plots. Oh, no, Will Playfair goes no more a gaming with a snare. He'll hunt in the open. *(Turning left)* But God 'a' mercy, whom have we here? Humph. Sir Peter and Sir Godfrey Gailspring. By the rood, if I thought that fatted fool did come a wooer for fair Cynthia's hand, I'd let his blood. Ah, the sight of him makes me sick; too young to be the dotard that he is, too old to be the clownish fool he looks. I'll away. *(Enter Sir Peter and Sir Godfrey Gailspring. Sir Godfrey is fat, short, red-faced, and far past forty. He clutches Sir Peter by the arm as they enter.)*

Sir Gailspring:
I pray you, hear me out, Sir Peter, I must apologize again.

Sir Peter:

But list to me again, Sir Godfrey. I speak truth when I say apologies do come unwelcome from your lips. You need none save for not coming sooner.

Sir Gailspring:

But dropping down upon a man at dead o' night without announcement and unasked.

Sir Peter:

Yourself announces you to us, Sir Godfrey, say no more.

Sir Gailspring:

I will speak on. It was all this way. I had no sooner got wind that there was to be a meeting of the maiden's suitors, then I cried, Gazooks, I'll have a try. I'm old I know, but I've looked on her since she was a little toddling babe, and she's grown as close to my heart as—as—as—well, as a filly that you have brought up by hand. So I got into my boots, called to my man to saddle my horse, and though I weigh more than I used to, and my years begin to tell, I came at hell's own pace. Damn me, I said, I'll be in at the death, and here I am.

Sir Peter:

I would you had been here last night to lay that coxcomb that I told you of. But 'twould have gripped thy gall to see his airs, but you shall see them for he comes again to-day.

Sir Gailspring:

Ah, would I had been there to lay him by the heels. I tell thee Sir Peter, though I do say it myself, I'm a man of parts.

Sir Peter:

Of most prodigious parts, ha, ha.

Sir Gailspring:

Hah, I'll hit.

Sir Peter:

Well, let us on.

Sir Gailspring:
Nay, nay, sir Peter, let us rest awhile, you know, I ride better than I walk.

Sir Peter:
Come, come, Sir Godfrey, if you fain would be a suitor for my daughter's hand you most of all must not be too late. I doubt not that the others are all there, even perchance Bob Herrick, who loiters by the way dreaming what words he'll woo my Cynthia in. Come, I've a rare joke to tell you when we're all assembled.

Sir Gailspring:
Ah, my poor shanks, ye do groan with your own prosperity, so it is in love. Stay, Sir Peter, let us moralize.

Sir Peter:
Art thou a suitor or no?

Sir Gailspring:
Suitor, yes, and would be husband, but if thou goest such a gait, thou'lt widow her at once, and make one of those jackanapes happy with both my fortune and herself.

Sir Peter:
Wilt come man?

Sir Gailspring:
Lead on. Oh my poor legs.
Thus age its folly and its wisdom shows,
When wooing changeful maids too slow it goes.
(Exeunt. Enter Herrick, dreamily and slow.)

Mr. Herrick:
How smilingly the sun looks on the earth,
Methinks, he's glad that Cynthia lives;
Glad with the gladness that I feel, when here alone
I do unbare my brow and know the joy
That she doth breathe this same perfumed air

Which laves my brow with its caressing touch.
Ah, Cynthia, 'tis thy breath perfumes the air.
Methought it was a rose. Ah, no, 'tis not,
No rose as sweet as thou ere sucked its life
And took its glory from the common earth.
If Heaven were a place for roses known
Thou wert a golden rose from Heaven blown,
And floating hither to this lowly place,
All other blooms would fade to see thy face.
And now a kiss to sun and day and air,
For they are glad with me that she is there;
Yes, 'tis the very essence of alloy
That mortals leap too soon unto their joy;
So, I will bide me here a little while,
Enjoy the morning and the morning's smile
And while I walk thy golden paths along
Weave to thee, Cynthia, my wooing song.
(Exit taking out tablets and writing.)
Scene ii: [setting] Same room as before in Sir Peter Temple's house. Curtain rises on empty stage. After an interval—enter Wetheridge and Hastings as from their stroll. They separate gladly and seat themselves on opposite sides of the room.

Mr. Wetheridge:
(Yawning) A fine stroll.

Sir Hastings:
(Yawning) Very fine.

Mr. Wetheridge:
I'm better for it.

Sir Hastings:
I was well at first.

Mr. Wetheridge:
I mean my spirits wear a brighter aspect.

Sir Hastings:
What, were they not so bright at first?

Mr. Wetheridge:
With such a rival in such a cause, the face of my spirits looked not too smilingly this morn.

Sir Hastings:
Ha, ha, my Wetheridge, thou liest well.

Mr. Wetheridge
And, thou, good Harry, art no poor dissembler. *(Rising)* Well, we are early in the field. Pray Heaven 'tis a good omen.

Sir Hastings:
(As Will Playfair enters) And not much earlier than Will Playfair. This earliness cannot be an omen for us all, e'en if it may be good.

Mr. Playfair:
Good morrow, gentlemen, how fare ye both?

Mr. Wetheridge:
With me as with a hunter who plies a hopeless chase.

Sir Hastings:
Methinks our Harlowe loses spirit.

Mr. Playfair:
So should we all who hunt with springes.

Sir Hastings:
Springes?

Mr. Playfair:
Aye.

Sir Hastings:
Methinks thy conscience comes to thee too late.

Mr. Wetheridge:
You do me wrong, Will Playfair, for 'tis not my method that doth sorrow me, but that every method seems to fail.

Mr. Playfair:
Then more's the pity.

Sir Hastings:
I fear we cannot join thee in thy moralizing, Will.

Mr. Playfair:
Thou wilt when thy wooing is done, but peace, here comes the lady's father. *(Enter Sir Peter and Sir Godfrey.)*

Sir Peter:
What, gentlemen? All here? You are most punctual, especially after last night's rout.

Sir Hastings:
We suffered no discomfort sir, our love did prove our shield.

Sir Gailspring:
All youth woos hotly.

Mr. Playfair:
And age should never woo at all.

Sir Peter:
Peace, Will, this is my good friend Sir Godfrey Gailspring, who will be thy rival too.

Sir Gailspring:
Ah, say not peace to Will, I'll take no harm of him. I knew his father, an out-

spoken man as ever tipped a cup. I was younger then, 'tis true, and his father was much older.

Mr. Playfair:
And for thy business should be younger now.

Sir Peter:
Will!

Sir Gailspring:
Anon, Will, anon,—thy hands, Wetheridge and Hastings there.

Sir Hastings:
Sir Godfrey.

Mr. Wetheridge:
I am glad to see you.

Sir Gailspring:
A lusty pair of bucks I have to fight in you. If I come not out from this encounter basted like a pheasant, then my little wisdom belies my whitened hair. Now, Will, thou dost object to me, but I—I'm not so old. I've as good a leg as the best o' ye.

All:
Ha, ha, ha, behold!

Sir Gailspring:
Oh, laugh, laugh, but I've an arm.

Sir Hastings:
Like an o'er fatted leg o' mutton.

Sir Gailspring:
And I can drink my cup 'gainst you all.

Sir Peter:
Ha, ha, well turned on them, Sir Godfrey, well turned, had you been here yesternight, we'd 'a' cropt the feathers of a strutting cock, but these youths—

Mr. Wetheridge:
We cry you mercy.

Sir Hastings:
Spare us my Lord.

Mr. Playfair:
Nay, tell not on us, we have weaker heads than Herrick, both as to what we may put in and what we may take out.

Sir Hastings:
Herrick—

Mr. Wetheridge:
What's that?

Sir Peter:
Bah!

Sir Gailspring:
Why, I must see this wondrous dog of whom Will Playfair speaks so well.

Sir Peter:
He's but a graceless scamp who needs trouncing to medicine his manners. But I promised thee a joke before he comes.

Sir Gailspring:
Aye, thou didst. *(They gather around.)*

Sir Hastings:
A joke on Herrick—good.

Mr. Wetheridge:
I hope 'twill be a bitter one.

Mr. Playfair:
It was last night.

Sir Peter:
Ah!

Sir Hastings:
Thou raven!

Sir Peter:
'Tis this. When that the Lady Cynthia comes to ply her needle in this present room, her Aunt Lucinda shall accompany her. Lucinda, now, has passed the age of choice and looks on Herrick with indulgent eyes. Remembering this, her have I told that Herrick loves her fondly, but still fears to speak, and bade her give him courage, hold him still apart in converse while you gentlemen do pay my Cynthia court.

All:
Ha, ha, ha, capital!

Sir Gailspring:
Body o' me! I've not laughed so since old Squire Avery's favorite mare was taken with the bots, ha, ha, ha!

Sir Peter:
Peace, peace, that's not all. When he is well engaged, we'll all slip out and leave him there alone with Lucinda. *(Cries "Good, Good!" Sir Godfrey explodes with laughter.)* And if he follow, why later on, Lucinda and her niece shall return where each may singly press his suit.

All:
(Except Will Playfair) Well planned.

Sir Peter:
If Cynthia will none of you, then back to the country she goes.

Sir Hastings:
(Starting forward) I have it.

Sir Peter:
Mr. Wetheridge:
(together)
What is it?

Sir Gailspring:
Egad, the boy startled me.

Sir Hastings:
We'll lay him by the heels. *(To Sir Peter)* If she refuses us and goes back to the country, your way is cross the moors?

Sir Peter:
Yes.

Sir Hastings:
Canst go at night?

Sir Peter:
At night? What is't? Thy question's strange when thou dost know that then the worst of all the robbers who do molest London and its confines plies his trade when he doth visit us i' the country.

Sir Hastings:
That's what I mean. Canst go at night?

Sir Peter:
That's what thou meanest? Art mad?

Sir Hastings:
Nay, canst thou not see? Will Playfair here, good Harlowe, Sir Godfrey and myself, we shall be Turpin and his men. Herrick shall be your guard. A lonely road, a night attack he flies disgraced, and then the lady will choose among us. This if our suit fail.

Sir Peter:
Good, 'tis worthy of thee.

Sir Gailspring:
'Twere a jolly game.

Mr. Wetheridge:
Your hand. I do agree.

Mr. Playfair:
Stop, I'll none of it. Will Playfair plays no more in such a game.

Sir Hastings:
Mayhap he'd rather play the tell-tale?

Mr. Playfair:
What sayest thou? I am no tell-tale, I can prove it at thy throat. I'll hold my tongue, but not my sword. *(They both draw.)*

Sir Peter:
Stop gentlemen, stop, you have no quarrel, put up your swords. *(They withdraw.)* No man can be forced into our game who likes it not. Will likes it not, so he withholds his voice from us from our enemy. We need no promise from his honest lips. *(Will bows.)*

Sir Gailspring:
Egad, the man hath taught my years a lesson. I'll not go in it. It smells too strong of trickery.

Sir Hastings:
Thou'rt zealous grown, Sir Godfrey, but then late zeal were ever zealous.

Sir Gailspring:
(Bursting into a laugh) Harry, thou art for all the world like a cock we killed the other day, he was young, but far too lusty for the barn-yard. *(Hastings makes a motion to draw.)* Ah, boy, keep thy temper and thy sword, or thou'lt have goodly cause to think upon thy mother and her ready hand.

Sir Peter:
Harry, thou art too hot of head.

Sir Hastings:
I have no quarrel with him nor any one.

Sir Peter:
But here, I cannot choose this Herrick for our guide.

Sir Hastings:
If she do say us no, we'll proffer still ourselves to be your guide, but she will choose him for herself.

All:
(Save Will P.) True, true.

Sir Hastings:
So Harlowe, you agree?

Mr. Wetheridge:
So be it, if my suit goes wrong.

Sir Gailspring:
What men will do to win a woman. I really do believe I'd be a rascal too if I were young and hot of blood. *(The door is flung open and Herrick enters.)*

Mr. Herrick:
Good morrow, gentlemen. *(Silence.)* You pause as though my name were lately on your tongue.

Sir Hastings:
So great a man must think his name on all men's tongues.

Mr. Herrick:
Witty as ever.

Mr. Playfair:
Good morrow, Bob.

Mr. Herrick:
Your servant, Will, good Harlowe and Sir Peter.

Sir Peter:
And my good friend Sir Godfrey Gailspring. *(They bow. Enter servant bringing embroidery frame.)*

Mr. Herrick:
How now, what have ye all been good or bad enough to say of me?

Sir Peter:
We'll speak of that anon. You see my daughter comes. *(They move toward door center, Sir Gailspring and Sir Peter, Wetheridge and Hastings together, and Playfair and Herrick near each other as Cynthia enters. They bow. Enter Lucinda.)*

Cynthia:
Good morrow, gentlemen.

Sir Hastings:
Let me arrange your chair.

Mr. Playfair:
And me this cushion for your feet.

Mr. Herrick:
I'll—

Lucinda:

(Hurrying forward) Ah, there is Master Herrick now. *(Taking him by the arm and leading him apart)* I have a word for thee, good Bob, thou naughty one. *(He goes reluctantly, his eyes turning to Cynthia, who has seated herself.)*

Mr. Wetheridge:

Madam, I can do no more than set your frame.

Cynthia:

I thank you gentlemen, but this cushion is not right.

Sir Gailspring:

I'll fix it better, I'm older and know how.

Lucinda:

(After talking in dumb show) Thou really art too bad.

Mr. Herrick:

(Always turning to Cynthia) And how?

Lucinda:

Thou'st hidden something from me. *(Hastings and Wetheridge watch her with smiles.)*

Mr. Herrick:

I?

Cynthia:

The cushion's better, but the chair doth hurt my back. *(They all spring to set the chair aright.)*

Lucinda:

Who would have thought thee half so timid as thou art?

Mr. Herrick:

I am not timid save 'neath the eyes of her I love. *(Looking at Cynthia.)*

Lucinda:
(Bridling) Oh, Robert, not so loud, they'll hear thee.

Cynthia:
There, I have dropped my skein of silk. *(They get down to search for it. Herrick looks at her in agony. Aside)* She keeps him over long talking. *(To the searchers)* Nay, I have it. 'Twas not dropped after all. The frame's not setting right. I cannot work this way. *(They spring to set in right.)*

Lucinda:
Come tell me all.

Mr. Herrick:
All what?

Lucinda:
Fie, fie, I know it all—thy secret.

Mr. Herrick:
Thou dost? Bless thee, but breathe it low here.

Lucinda:
Ah, yes, I'll breathe it low.

Cynthia:
'Tis not right yet. Ye all are clumsy. Bob, wilt thou come and set my frame? *(He rushes away from Lucinda, she following and clutching his arm.)*

Lucinda:
Come away.

Mr. Herrick:
An' it please thee, Cynthia. I'll set thy frame. *(Hastings and Wetheridge turn away. Will Playfair holds his place behind her chair. Herrick sets the frame.)*

Lucinda:
Come away now.

Mr. Herrick:
Is't right?

Cynthia:
Aye. Wilt thou not stay and hold it so?

Mr. Herrick:
An' it please thee. *(Lucinda retires.)*

Sir Peter:
Cynthia, thou art petulant to-day.

Cynthia:
Nay father, I am very satisfied.

Sir Gailspring:
Body o' mine, but she looks it.

Cynthia:
(To Herrick) Wilt hold this silk?

Mr. Herrick:
(Their hands touching) Aye, at my life's cost. *(Re-enter Lucinda with her frame.)*

Lucinda:
Wilt thou set my frame, good Bob, thou art so good at it? *(Nods, smiles, and nudges passed among the conspirators, and Sir Gailspring holds his lips to keep from laughing.)*

Cynthia:
I cannot spare him. *(With consternation)* Go, thou, Sir Harlowe Wetheridge, set Aunt Lucinda's frame and see thou dost it better than thou didst mine or sir Harry, here, shall rival thee. *(Wetheridge goes reluctantly. Cynthia works on.)*

Sir Peter:
The devil!

Sir Hastings:
(Aside) The game goes all awry. 'Tis time for me to play. *(To her)* At last thou findest thy vocation, Bob.

Mr. Herrick:
Thou still hast far to hunt. *(Sir Gailspring scarce restrains his mirth, while Sir Peter is fuming.)*

Sir Hastings:
The sign of my vocation's here. *(Tapping his sword)* And thou, I see, dost wear thy sword.

Mr. Herrick:
Aye, and an unaching head, dost thou wear both?

Sir Gailspring:
Ha, ha, ha, true, true, he had thee there, Sir Hal, he had thee there. *(Hastings starts angrily, but Playfair restrains him.)*

Sir Peter:
Hush, thou old fool, dost thou not see that this game goes wrong?

Sir Gailspring:
I cannot help it, 'tis too rich, 'tis too rich.

Sir Peter:
Ninnies, dullards, cannot they answer him? She smiles at him, he grows apace in Cynthia's eyes.

Mr. Wetheridge:
(As if to Hastings in a loud voice) Our poet wears his sword awry.

Mr. Herrick:
Perhaps, but like my heart, still at the command of this, the fairest lady in the land.

Sir Gailspring:
The dog! I'll have a try at him myself. You know, Sir Peter, I used to be accounted a man of some wit.

Sir Peter:
Well, don't bungle, it's bad enough.

Sir Gailspring:
(Approaching her) What wearest thou that butcher's career for?

Mr. Herrick:
For killing fatted oxen in their time. Art ready? *(Sir Gailspring turns away in amazement at first, then bursts into a shout of laughter.)*

Sir Gailspring:
Why, damme, damme, the fellow's got a pretty wit.

Sir Peter:
Hush, you fool. *(Sir Gailspring subsides.)* Come gentlemen, I've promised you a game or two, come let us go and let the ladies work, and as we play, we'll find who first comes back to win my daughter's smile. *(Exit severally. Herrick still holding frame. Sir Peter returning.)* Master Herrick, we await you.

Cynthia:
(With a sigh) You may go Bob.

Mr. Herrick:
I go reluctantly.

Lucinda:
Ah, Bob.

Mr. Herrick:
Anon, anon. *(Exits with Sir Peter.)*

Cynthia:
Now must I be all industry, and thou, good Aunt Lucinda, all discretion. *(They work.)* Am I not like a lady in a tower? *(Works.)* With suitors warring beneath her casement to win her smiles? Ah, the victorious one will soon be here, and thou must have no ears.

Lucinda:
Oh, I'll be deaf, thou minx, for I've a suitor, too.

Cynthia:
(Laughing) 'Tis time.

Lucinda:
Out on thee, sauce box.

Cynthia:
(Dreaming) Look how I work.

Lucinda:
To thy task, girl. Thy father will come upon thee idling.

Cynthia:
(Falling to) He must not. Oh, but I will work. *(Pause)* Is't not quite like Penelope?

Lucinda:
(Shocked) You shock me child. Penelope was married.

Cynthia:
Ah, so she was. *(Sighing)* But I mean, am I not like her, that I work while my suitors wait for me and when my work is done, I shall be done for? *(A step without.)* One comes, even now. Oh, this is martyrdom. *(She works feverishly. Enter Wetheridge.)*

Mr. Wetheridge:
Ah, Cynthia, fair Cynthia. I've drawn the lot that gives me right to be the first to tell thee of my love.

Cynthia:
Thou art unfortunate.

Mr. Wetheridge:
Unfortunate, and why?

Cynthia:
For hadst thou come the last, thou hadst been the last refused.

Mr. Wetheridge:
Refused?

Cynthia:
Aye, Harlowe, thou art so good a friend I'll keep thee where thou servest best. I'll not make a bad lover of so good a friend.

Mr. Wetheridge:
This is thy final word good lady?

Cynthia:
My final word. *(He bows himself out in silence.)* One!

Lucinda:
(Wiping her eyes) Poor young man, he's quite heart broken. It was so sentimental.

Cynthia:
I thought that thou wert deaf?

Lucinda:
I am, and blind as well, but still I have my intuitions.

Cynthia:

True, true, that's what the housemaid useth at my chamber door. Fie!

Lucinda:

Back to thy work, chatter-box.

Cynthia:

(Working and singing)
> Within my 'broidery frame,
> I'll weave my true love's name,
> Ere he comes a wooing.

Lucinda:

Thou art so frivolous.

Cynthia:

When men woo, need women weep? *(Enter Will Playfair.)*

Mr. Playfair:

I only come Cynthia, to give thee full assurance of my love. I know my answer e'er thou givest it, for I have seen thy look of love and know on whom it rests.

Cynthia:

(Rising and seriously) Good Will, I would my answer might be different to thee, for thou of all who ever sought my hand hast touched it more than any man save one. Thou sayest thou knowest who this is. I give thee leave, my love is not ashamed to face thy honesty. I like thee for thy truth, for thy plain-spoken truth. Wilt be my friend? *(Offering her hand. He kisses it.)*

Mr. Playfair:

Ever and always, good my lady. My heart and hand are thine still to command. *(Exits.)*

Cynthia:

Now mayest thou weep, aye weep for him. There went a man. *(Door is impetuously thrown open and Hastings rushes in.)*

Sir Hastings:

At last, Cynthia, my love, I come to thee. I have fair burned to throw me here before thy feet and tell thee how I love thee. Thou canst not refuse.

Cynthia:

Ah, can I not? *(Works on.)*

Sir Hastings:

Nay, do not flout me dear, my heart—

Cynthia:

How is thy head?

Sir Hastings:

My head?

Cynthia:

On yesternight 'twas fuller than thy heart.

Sir Hastings:

    Nay, do not jest but hear me.
        Ah, darling, say not nay
        Thou art my sun, my day
        If thine eyes did not shine,
        Eternal night were mine.

Cynthia:

        The hero of our idle hours,
        Who twangs his lute in ladies' bowers,
        His only pride is to be strong,
        His only strength lies in a song.

What, dost thou dare to woo me in the words of him thou feign'st to scorn? Rise up, Sir Harry Hastings. Go thy ways. Already have I seen thee at too close a range. *(He rises reluctantly, going.)*

Sir Hastings:

Ah, well, mayhap thou'dst rather have the author speak his lines?

Cynthia:

Mayhap. *(Exit Hastings.)* Aunt Lucinda, an' I were a man I'd kill yon churl for the good of his soul.

Lucinda:

Oh, thou wert ever bloodthirsty niece. Just think, when thy wert a little maid I saw thee kill a beetle.

Cynthia:

Hum, with less scorn than I'd have for letting Hastings' blood.

Lucinda:

But whom wilt thou accept my dear?

Cynthia:

None if they come not better than he. *(Noise outside.)*

Lucinda:

Another. To thy work. *(Enter Sir Godfrey slowly. He comes down to Cynthia. She puts her face close to her work. He deliberately and somewhat painfully gets down on one knee, and then on the other. Cynthia has been trying not to laugh, but when Sir Gailspring finally plumps down on both knees, she bursts into a peal of laughter. Sir Gailspring looks at her a moment and then joins her. He rises and holds his sides. She rises and holds hers. Miss Lucinda gives every evidence of being shocked.)*

Cynthia:

Oh, Sir Godfrey. *(Breaking out again.)*

Sir Gailspring:

Child, child! *(He breaks down. They laugh every time they look at each other.)*

Cynthia:

Your pardon. Ha, ha, ha.

Sir Gailspring:
That's right, child, child, child, ha, ha, ha. I'm an old fool. I knew thee when thou wert a baby, and now come a-wooing thee, ha, ha, ha. Well, never mind, good wine and a good table are better than many damsels. *(He goes to the door but turns to look back, they both laugh and his shouts can be heard long after the door is closed.)*

Lucinda:
I think it was perfectly shocking. A wooing should be a very serious affair. *(Still laughing.)*

Cynthia:
I should think it would be with you, Aunt Lucinda.

Lucinda:
Thou shalt see how I behave when my suitor comes. *(She arranges her skirts and sits primly as the door opens. Enter Herrick. Lucinda drops her head and alternately simpers and sighs in the moment he pauses at the door. Then he comes to Cynthia.)*

/

Mr. Herrick:
Cynthia, at last!

Lucinda:
(Running over to him) Thou base man, thou deceiver.

Mr. Herrick:
Deceiver?

Cynthia:
Good Aunt Lucinda, give us leave.

Lucinda:
But this is my lover, thy father told me so.

Mr. Herrick:

Thy lover? Her father? And who shall speak for Herrick save Herrick's self?

Cynthia:

Pray, give us leave, good Aunt Lucinda. *(Lucinda goes toward door, still weeping, when it is suddenly thrown open and Sir Peter enters, followed by the rest.)*

Sir Peter:

I pray thee Master Poet, is thy wooing done?

Mr. Herrick:

How now, Sir Peter, I have but come in.

Sir Peter:

No matter, we must go. The lady Cynthia returns her to the country.

Mr. Herrick:

A trick. She shall not go.

Cynthia:

Nay, nay, not that, I love thee, hush.

Sir Peter:

What man says shall not to her father's face?

Mr. Herrick:

I crave your pardon sir. You drove me mad. I do submit!

Mr. Wetheridge:

But good Sir Peter, if you start e'en now, the night will find you on the moor where Turpin and his robbers ply.

Sir Peter:

I care not, I will go.

Mr. Wetheridge:
Then let me be your daughter's guard, good sir.

Sir Hastings:
Nay, let me go.

Mr. Herrick:
I proffer thee myself. *(Sir Gailspring and Will Playfair silent.)*

Sir Hastings:
(Aside to Wetheridge) Note her flashing eye. The poison works. *(To all)* Sir Peter hesitates. Let us then all draw lots.

Sir Peter:
Aye, that will do. You four. *(Indicating Hastings, Wetheridge, Playfair, and Sir Gailspring.)* Draw lots and he whom Fate allows shall be the guard. *(They are grouping themselves together.)*

Cynthia:
Stay!

Sir Peter:
Tut, tut!

Cynthia:
I'll have my say though Temple Towers come tumbling round my ears.

Sir Gailspring:
Whew! My single blessedness remains to me.

Cynthia:
Is this the way to storm a woman's heart, by tricks, by insult, and by foul deceit? Oh, fie! Shame on ye, and most on you, my father. What are these friends that you have gathered here, buyers and sellers of our woman-hood? Out on ye all, I'll have no more of it, what—what am I, the Mistress Cynthia, to be played and bartered, schemed and bargained for? I'll have no more of it. My

escort back into the country I will choose and choose him for myself. And he'll go with me, I'll have no one but him—Bob Herrick. *(Herrick takes her hand.)*

Lucinda:
Shocking!

Sir Gailspring:
Blessed bachelor-hood!

Sir Peter:
Damn!

Curtain

Act III

Scene: [setting] A lonely road with a forest bordering on it. Wetheridge and Hastings discovered lurking on one side. Both are masked.

Sir Hastings:
'Tis a lonesome night and methinks my lord and lady devilish slow.

Mr. Wetheridge:
Mayhap the real Dick Turpin and his men have met them further down the road and mean to spare our pains.

Sir Hastings:
I would not have it so, for I've an old account to settle with this Herrick.

Mr. Wetheridge:
Our present venture, tho', is for our mirth and his discomfiture.

Sir Hastings:
The way to pay old scores is on the earliest chance.

Mr. Wetheridge:
Thou wouldst not really harm the man?

Sir Hastings:
Watch then and see. I hate him, my sword doth know my hate, and even tho' I felt constrained to let him go unscathed, 'twould leap forth undirected to his heart.

Mr. Wetheridge:
We have as good as promised tho' he shall not come to harm.

Sir Hastings:
What the lips promise the sword may break. My good sword promised naught.

Mr. Wetheridge:
Well, as you will. *(Unmasking)* I prithee Hal, unmask. 'Tis ghastly seeing but that sombre patch in all this sombreness.

Sir Hastings:
What if he come upon us and we bare of face?

Mr. Wetheridge:
We can soon mask.

Sir Hastings:
(Unmasking) Then too, we'd note their near approach by warning of the coach's wheels.

Mr. Wetheridge:
That's better. 'Tis a gruesome watch without our faces being covered from each other.

Sir Hastings:
I do confess I do not like the place.

Mr. Wetheridge:
'Tis such a place as the real robbers whom we feign, would choose.

Sir Hastings:
(Starting) Methought I heard a horse neigh.

Mr. Wetheridge:
I heard naught.

Sir Hastings:
My expectation doth outride my sense. I hear my Herrick ere he comes.

Mr. Wetheridge:
Hush, was that hoof-beats on the turf?

Sir Hastings:
Nay, I heard naught. Fie, are we women to be so alarmed?

Mr. Wetheridge:
I like it not.

Sir Hastings:
Then look thee to thy sword. What's that? *(They draw close together.)*

Mr. Wetheridge:
Come, come, we are unnerved.

Sir Hastings:
Not I, but then, I do not like this place. *(Suddenly enter two robbers.)*

Robbers:
Yield, yield.

Sir Hastings:
Turpin's men, fly, fly! *(They rush out followed by robbers. Re-enter robbers, laughing.)*

1st Robber:
Egad, they did run like frightened deer when the huntsmen to the windward.

2nd Robber:
Aye, and did bellow like young calves.

1st Robber:
What did they loitering here?

2nd Robber:
From what I overheard, they wait some one whose coach is due to pass this way.

1st Robber:
And what of that?

2nd Robber:
I do not know whether they are a pair of blades who have a mind to take a taste of our trade or whether 'twas a prank in mind.

1st Robber:
In either case, we'll take their place and do their work better.

2nd Robber:
Aye, 'tis plain we've had more practice. *(Coach wheels heard, then shouts, and a loud noise as if the coach had broken down.)* But listen, methinks our game approaches. Let's retire a little distance and stalk it.

1st Robber:
Our devils have been good to us and thrown the prey into our very hands. *(They retire a little up the woodland path. Enter Sir Peter, fuming.)*

Sir Peter:
'Tis the devil's own work that we should be wrecked just here.

1st Robber:
(Aside) Just what I said.

Sir Peter:
It couldn't have been at a worse place, and not a sign of those other two fools. *(Turning around)* Come on, come on I say. Cynthia, why do ye lag behind? Lucinda! *(Enter Lucinda.)*

Lucinda:
Ah, is this not romantic?

Sir Peter:
Ah romantic! Body o' me. Out upon thy romance. What would you? Be upset in a morass and then talk to me of romance? *(Turning again)* Cynthia, why dost thou lag? Art helping that dolt to mend the coach? Thou wouldst better mend thy pace. *(Enter Cynthia escorted by Herrick.)*

Cynthia:
I was so frightened that I needed help and Bob was kind enough to help me.

Sir Peter:
Oh, Bob is wondrous kind. I would he had been kind enough to kill yon coachman ere I took him forth.

Mr. Herrick:
Sit here, upon this hummock, ladies. *(To Sir Peter)* I'll kill him now an' it please you.

2nd Robber:
I like him not, 'tis a blood-thirsty blade.

1st Robber:
If he drink blood he'll bleed the easier.

Cynthia:
Oh, talk you not of killing, it makes me shudder.

Lucinda:
And me.

Sir Peter:

When will that fool get the coach aright?

Mr. Herrick:

'Twill take an hour.

Sir Peter:

If curses were wasps I'd let a flock on him and sting him into better sense.

Mr. Herrick:

I have some knack of hand, I'll go and help him.

Cynthia:
Lucinda:
(together)
(Seizing him) Oh, leave us not.

Sir Peter:

How all the fiends seize me! Dost think I am too old to keep you safe?

Cynthia:

Nay, father, but—

Lucinda:

Nay, nay, but—

Sir Peter:

But me no buts, I'll not drink shame from out your cup of fear. Herrick go on.

Mr. Herrick:

But—

Sir Peter:

But me no buts I say, go on. *(Herrick bows and starts.)*

Cynthia:

Oh!

Lucinda:
Oh!

Sir Peter:
What is't?

Cynthia:
Methought I heard a noise.

Lucinda:
Methought I saw a shape.

Cynthia:
Lucinda:
(together)
Oh!

Cynthia:
Ah, 'tis a fearsome place.

Lucinda:
Just the spot for a murder. Oh!

Cynthia:
Oh!

Sir Peter:
Stay, Herrick, those women make me nervous.

Mr. Herrick:
It is most natural, Sir Peter, 'tis the nature of the sex.

Cynthia:
Nay, I'm not afraid.

Lucinda:
Nor I.

Both:
(Shuddering) Oh!

Cynthia:
The mishap's most amusing.

Lucinda:
And passing sentimental.

Sir Peter:
Oh, that sentimentality of yours again. *(Aside)* I wonder where those two fools are? *(Looks off.)*

Mr. Herrick:
From yon poor fellow's face, the coach mends slowly. Mayhap I'll find a place comfortable, let me explore. *(Walks direct toward place where robbers are hiding. They rush forth upon him.)*

1st Robber:
Stand ho! *(Herrick draws.)*

Cynthia:
Lucinda:
(together)
Oh!

Sir Peter:
They come at last. *(Herrick engages first robber and keeps him in play while he turns over from the thrust of the second.)*

Sir Peter:
(Chuckling) Fly, Herrick, fly, and leave us to our fate.

Mr. Herrick:
If I do may I be damned.

1st Robber:
Why playest thou, Roderick? Come in.

Mr. Herrick:
I'll prick thee ere he come.

Sir Peter:
Stop, stop, you know not what you do.

Mr. Herrick:
I'll learn ere I am through.

2nd Robber:
His point is everywhere.

1st Robber:
(Staggering) Oh, I'm hit. Fly Roderick, he is the devil's own. *(Falls.)*

Mr. Herrick:
(To 2nd robber) Have at you fellow, point to point. *(They fight.)*

Sir Peter:
I bid you stop, stop!

Mr. Herrick:
I'll never stop while I can breathe.

Sir Peter:
Look what you've done, they're friends.

Mr. Herrick:
I'll test their friendship.

Sir Peter:
'Tis but a joke, I tell thee, but a joke.

Mr. Herrick:
'Twill have a bitter tag. Look to thyself. *(He exits fighting with robber.)*

Sir Peter:
Oh, how the joke turns out, he's done for one of them.

Cynthia:
Art not thou glad, and will he not be hurt?

Lucinda:
Ah, but he is a gallant gentleman.

Sir Peter:
Silence, ye do not know. *(Seating himself on the hummock his head in his hands.)* Two gallant gentlemen, so young, so brave, ah, me!

Cynthia:
What is it father?

Sir Peter:
(Pointing to robber) Look, there lies either Harry Hastings or Wetheridge, pinked like a fowl at Michaelmas.

Cynthia:
Hastings?

Lucinda:
Wetheridge?

Sir Peter:
Look.

Cynthia:
I dare not, but how came they here in such a guise?

Sir Peter:
'Twas but a joke to take Bob Herrick down, oh me!

Cynthia:
A joke, fie, father, fie!

Sir Peter:
Look on the poor man's face and tell me which it is.

Cynthia:
I cannot look.

Sir Peter:
(To Lucinda) Do thou.

Lucinda:
I dare not look.

Sir Peter:
Nor I. We'll let Bob Herrick note for himself if he returneth whole of skin.

Cynthia:
He had the best of the whole fight.

Lucinda:
He is a gallant gentleman.

Sir Peter:
He is the very devil.

Cynthia:
Look how he comes bloody and raging back. *(Re-enter Herrick, bloody and wild.)* Bob!

Mr. Herrick:
He did escape me, he did escape. I pricked him in the arm and then he fled. My blood boils like a cauldron. This it is to fight, to fight! Ha, ha! He would sing sweet songs and twang his lute when his strong arm and his good sword speak better, sweeter than his tongue? Oh, music of the steel when it clashes steel, and the soft feel when it striketh flesh, 'tis dearer than the touch of

maiden's hand. Oh, sword of mine, thou wert athirst, but thou has drunk, drunk, drunk!

Cynthia:
Bob!

Mr. Herrick:
(Dazed, but recovering) What—ah Cynthia, art thou safe?

Cynthia:
Yes, and thou?

Mr. Herrick:
Unharmed.

Cynthia:
But—

Mr. Herrick:
Why look ye all so pale?

Sir Peter:
I bade thee stop in time.

Mr. Herrick:
What dost thou mean?

Sir Peter:
Thy hot head hast laid low a friendly soul.

Mr. Herrick:
I do not understand.

Sir Peter:
'Twas but a plot to frighten thee. These were no robbers, but our worthy Hal Hastings and good Wetheridge.

Mr. Herrick:
What?

Sir Peter:
(Sadly) One now lies there.

Mr. Herrick:
God a' Mercy! *(Rushing to robber and tearing off his mask. He starts upright. Sir Peter turns away in grief.)* I have forgot the faces of our friends if this be one. *(Sir Peter starts and looks.)*

Sir Peter:
'Tis neither one. Thy sword hath saved us.

1st Robber:
(Groaning) Oh, I am badly hurt.

Sir Peter:
What art thou fellow?

1st Robber:
An honest robber, one of Dick Turpin's men.

Cynthia:
Turpin, ugh!

Lucinda:
How very romantic.

Mr. Herrick:
This is the friend whom thou wouldst have me spare?

Sir Peter:
Lay not the measure of thy scorn so strong upon me, Herrick.

1st Robber:
Water.

Mr. Herrick:
He craves drink.

Lucinda:
I'll go fetch it, poor man. *(Exits.)*

Cynthia:
Thou has saved us after all, good Bob, in spite of all that they would put on thee.

Sir Peter:
And now I wonder where the others are. I'll call, they may be further up the road.

Cynthia:
Nay, call not, mayhap it will attract more robbers and Robert is already spent with fighting.

Mr. Herrick:
Nay, my lady, I am but heated to the fray.

Sir Peter:
Robert, Robert, body o' me, ye'd think no one was here but Robert. What, healthy father lost his arms that he can no more wield a sword? Let Robert be. If he be spent I am not.

Mr. Herrick:
Nor am I Sir Peter. If more come on us, back to back, shoulder to shoulder, heel to heel, we'd keep a score at bay.

Sir Peter:
Eh? Now, thou speakest like the man thou art. *(Catching himself)* Oh, a murrain on thee, thou wilt win me ere I know. Go to, what thou has done, nigh any man could do.

Mr. Herrick:
Aye, any man with a strong arm made stronger by the glance of his lady's eye.

Sir Peter:
Ever, thy oiled tongue.

Cynthia:
It leaps not quicker than his valiant sword.

Sir Peter:
Cynthia!

Mr. Herrick:
My love!

1st Robber:
Water. *(Re-enter Lucinda, with cup.)*

Lucinda:
I come. *(She holds cup to the wounded man's lips.)*

1st Robber:
Thou art an angel.

Lucinda:
Ah, he calls me an angel.

1st Robber:
An' hast been one for a long time.

Lucinda:
(Softly) I have been one for a long time. *(Suddenly)* How, now, what meanest thou?—a long time? Oh! *(Rises and moves away.)*

Sir Peter:
The coach mends slowly. I will call and see if Hastings and our Harlowe be about. *(Goes up stage calling)* Hollo, hollo, hollo! Hastings! Wetheridge!

Voices Without:
Hollo! Hollo!

Sir Peter:
They come. Hollo!

Voices:
Hollo! Hollo! *(Enter Hastings and Wetheridge. Hastily.)*

Sir Hastings:
We waited for you up the road.

Mr. Wetheridge:
Aye, up the road.

Sir Peter:
Why, we have been attacked.

Sir Hastings:
And we ourselves, have had a fierce encounter.

Mr. Wetheridge:
Aye, most fierce.

Sir Hastings:
A dozen at the least, set on us here.

Mr. Wetheridge:
A dozen, yes.

Sir Hastings:
Or more. But one point facing many, did we drive them off.

Sir Peter:
Brave fellows.

Sir Hastings:
And waited for you where we saw the last one go, lest they should attack you. Mayhap some didst return.

Sir Peter:
My brave boy. Thou seest Herrick, thou didst fight with two, but these with six.

Mr. Herrick:
(Gravely) I envy him his chance.

1st Robber:
(Raising himself upon his elbow) How he lies. *(Hastings sees him for the first time.)* We met them two to two while they were waiting for thy coming coach and with small show of fight, they fled like frightened does. A yearling buck had shown more blood than they. Had it not been for that brave devil there *(points to Herrick)*, we had been drinking now the contents of thy purse.

Cynthia:
Ah!

Sir Peter:
How now?

Sir Hastings:
He lies! *(Starting toward 1st robber. Herrick intervenes.)*

Mr. Herrick:
Back, let the fellow speak.

1st Robber:
I do not lie. What cause have I to lie for him who gave me hurt? Ye trembled ere we came, and when we came, ye fled.

Sir Peter:
Yon gallant gentleman—

Sir Hastings:
Sir Peter—

Sir Peter:
Silence! I will have no word from you. I am a plotter and deceiver, but no coward I. Gad, have I wished an hour since to trust my daughter with such as you? Where are my eyes? I see you now in your full infamy. Out on you for a coward pair unworthy of your names. Herrick, your hand, I crave your pardon for my witlessness, but 'tis an old man's right.

Mr. Herrick:
Sir Peter, say no more.

Sir Peter:
Come, Cynthia, thy hand in his.

Mr. Herrick:
My love.

Cynthia:
Bob!

Lucinda:
It's so affecting.

Wetheridge:
Sir Hastings:
(together)
Oh, damn!

Sir Peter:
Is that coach yet repaired? We'll leave yon robber for his friends.

Coachman's voice without:
'Tis ready now.

Sir Peter:
Then to it and turn back. Our journey needs another end.

Mr. Wetheridge:
Thou wilt forgive me and still call me friend?

Sir Peter:
> When thou hast shown thy liver is not white
> I'll then forgive thee what thou has done to-night.

Sir Hastings:
> I bid you fare ye well, good sir, with awe,
> And wish you pleasure of your son-in-law.

Sir Peter:
One word against him and I'll void your veins.

Mr. Herrick:
> Useless, Sir Peter, you may spare your pains,
> My Cynthia says that we will slowly trace
> Our way to suit these wandering bravo's pace,
> Lest something in the guise of man or maid
> Should cross their path and render them afraid.

Sir Hastings:
Egad! *(Draws.)*

Mr. Herrick:
(Drawing) Go on, good Hastings, tempt my ire no more, I've had enough, our comp'ny waits, go thou before. *(Stands with sword drawn pointing toward coach.)*

Curtain

1898, The Papers of Carter G. Woodson, Reel 6, Box 9, Library of Congress.

The Gambler's Wife

Act I

Scene: [setting] *A room furnished with careless elegance. Madge seated alone.*

Madge:
I am tired of this life, and what sensible woman would not be? I am in a continual state of doubt and anxiety. Miserable wretch that I am, that most accursed thing—a gambler's wife—continually vacillating from sudden wealth to more sudden poverty. One day greeted by a husband's smile; the next, spurned by a demon's curses. My life is regulated by the drift of the cards: when they are favorable, the smile; when they are unfavorable, the curse. Bah! I am tired of it. So as Ralph Darrell no longer sees fit to make it pleasant for me, why should I not enjoy myself as well as possible in his absence? When he has ceased to be a lover, why should I not find another? Ha! Ha! Thus the husband's cruelty teaches the wife deceit. Humph! Ralph Darrell, husband: but Arthur St. Clair, lover, ha, ha, ha! The cruel world would call me wicked; but no, I am not wicked, but a woman scorned and abused. Scorn turns the honey of a woman's smile to gall, her blood to fire, her love to hate. *(Looks at her watch.)* It must be time for Arthur to come—it is almost eight. *(Enter Caesar.)*

Caesar:
Miss Da'l, da wuz a note come fo' you dis mo'nin', but fo' de Lawd, I fo'got to deliber it.

Madge:
You forgot, Caesar?

Caesar:
Yes, I fo'got. You don't s'pose my memory's disfallible, case I's a sarvant, does you? *(Aside)* I don't know, white folks is awful to wuk fo'.

Madge:

Give it to me, Caesar. *(She takes the note, reads)* God in heaven! Your unlucky negligence has ruined me!

Caesar:

How, missy, how? Is it very bad?

Madge:

I am in sore danger.

Caesar:

In dangah? Lawd, I'll stand atween you an' dangeah, any time.

Madge:

Would that a man's broad shoulders could bear my burden, but they cannot; it is for me alone to bear. Go, Caesar, go.

Caesar:

Caesar, doggone your ole black hide. You see de cause o' dis, an' you's got to pay fo' it. *(Exit.)*

Madge:

My husband's coming tonight, and he will come probably at the same instant when Arthur arrives and then, what will become of me? One or the other will be killed and probably myself. Heavens, it is awful! Why could not Ralph Darrell have remained away a day longer? Curse him he always turns up at the wrong time. Had he but given me a day longer I should have been out of his reach, and with half a chance I'll inveigle that fool Arthur St. Clair into an elopement and triumph yet, ha, ha: you are pressing close upon my track Ralph Darrell, but the most keen scented hounds have before been baffled. I will go and watch at a window to see which comes first, the husband or the lover. *(Exit. Enter Caesar.)*

Caesar:

Humph, Miss D'al's gone. Spec she's done gone to 'mit, 'mit, dat is to kill herself, well dat's nuthin' we'se all got to die some time or 'nuther, an' don't make much diffunce how we goes; but I tell you dere's lots a consolation on arth, d'ain't nuthin' like takin' off yo' shoes an' stockins an' sittin' down befo' a good wa'm fire wid a glass o' whiskey befo' you. When, but dat is fine! Don't you know since I come to dis place I'se got right musical? When I come heah I didn't know a note, now I kin sit down to de pianner and play right sma't, don't you b'lieve me, jes listen *(plays and sings, knock at the door)* now I know dat ain't no visitor or dey neber would knock dat way. *(Goes to the entrance.)* Jes walk right in. *(Enter Sister Gabriel.)* Why sister Gab'el, howdy, how is you any how?

Sister Gabriel:
I'se right sma't, how's you?

Caesar:
O, jes' tolable. Ain't feelin' any too well.

Sister Gabriel:
Yas, honey, I was jes comin' fum ma'kit an' I thought I'd drap in. I had to go to ma'kit to see about gittin' some ducks an' chickens.

Caesar:
Lawd, how times hab changed sistah Gab'el.

Sister Gabriel:
Dat's so! Uh huh! Dat's so.

Caesar:
Now when I libed on ole massa's plantation, long about Christmas, all I had to do was to jes take a sack an' go out an', sistah, fo' de lawd, I could jes get all de chickens an' ducks I wanted fo' nuthin', I tell you sistah.

Sister Gabriel:
I belieb you brother.

Caesar:
Dem was times; now ev'ry little chicken feather you gets, you'se got to buy.

Sister Gabriel:

It's a shame fo' Moses.

Caesar:

'Deed it is. Chickens was de count o' me leabin' de ministry.

Sister Gabriel:

Why brudder Caesar, did you ever preach?

Caesar:

Why, cose I used to be a preacher, had chawge of a chu'ch down heah in Punkinville, but de niggas jes car'ed on so I had to quit'em.

Sister Gabriel:

But how'd de chickens cause it brudder?

Caesar:

Why you see dem ornery coons got to sayin' dey could allays tell when I was aroun' case de chickens roosted high, an' dey said dat when eber I came aroun' dey allays missed one or two pullets, and dey axed me to resignate so I jes gots 'gusted an' ups an' quits 'em, though, I spec' it warn't very christun like.

Sister Gabriel:

You was jes right, brudder Caesar, you orter quit people, if dey was so ornery dey grudged their pastor a few po' little pullets, but der're meaner people in dis world dan you an' me'd think fur.

Caesar:

Cose dere is, don't I know it. 'Spec you don't 'member when I was delegate to de prohibition convention? Well, you know 'fo' de meeting took up all de delegates went out to take a little dram; well I kep' on drammin' until somehow I got dizzy an' went to sleep, an', sister Gab'el, when I woke up, I found myself in a tub, wid my coat painted red an' a prohibition sign over my head. Now dats what I call mean. I wouldn't cared for dere paintin' de coat, case red's a mighty pretty colah, an' it was a prince albert coat, a bran' new second handed coat, and I wouldn't a cared fo' de tub but de prohibition sign over me; dat was too much.

Sister Gabriel:
You're right brudder.

Caesar:
So after dese tricks I gib up preachin' an' politics altogether, an' me an' Bob Nevin's runnin' a little mission Sunday school out in Miami city, that's my 'sperience.

Sister Gabriel:
Well, I'se got to be goin'. Ain't got long to stop 't one place.

Caesar:
Don't be in a hurry.

Sister Gabriel:
Oh, I mus' go!

Caesar:
Well, drap in agin.

Sister Gabriel:
I will. I like to drap in on de brethren and sistern an' talk about 'ligion.

Caesar:
Yes an' I like to hab de sistern drap in. Good bye.

Sister Gabriel:
Good bye. *(Exits.)*

Caesar:
Wonder what dat ole debbil come here fo'. I'm gwine out an' sprinkle salt after her. *(Exits.)*

Madge (enters)
. . . So it is the husband . . . and not the lover . . .must get him away before Arthur comes; in that lies my only hope of safety. Some trumped up story must send him away on a wild goose chase, ha, ha, ha. Necessity is the mother of

invention; shall I be very sick and send him for a doctor eight blocks off? Ah, that will hardly do, as I want plenty of time to talk to Arthur—he must be conquered tonight. Why not a dreadful headache combined with wifely advice to return to the club, ha, ha. That will do excellently; that will touch him, and he will leave me free to receive what company I will; but he is coming. *(She seats herself languidly; enter Ralph Darrell.)*

Darrell:
Madge, I am in luck—what, are you ill?

Madge:
A dreadful headache.

Darrell:
Then I won't bother you.

Madge:
I am going to retire soon, and it will be so lonesome for you here without me. Hadn't you better return to your club?

Darrell:
I will, Madge, if I can do nothing for you.

Madge:
No, nothing; just go.

Darrell:
Don't you want—

Madge:
I want nothing; just go, go at once.

Darrell:
(Going) Good-bye, Madge. *(Aside)* There's mischief in the wind; you're too anxious, my fair lady, to have me out of the way, so I'll just hang around and await developments. *(Exits as far as to be concealed from her by the portiers.)*

Madge:

'Twas well done; he suspects nothing, ha! But that was close work, but for once the lynx is baffled, his eyes are closed by my fancied illness. Once surrounded by the pleasures of his club, he will forget me and lead me to forget him in the pleasures of another's love.

Darrell:

(Aside) Ha, madame, it was a sharp trick you played. Your headache was soon over. My absence proved a specific remedy. Madge Darrell, you are playing a shrewd game, but so far we are horse and horse. Be careful madame, you are playing with a fire that burns deep and leaves an everylasting scar! *(Exits.)*

Madge:

Ah, it is glorious to be loved, to see the glance of silent adoration flit from a lover's eye, to hear his pleading tones and see his face light up at every smile that he receives. Oh, who could blame a woman for clinging to him who loves, rather than to him who should, but does not. *(Enter Arthur St. Clair.)*

St. Clair:

And so the fair Juliet awaits her Romeo.

Madge:

Ah, Arthur, you are here.

St. Clair:

And are you glad to see me?

Madge:

Yes, Arthur, more than I can tell you—but what am I saying?

St. Clair:

Only what a woman has the right to say to the man who loves her, as I do you.

Madge:

Arthur.

St. Clair:

It is true, Madge, you must have seen that I adored you, as I sat at your side drinking in the glory of your presence. I have lived and longed for this moment when I might tell you that I loved you, and ask you, darling, to be my wife.

Madge:

Enough, enough!

St. Clair:

(Taking her hand) Have I been wrong, Madge; do you or don't you love me?

Madge:

Yes, with my whole heart.

St. Clair:

Then, darling, saying that one little word will make me infinitely happy.

Madge:

It can never be.

St. Clair:

What!

Madge:

No, never; listen Arthur, you know my meetings with you have all been clandestine. My father does not know of them. He wishes me to marry another and he will never consent to this.

St. Clair:

Stop, do you love me?

Madge:

Oh, yes, yes.

St. Clair:

Then that is enough. Fate has given this hand to me, and let no man dare to snatch it from me. You are mine by the gift of heaven; mine to keep. Can you dare a little for my sake?

Madge:
For your sake, I can dare anything.

St. Clair:
Then, tonight I will return and we will go to the nearest minister and bind our hearts and hands by that tie which no man can break asunder.

Madge:
This is too rash.

St. Clair:
No, darling, no. Think how I love you. I will take you to my home where I will surround you with splendor. I am rich and you shall not have a care.

Madge:
(Aside) Ha, now he talks, I must hear him out. *(To St. Clair)* But how can I know that you are sincere, that you will not some day desert me, and I should be left friendless, poor and alone.

St. Clair:
Desert you? Never! I could not do that, love, for you are my heart, my very life; and as for being poor, you never shall. As soon as we are married, I will settle thirty thousand upon you.

Madge:
You are too kind, Arthur, too kind . . . I do not deserve it. *(Aside)* Whew! a cool thirty thousand.

St. Clair:
You deserve far more than I can give, Madge, and I shall be grateful if you are satisfied with these terms. So tonight I come for you, my little love, until then, good bye. *(Embraces her.)*

Madge:

Good bye, Arthur, the hours shall drag till you return. *(Exit Arthur.)* Capital, capital, capital! What! a cool thirty thousand! That touches my heart. The nearest way to a woman's heart is through her pocket. Farewell, my dear husband, farewell; I am tired of you and am going to a more congenial place. You have kept me here in the country, for fear other men should see my face; but fate out played you and I met Arthur St. Clair with his thousands, and now I am off with him. Once in the heart of that great city, which he hardly allowed me to think of, it would take Ralph Darrell a decade to find me. But I hardly think he cares enough to hunt me that long. *(Enter Darrell unobserved.)* Ah, I have played a long and deadly game, but my triumph is now.

Darrell:

And mine is yet to be.

Madge:

(Aside.) The game's up. I thought you were at your club.

Darrell:

I returned to see if your headache was better.

Madge:

Yes, thank you, I am much improved.

Darrell:

You are a cool woman, Madge Darrell, under the circumstances, while I am away night after night, gambling to support you, you are here entertaining a lover.

Madge:

So wags the world.

Darrell:

Don't trifle with me. What is to hinder my strangling you here like a rat?

Madge:

Nothing, Ralph Darrell, but your own natural cowardice. Your cruelty and neglect made a false, scheming woman out of a true loving wife; now take the consequences. When I compare you with Arthur St. Clair, my whole heart goes out after him, and yearns for him. He is as far above you as heaven is above the earth.

Darrell:

You are not complimentary to your husband, but tell me, do you love Arthur St. Clair?

Madge:

Yes, deeply.

Darrell:

How fortunate! He will then have a wife who loves him; quite extraordinary.

Madge:

I shall never be his wife now.

Darrell:

Oh, yes you shall, do you think that I am going to let this chance to handle that cool thirty thousand which St. Clair settles on you, slip by? Oh, no, I'm going to finger Arthur St. Clair's money.

Madge:

What do you mean?

Darrell:

You are not well enough known here for your sudden departure to cause any excitement so play out your little game of eloping with Arthur St. Clair, and when you are married and receive your settlement of thirty thousand I shall ask you to give me ten and to fill whatever subsequent demands I may make. This is the price of my silence.

Madge:

I will never do it.

Darrell:

Oh yes you will, you have gone too far in the maze to think of returning, so you must go on to the end. You dare not refuse. Will you consent?

Madge:

(Aside)—It is my only way out.—I consent.

Darrell:

I thought you would and now I will not detain you longer as you no doubt wish to prepare for your elopement; good-bye, my wife, you have shown me how false a woman can be and I go out from this house tonight to be from this time henceforth to you a stranger, to the world dead.

Act II

Scene: A garden at St. Clair's house. Cedar Ridge. Enter old George St. Clair.

George St. Clair:

The longer the world rolls, the bigger fools men get to be; the idea of my son Arthur eloping with a strange woman, and bringing her here. Now, six weeks after his marriage a strange man is seen loafing about the place. It looks suspicious, and that wife of his, I've studied her deeply and my knowledge of human character tells me, that though women are at best a bad lot, Madge St. Clair, my son's wife, is the worst of her sex. Why she's got a bad eye. Any man with common sense could see that she is wicked. Her very voice betrays her. They say that love is blind and I am half inclined to believe that it is deaf and dumb also, poor son, my poor son! It's a shame that Arthur should throw himself away on such a miserable outcast, for he is a handsome fellow, he resembles me very closely, he's a fool—You Jerry, Jerry, you Irish dog. Do you want to pull up every flower in that garden? Hey there! Put that damn dog out of the garden, do you hear? Jerry, confound your body, stop racing after that dog, you'll ruin every bed in the garden, come here, you rascal. *(Enter Jerry.)*

Jerry:

Faith master, it was sech jolly foon, to see that dog git up an' dust.

George St. Clair:
Yes and to see my garden beds flying skyward under your feet.

Jerry:
Under moi feet?

George St. Clair:
Yes, yours and the other dog's together but you rascal, how came your coat tail gone?

Jerry:
Well, oi'll jest tell ye: last noight oi wint to say Kitty Maloney, an' faith oi had no more'n stepped into the yard whin their big bull dog begun to sing me a bass solo. Says oi to him, your song's first rate for milody, Mr. Towser, though you be a thrifle hoarse, and thin without hadin' the compliment except fur a grin which he gave me, he began to sing louder. Be aff wid ye, sez oi, oi'm on me way to say Kitty Maloney, an' faith she'll sing me a swater song than iver you can; wid that oi turns aroun' to go. But the miserable spalpeen made for me. Thinkin' we'd have a little friendly chat, oi jumped for a palin'fence, to sit down av course, but I wint clane over it, all ixcipt me coat tail, that oi lift instid of a card.

George St. Clair:
Ha, ha, ha, Jerry, Jerry, Jerry, the fools ain't all dead yet.

Jerry:
Not by a long shoot!

George St. Clair:
Come on, let's take a drink on it. *(Exit; and enter Nellie.)*

End of Fragment

Dayton, Ohio, *Dayton Tattler,* December 13, 1890.

The Island of Tanawana

Act I

Scene i: [setting] Market Place on the Island of Tanawana. Assembled there are part of the populace and the officials of the Cabinet, the Treasury.

The Treasurer:
We regret very greatly that the treasury is bankrupt. We have no money and no prospect of getting any.

The Lord High Chancellor:
But we must get money, and get it quickly, or there will be an insurrection of our people. It is all the fault of Prince Jujube. He has been to the United States and he has learned the ways of the Yankees, and latterly he has broken every Cabinet Officer.

The Treasurer:
Ahem!

The Chancellor:
(Resumes) I say every Cabinet Officer; our good Treasurer not excepted, at a vile and wicked game popularly denominated, "Poker."

Chorus:
Poker? It seems we have heard of that.

The Chancellor:
(Coming down center) It seems you have heard of that? *(Takes the song)*

> It seems we have heard of that,
> From Denver to Poker Flat.

The Secretary of State:
Gentlemen, you understand there is something more to consider. We are in-debted to the United States for four million dollars, and every minute we are expecting a warship here to enforce the payment of that debt. *(All of a sudden [a] bugle [is] heard off left. A native runs in wildly.)*

Native:
(Crying) The Americans! The Americans! *(Utmost confusion among the natives. They huddle together.)*

The Chancellor:
(To the Treasurer) Just what I expected from your extravagance, sir.

The Treasurer:
(To the Chancellor) Just what I should have expected from your manipulations, sir.

The Treasurer and the Chancellor:
(To the Secretary of State) Just what we should have expected from your diplomacy, sir. *(They are engaged in a heated discussion when a body of American Marines enter, accompanied by the sounds of the bugle. They advance to center stage, and, after saluting the girls who are gathered in the marketplace, sing:)*

The Marines:
> We're sure you're very small,
> But we'll take your king and all.

(And the girls begin making eyes at the marines. Entrance Song for the King. [King enters.])

The Marines:
(In a jocular manner turn to him and sing:)
> We bow before your sovereign Grace,
> Though you have pimples on your face.

(Recitative for:)

The King:

> Dear gentlemen, I pray you, stop and hear me,
> The argument I now will make I am sure will clear me;
> I own, alas, a scape-grace of a son,
> Whose wickedness the whole base deed has done.

The Marines:

(Breaking in)

> We own you have a very taking way,
> But what we want is pay—just pay.

The King:

(Expostulates in dumb show)

> But pardon me, my story, kindly friends, it still awaits;
> He gambled, yes he gambled, in your own United States.

Chorus:

(Taking up recitative:)

> He gambles, yes he gambled in their own United States.

(Shrieking:)

> Ain't it awful? It must be Poker.

Quartet of Marines:

(Fingers to nose.)

> It seems we have heard of that,
> From Denver to Poker Flat.

Chorus:

(Takes up refrain:)

> It seems we have heard of that,
> From Denver to Poker Flat.

The King:

Gentlemen, while my treasury is bankrupt—while my Treasurer—

The Treasurer:

Allow me to turn pale, your Majesty.

The King:
My Chancellor—

The Chancellor:
Please may I fade, your Majesty?

The Advisor:
And now your Majesty ascend the throne. *(Myer ascends the throne.)* Now, people, shout and hail your king!

The People:
Hail! Hail! Hail! To the king.

Myer:
(Myer after ascending the throne rises, stands on the steps and bows right and left and shouts:) I vish you all vell. I vill rule you as you haf nefer been ruled before, and I vill make a present at once and immediately, of ten thousand cakes of my famous soap which I make in Hoboken, New Jersey.

Chorus:
Hail! Hail! Hail! To the king.

Myer:
Van you vant to hail me for? First thing you know you vill be stonin' me. Now, quit dat.

The Advisor:
Your Majesty, it would be a good thing to distribute a little largess among the people.

Myer:
A little largess? Next ting you vill ask me for de whole alphabet.

The Advisor:
I mean, your Majesty, some little gratuities.

Myer:
Oh, if dat is what you vant I vill distribute gratthreeities.

The Advisor:
Still you misunderstand me. It would be well to give them a little money that they may go forth and celebrate your ascension to the throne, and sing a mass for the dead king who is your predecessor. *(Suddenly straightening up about the king; chorus comes forward. Enter Courier, hurriedly.)*

The King:
But who comes here?

The Courier:
My lord, my lord, I have an announcement to make. There have arrived upon our island a great American Millionaire, Mr. Julius Myer of Hoboken, New Jersey, and he has with him in his party, his daughter and relatives, their relatives, and their relatives, and their relatives, and they are at your gate.

The Chancellor:
(To the Secretary of State) See to it that your diplomacy is a little bit better.

The Chancellor:
The Secretary of State:
The Secretary of the Treasury:
(together)
(To the King) You have used up that last cask of wine, and now—*(Enter the yachting party, Mr. Myer in the lead.)*

The Courier:
(As they enter singing) We are out on a little frolic. *(He introduces the Chancellor to Mr. Myer. The Chancellor introduces Mr. Myer to the Secretary of the Treasury, and the Secretary of the Treasury introduces Mr. Myer to the Secretary of State. To each one he gives a hearty hand shake, and . . .)*

Mr. Myer:
How do! Haf a cake of my soap? I make it up in Hoboken.

The Secretary of State:
Oh, King, will your Gracious Majesty permit me to introduce you to one of the citizens of the great United States, Mr. Julius Myer?

The King:
Hail, Mr. Myer!

Mr. Myer:
How do, King, haf a cake of my soap? Ah, dis iss a beautiful island you haf. I vish I had it myself. Ah, girls and boys come here and meet de King. King, dese iss my relatives my daughters and dere cousins, and dere cousin's cousins, and der cousin's cousin's cousin, and all of dere schentlmen-fren's, and we're all out on a little yachting cruise, and we don't gif a dam. King, shake!

The King:
I welcome you, most noble Mr. Myer and all your relatives and friends.

Yachting Party:
He welcomes us—a real king welcomes us. *(They talk among themselves.)*

Myer:
Say, Monarch, how does it feel to be a King? Haint you got a sort of inflated feelin' like when ye floated a lot of stock and ye know ye're goin to get out der hole and der oder feller's goin to be in de hole?

The King:
Ah, Mr. Myer, there are sad things that happen to a king.

Myer:
Get out, now, you're jokin'. Why, you could corner a whole dry goods or soap market in de whole island.

The King:
Yes, but I wish I could corner my son.

Myer:
Vat iss he—a bull or a bear?

The King:
I fear that I do not understand your country's tongue.

Myer:
Vell, in a bull or bear market, it is mostly lamb's tongue. Oh. Vas your son a lamb?

The King:
No he was worse than a lamb—he was a poker fiend.

Myer:
I congratulate you, sir. You are in luck. I thought maybe he vas on Wall Street or vas running a newspaper.

The King:
No, it is not so bad as that, but I am broke by his experiences.

Myer:
Broke! Vat, a king broke? How much money you vant? Vat vill you pawn de island for? I haf always vanted to be a King.

The King:
Six million dollars will pay me out, while you may not be the King, as the office is hereditary, you may be the Prince Presumptive.

Myer:
A Prince Consumptive? Dat's taking a whole lot on myself. Suppose ven I got rid of de job I didn't get rid of de disease?

The King:
Oh no, I mean that you shall be an Heir Apparent.

Myer:
But vasn't my hair apparent?

The King:

My dear sir, you don't understand me—you shall be next in succession and all your relatives will be princes and princesses.

Myer:

Ah, girls you vant to be a Prince and a Princess?

The Girls:

Yes, father, but which will we be.

Myer:

It don't make no difference; you yust vait. I don't believe King, dat I haf six million in my pocket yust now, but I vill take great pleasure in giftin' you four million on account.

The King:

Good! Good! Mr. Myer, that will do finely, and as the cabinet is already assembled we will proceed at once to crown you as my Heir Apparent, Prince Jujube of Tanawana. *(Let the orchestra take up the march. King calls for the Grand Chancellor.)* Go hither and bring the crown of the Prince who has proved renegade to his trusts. *(Enter Prince Jujube.)*

The King:

There is the scape-grace now. *(The chorus are gathering round him with pleasure and joy. They pour him a stout of wine and he throws himself into a chair, laughing carelessly, but his eyes following Myer's oldest daughter. He raises his cup and sings recklessly.)*

Prince Jujube:

My castle of dreams. Ah ha! That for my kingly dad; I am glad that he sent me to the old United States to learn statecraft, for I learned lot more things. *(Glances at Myer's daughter. Grand Chancellor passes him superciliously, and in a little while returns with a crown on a velvet cushion. He bows low before the King and presents the crown.)*

The King:
Secretary of State, bring hither our royal mace. *(The Secretary exits and re-enters with a club.)* Bow before us, most noble Myer, we anoint you Prince Jujube of Tanawana *(smashes him with a club)*, and invest you with this Princely Crown. *(Places crown upon his head. All kneel while the king hands the money to the Treasurer which he passes among the members of the Court. The chorus still kneeling.)*

Chorus:
It is really too good to be true,
But we'll see what the new Prince will do.
(In the meantime unostentatiously, the real Prince Jujube and the oldest daughter of Myer have disappeared. The chorus is hardly ended when a courier rushes in again crying.)

Courier:
They fly! They fly!

Myer:
Oh, shut up, vhy don't you get a gun and shoot 'em?

Courier:
It is your daughter and Prince Jujube.

Myer:
How can it be Prince Jujube, ven I am Prince Jujube. I am not flyin' with my own daughter; I ain't no eagle.

Courier:
But it is the King's son who flies with your daughter.

Myer:
Vat, my daughter? Oh, my daughter! Call out de army! *(The King motions to his Secretary, runs to door and shouts.)*

The Secretary:
Army, come in here! *(Two ragged soldiers appear and salute.)*

Myer:
Is dat de army?

The King:
It is.

Myer:
(Collapsing, then reviving suddenly.) Call out de navy. *(The King again motions to his Secretary. A moment later a sailor comes trundling in a toy ship on a little wagon.)*

Myer:
Mine Gott! Is dat de navy?

The King:
It is.

Myer:
(Collapsing entirely) Vell den, I suppose dey vill haf to keep on flying. *(Here the populace gather round him.)*

Populace:
No, no, we will find them for you. We will go with you and trace them to their lair.

Myer:
Mine Gott! Haf dey got a lair too?

Populace:
They must have or they would not have fled. We will be the army, we will be the navy; we will soldiers be. *(They gather round Myer and take up the chorus.)* We will soldiers be.

End of First Act

Act II

Scene: [setting] *Throne room of the Principality of Tanawana. Chorus discovered in great grief. Funeral chorus. Eleven days have passed. Enter Myer and Courier.*

Courier:
Oh Royal Sir, while you were coasting about the shores of our island, our royal lord departed this life and has been placed in the tomb of his ancestor.

Myer:
Good economy. Vat wass de matter wid him?

Courier:
Good sir, he died of spleenitis.

Myer:
And vat is spleenitis?

Courier:
Why, angered at the flight of his son and your daughter, he fell into a fury.

Myer:
Vat did he leaf de fury open for?

Courier:
You don't understand me, sir; he grew terribly angry an died in a paroxysm.

Myer:
Oh, to tink of a man dying in a paroxysm. Why didn't you put him to bed?

Courier:
We did, but it was of no use, he was foredoomed to dissolution.

Myer:
Ach, dat is awful, dat is awful! Couldn't you cut it down and make it three-doomed?

Mr. Chamberlain:
Noble sir, we beg that you will here, in the sight of the populace, ascend the throne of Tanawana, as you, according to our gracious master's will, are the heir apparent.

Myer:
Ascend de throne! Ach, dat ain't much to do—I could jump up dere.

The Chamberlain:
But, sir, first allow us to take you out and to array you in royal robes.

Myer:
Vat did you pay for dem?

Courier:
It will be no cost to your Majesty.

Myer:
Your Majesty! Dat sounds nice. Come on. *(Exit Chamberlain, Myer, and Cabinet.)*

Chorus:
He goes to be arrayed. *(Enter stranger.)*

Chorus:
Who is this? *(They talk among themselves. He comes down center and introduces himself. A recitative.)*

Stranger:
    I am the King's advisor
    I shall try to make him wiser
    Than he is.
    Of course you may not know me,
    But I'll thank you if you show me
    Which he is.

Chorus:

> Of course we may not know him
> But we're very glad to show him
> Which he is.

The King's Advisor:

> I have sailed on every ocean,
> And I think I've got a notion what to do,
> I will show the King his duty,
> With an advisorial beauty,
> And always keep him up to what is new.

Chorus:

> He will show the king his duty,
> With an advisorial beauty,
> And he'll always keep him up to what is new.

(Blare of trumpets; enter Courier)

Courier:

Behold! the King arrives. *(The Advisor steps up and whispers in the Courier's ear. Enter the advance of the King's court.)*

Chorus:

Hail to the King! *(Enter the King dressed in royal robes.)*

Courier:

Oh, King, behold the advisor whom your predecessor has left for your enlightenment.

King:

How do, Advisor. Haf a cake of my soap. *(Hunting in vain for his pocket, which is absent in his royal robes, and calls to one of the girls.)* Oh, Isabel, go bring a cake of my soap out of my jacket!

Advisor:

Your Majesty, bid all the people bow.

Myer:
Bow down you geysers. *(They all bow.)*

King:
And my Secretary of State—

The Secretary of State:
May I ask that there be no flowers at my execution?

King:
Have lost all the kingdom owned at Poker. I can do nothing but give you the last courtesy of a dismantled Monarchy. I ask the pleasure to bring you my last cask of wine that has lain in my cellars since my father reigned a happier and richer kingdom. *(Blare of trumpets. Four men enter bringing cask, while the marines talk apart with the girls. The wine is poured out and the men and the populace drink. Raising their cups—quartet of Marines.)*

Marines:
As kings go now-a-days he's not so bad.

King:
Gentlemen, I have nothing to offer you further except my kingdom, and that under the stars and stripes would be badly ruled.

Chief of the Marines:
My dear, sir, we have orders from our government not to be harsh with you and therefore, we will wait a little while.

King:
I thank you, gentlemen, and give you the freedom of the Island of Tanawana. *(Marines exit saluting.)*

The Chancellor:
Very, very badly managed. Secretary of State, I should have done it so differently.

Treasurer:

Why, I should have had another loan from them.

King:

If there is more argument I shall call the Lord High Executioner.

The Three Couriers:

Your Majesty we beg a thousand pardons.

Myer:

Haf de fugitives been caught yet?

The Chamberlain:

They have not, your Majesty.

Myer:

Has de army searched on de land?

The Chamberlain:

It has, your Majesty.

Myer:

Has de navy searched on de sea?

The Chamberlain:

It has, your Majesty.

Myer:

Vat about de air ship brigade? Dey ought to catch dem i' de air some place, since dey are flying.

The Chamberlain:

They have had no better success, your Majesty.

Myer:

Still, still dey fly.

The Chamberlain:
I am sorry, but it could not have been avoided your Majesty.

Myer:
Well, cut off de heads of de army.

Chorus:
Oh—h-h-h!

Myer:
Hang all de navy.

Chorus:
Kill de air ship brigade and execute yourself.

The Chamberlain:
Ah, my lord and master—

Myer:
Speak not wid me. I am in a fury. My royal highness is in one fury passion.

The Chamberlain:
Ah, but you know, your Majesty, that our late king died in just such a paroxysm.

Myer:
Vat iss dis? Do you ting I vill die in a paroxysm? Diss iss too much; I countermand the order. Gif de air ship a pension, gif de navy a pension, and gif de whole air ship brigade a pension.

The Chamberlain:
(Smiling) And, your Majesty, as for myself—?

Myer:
And execute de whole dam cabinet. *(Down below like a lot of barking pups; he sitting up there where they cannot reach him. Seems to be somewhat of a*

chasm between them and they cannot cross it and only he knows the way to get across that chasm and he won't tell them and they are threatening him with everything dire, and Myer is running around like an old fool, but the King is still his old dignified self.)

The Prince:
Myer:
(sing duet)
With love, I own the world.

Myer:
Oh, you son of a gun. If you did own the world, you'd pawn it.

The Prince:
Not to you, not to you.

Miss Myer:
Oh father, forgive us!

Myer:
Ach yes, yust gif me a chance. *(Enter Fat Priest.)*

Fat Priest:
    My friends, I pray you, cease your strenuous agitation,
    You all must recognize the holiness that doth surround my station,
    Before you come this anxious girl,
    The King's son and the Merchant's daughter,
    If aught you have to do so long left in the lurch,
    Why, give a few gold eagles to the church.

Chorus:
(Speaking) Impudence!

    *(Singing)*If aught we do since so left in the lurch,
    We must not give gold eagles to the church.
    (Stamping their feet and speaking) Impudence!

Myer:
Vat you vant? *(Shaking his fist.)* You want me to make my daughter a saint and build a shrine fo' her? Come down, come down, oh, say, come down, and I vill set 'em up.

End of fragment

Original manuscript, undated, in Paul Laurence Dunbar Collection, Reel IV, Box 12, Ohio Historical Society (hereafter OHS).

MUSICALS

Uncle Eph's Christmas

A One Act Negro Musical Sketch

CAST OF CHARACTERS:
Uncle Eph
Aunt Chloe
Eph Jr.
Village Gossip
Parthenia
Chorus
Darky Dan/Czar of Dixie Land
Parson Jones
Expressman
Slob Coon

Scene: [setting] Kitchen, full stage, practical door to the left, prospective window to the right. Christmas Tree in three left. Old fashioned Fireplace in two right. Chairs, tables, etc., curtain music. Aunt Chloe and pickanninnies discovered fussing about the tree, putting things on it, lighting candles, etc.

Aunt Chloe:
Now I want you children to keep away from that tree, you hear me, Abraham? I want you to be real good, 'cause if you don't, Santa Claus won't treat you right. Go right away and wake up your dad, wake him up and tell him to be sure to put on his biled shirt. I don't know what's the matter with de old man, dis time o' evenin' sleeping mention names and reason why. *(Turning to Ephram, Jr.)* Eph, did you grease your pappy's boots?

Eph Jr.:
Yes, ma, but I left 'em outdoors.

Aunt Chloe:
Go, bring 'em in, do you spose your dad gwine put his boots on outdoors? *(Eph Jr. brings in boots. Abraham goes to wake up daddy. The children call, "Pappy, pappy. Christmas gift, Christmas gift." Soft music. Enter Uncle Ephram. Children cluster around him. He is dressed in his wife's waist. Children bother him, crying at him.)*

Aunt Chloe:
Law, Ephram, what you doing with my waist on?

Uncle Eph:
Go way from me now, chillen, don't bother me now, don't bother me, cose I knows it's Christmas, Christmas gift, Christmas gift. *(Snorts in derision. Turns to Aunt Chloe.)* In de name of de Lawd, old ooman, what did you do with my biled shirt?

Aunt Chloe:
Your biled shirt is right in de chist—

Uncle Eph:
Well, why didn't you say so. You done grease my boots right, eh? You done grease my boots right? Right?

Aunt Chloe:
Cose, Eph grease your boots right. Ephram, 'and your pappy his boots—

Eph Jr.:
Here dey is, pappy—*(Uncle Eph takes boots and stares hard at Eph Jr.)*

Uncle Eph:
(To Aunt Chloe) Blessed Moses, old ooman, what you been greasing dat chile's face with?

Aunt Chloe:

I done grease it with mutton taller.

Uncle Eph:

Mutton taller, mutton taller. Don't you ever grease no chile's face with mutton taller, You must just grease it with de marrer of de bone.

Aunt Chloe:

But I don't know de ingrejents.

Uncle Eph:

De ingrejents is just this. You take de bone of de hog jole and you bile it down twell you git de marrer from de bone, den you mix dat with dis here contemplanous oil and bile dat clar down to a salve. Den you comply dat to de face. Why, that little darky's face will be so cracked dat it will look lak an earthquake. Go fill my pipe, you young scoundrel, and don't you put no powder in my pipe this time. Old ooman, I just pintedly got to whup that boy. I got to whup him. De last time I told dat young rapscallion to fill my pipe he went out and broke one of dem firecrackers and put de powder in de bowl and mixed it up with the baccer. Here I stands, I take my coal of fire and draps it in the baccer and Lawd a mussy, pouf. It liked to blow my head off. *(Music chorus of voices in the distance, children run to window. They cry, "Look pappy, listen pappy.")*

Aunt Chloe:

Git on out of here, Ephram, git on out of here, don't you hear de people coming?

Uncle Eph:

(Going to window) Heish your mouf. I ain't a going. I's gwine to stay right here and excuse my guesses.

Aunt Chloe:

You ain't gwine to 'scuse no guesses in my waist. I tell you to clear out of here.

Uncle Eph:
Here, I'm de head of dis fambly, you just organize dat fact. I'm de head of this fambly.

Aunt Chloe:
Yes, and you's de foot of it too.

Uncle Eph:
Hold on, old ooman, hold on. I's been de head of this fambly for des many years. How long we been married, old ooman, does you remember de year we was married? Dat was de year de watermillions was scarce and de chicken roosted high. Dat was in eighteen skinty-four.

Aunt Chloe:
Eighteen skinty-four, dey ain't such no number. Clear out from here. Dem peoplers right on you. *(Starts to run him out. Uncle Eph, rushes to door and throws it open. Sleigh bells stop, old folks chorus, "We's a comin'." Enter old folks singing "We's a comin." General jabber, pulling off comforts, etc. Different voices calling, "Howdy Unc Eph.")*

Uncle Eph:
(Shaking hands generally) Howdy children. Howdy children, Evening Parson Jones, Sis Brown. How you come on?

Sis Brown:
I's right smart. Uncle Eph, how you?

Uncle Eph:
Just as peart as a spring chicken, honey.

Village Gossip:
(To Uncle Eph) Has anybody told you 'bout dat Lizy Ann Gibbs?

Uncle Eph:
Yes, yes, Sis Smif. *(Turning away from her)* Parson Jones, just git out dat coat and make yourself at home. I just want you all.

Village Gossip:

(Interrupting) De way dat ooman is carrying on is jest owdacious.

Uncle Eph:

Yes, yes, yes, I know. I know. Sis Brown, take dat split bottom chair and . . .

Village Gossip:

And brother Ephram, she come down to church the other night and, . . .

Uncle Eph:

Yes, yes, I reckon you all must a had a mighty time coming through this snow. It's wuss den de winter was I remember when Chloe and me married. Hit was.

Village Gossip:

And she walked in dere and sot down, and listen to me. Listen to me, man.

Uncle Eph:

Oh, ooman, do stop your talking. Go on and talk Chloe. She's got time to listen to you. *(Aside)* Never saw a ooman talk so much in all my life. *(Music pianissimo [soft music] growing from a distance imitating sleigh bells, horses' hoofs, etc. leading up to carol.)*

Village Gossip:

Listen to me, brother Ephram. *(Uncle Eph talking at the same time to Parson Jones.)*

Uncle Eph:

I tell you Parson Jones, it was so cold that winter.

Village Gossip:

(Raising her voice) Listen to me, Ephram.

Uncle Eph:

I ain't gwine to do it. I's gwine to talk just as loud as you is and I's gwine to be heard. I never did see a ooman talk so in all my life. *(Shouting at the top of his voice)* And that winter was so cold that our old cow swung her tail agin de fence and it froze so hard dat it broke short off.

Village Gossip:
(Raising her voice also) And as I was saying, she come in dar and sot down.

Uncle Eph:
Oh, go to the devil.

> *Opening Chorus:*
> Christmas fun is in the air
> Heigho, heigho,
> Christmas doings everywhere,
> Heigho, heigho,
> Don't be foolin' roun' dat gate,
> 'Possum he don't like to wait,
> Hurry up or you'll be late,
> Heigho, heigho,
> Hear the bells across the snow,
> Heigho, heigho,
> Christmas everywhere you go,
> Heigho, heigho.

([At the climax of the music] Young folks rush on stage, singing carol. Picture lying too.)

Uncle Eph:
Well, young folks and old folks, Uncle Eph bids you all well welcome. I want you to make yourself at home. Just tear up de house if you want to, case in de old times, I allus hyeahed it said dat the immoral Shakespoke writ "Christmas comes but once a year. Let us have our gin and beer. White folks pour your whiskey in. Give us colored folks our gin" *(Laughter and applause)* But where's Parthenia? Didn't she git an incantation to dese here festivities? Dey ain't no good time less'n dat gal's around.

Aunt Chloe:
Seems to me like he's mighty bothered about da gal.

Uncle Eph:
Oh, you go old ooman, you's gittin' too old. Don't bother me. *(Looks slyly around. Someone whispers to him)* Humph, what you say? Where is she? Hiding behind dat gal Minty? Never mind, I'll find her. Ain't gwine to have

her playing no congeatment tricks on me. *(Dodges about finally catches her)* Ha, ha, ha, I cotch you, I cotch you. *(Brings her down center. Parthenia very bashful)* Here she is, here she is. You all know Parthenia. Dis is Parthenia Jenkins. Sis Jenkins daughter. Did you ever hear about Parthenia, about de time she went to skollege? She made up her mind to make her exit into skollege and git an ejimuncation, well, she gits up and makes her debut into did here vaseline skollege. *(Someone corrects him in a whisper)* Humph? Yes, yes dis gassar's skollege dats what I mean. White folks don't ax her whether she black or ha, ha, ha. So she goes to dis her gasoline skollege. *(Someone whispers, correcting him)* Yes, yes, dat what I mean. Dis here skollege and gits an ejimuncation herself and de final cousemquences is dat she gradumungates at de head of her class and de white folk dey don't know she's a brudenette case she looks jest like dem, 30 deys tickled to death when she come out of dis glycerine skollege. *(To Parthenia)* But tell 'em about it honey, I can't tell 'em.

Parthenia:

Oh, Uncle Ephram, I'm so ashamed, but I'll tell 'em the best I can. *(Sings one verse, "I'm the colored girl from Vassar," two verses "Lover's Lane." Through all the preceding scenes a deaf deacon has been rushing about making frantic efforts to hear, saying "Eh? Eh?" hands to his ear. After Parthenia song)*

Aunt Chloe:

Ephram, Ephram. *(Beckons him to one side. Others talk among themselves.)*

Uncle Ephram:

What you want, Chloe? I wish you wouldn't bother me when I'm talking to Parthenia.

Aunt Chloe:

You better let Parthenia alone and go out and git some pro-visions for these here people. You ain't got no idea of hospumunality. Go on out of here and git a possum and a jug of gin and don't you be gone no time, and we'll be 'stributing de presents so's to keep 'em busy.

Uncle Ephram:

Oh, Lord, Lord, Lord. Old ooman, I wish you'd go yourself.

Aunt Chloe:

Go on, go on. *(Exit Uncle Ephram hurriedly makes excuse.)*

Aunt Chloe:

Now folks, I done sent Uncle Ephram on a little errand and while he's gone, we just as well 'stribute dese presents. Dere's something on that tree, I reckon for most everybody. *(Stamping heard outside. Knock at the door. And Chloe says, "Come in." Chorus says, Music of "Darky Dan" or "Czar of Dixie Land." Enter Darky Dan.)*

Czar of Dixie Land

You white folks don't 'lect no man
    Less he's of yo' nation.
What you want to do's to keep
    Black folks in dey statien.
But dese black folks boun' to have
    Some one go a starrin',
So in Dixie Land, I spend
    All my time a Czarrin'.

    Chorus:
    I am de finest thing
    From near or far;
    Black folks in Dixie sing
    Dis is de Czar,
    You see my make up fine
    Lawd folks, but I'm line,
    Go way, de world is mine
        I am de Czar.

All you people note my dress
    And my royal manners,
Try me anyway you please
    I take off de banners:
No white man can pace wid me
    When I'm fixed hobby,
Playin' high society
    Is my only hobby.

Chorus:
Oh, it's Dan, Dan, look at Parthenia blushing.

Darky Dan:
Ah, Ladies and gentlement, good evening, good evening. I am most happy to join in your festivities. I shall be very glad to help in the distribution of the presents as I see you are about to do something of the kind. But first I think it proper to announce myself to you in my real character. Miss Parthenia knows me, but I hardly think the others know who I really am. *(Sings either Darky Dan or Czar of Dixie Land. At end of his song, distribution of presents begins. Business of unfolding packages, exclamations, etc.)*

Parthenia:
And not a single present for me and everyone else has one.

Parson Jones:
I'll give you something. *(Hands her a wish bone.)*

Parthenia:
What can I do with a wish bone?

Parson Jones:
Take it and hang it in your door-way and the first man who comes in under it will be your husband.

Parthenia:
Perhaps Christmas will bring me a husband after all, if nothing else. Well, that's something. *(The wishbone is hung over the door.)*

Darky Dan:
Well, I wish I had arranged to come a little later. *(Orchestra music, horses' hoofs, etc. Enter Expressman with big box.)*

Expressman:
A package for Miss Parthenia Jenkins. *(Parthenia signs book and thanks him. Box is dragged to center of stage. Everyone crowds around Parthenia anxiously.)*

Parthenia:

I know it's something nice.

Girls:

Oh, my. *(Exclamations, gestures of wonder, etc.)*

Parson Jones:

I told you your wish bone would bring you good luck.

Eph Jr.:

How about a hog's wish bone?

Parson Jones:

Go 'long, hog, ain't got no wish bone.

Eph Jr.:

Well, how about a chicken's instep?

Parson Jones:

Oh, go 'long with you boy. *(Box opened. Business of breaking box open. Exclamations from chorus, "Oh, I wonder what it can be!")*

Parthenia:

Oh, I know it's something sweet. *(Box finally opened. Slob Coon is discovered.)*

Parthenia:

(Starting back) Just to think that that came 'n under my wish bone.

Slob Coon:

Well, I'm here.

Village Gossip:

I believe that's the same man that used to live in this here town. He's got a wife and seven children, and, and . . .

Slob Coon:
Oh, missus, missus, you mistake me. But who's the fair lady that I come to as a gift?

Darky Dan:
The fair lady is Miss Parthenia Jenkins. *(Introduces them.)*

Slob Coon:
Miss Parthenia Jenkins. Well, I'm happy to make your acquaintance. *(Hunting for her hand to shake it, his hand low down, Parthenia's high up in the air.)*

Slob Coon:
(To Darky Dan) Why-er-er. I thought it was allus proper to shake hands. *(Still bowing.)*

Darky Dan:
Higher, higher.

Slob Coon:
I don't believe she is for hire.

Darky Dan:
Higher up, higher up.

Slob Coon:
Tie her up, dat's just what I want to do.

Darky Dan:
Shake higher, man, shake higher.

Slob Coon:
I can't shake at all. I must have missed connection somehow. She ain't a bit glad to see me.

Darky Dan:
Her hand's up high.

Slob Coon:
(Finding Parthenia's hand) Oh, yes, I see you're used to grabbing the chicken by the head instead of by the foot.

Darky Dan:
The idea of talking to Miss Parthenia Jenkins that way.

Slob Coon:
(Imitating Darky Dan) Oh, yes I see you somewhat interested in the lady yourself?

Darky Dan:
I has the honour to be, sir.

Slob Coon:
Well sir, so am I, and all I got to say is dat heavy, heavy hangs over your head.

Darky Dan:
Do you mean that for an insult, sir?

Slob Coon:
Insult or result sir, take it as you wish.

Darky Dan:
Sir, this insult must be washed out with blood.

Slob Coon:
Use any old washing material you want. It's all the same to me.

Darky Dan:
Name your seconds.

Slob Coon:
Yes, yes, I'll make it an hour.

Darky Dan:
No, no, name your seconds.

Slob Coon:

I'll make it a minute. Let me git at him. *(Pulls a razor.)* I'm ready now.

Aunt Chloe:

You'll have to git out of here. *(Chorus frightened.)*

Slob Coon:

I'll go. I'll go. I'll make my debut. But, remember, I'll return with this. *(Pulls gun. Chorus screams and runs about. "Oh, stop him, oh, stop him." Exit Slob Coon. Business of chorus surrounding Darky Dan. Re-enter Slob Coon with a big pick.)* I'll go on gentlemen but when I go I want to take somebody with me. *(Chorus screams. Exit Slob Coon. Returns with an ax.)* I don't want any trouble. I don't want any trouble, but just let me git at that nigger. *(Chorus huddling together. Exit Slob Coon. Returns with a big basket of tools, picks up saw and sharpens it on stage.)* I don't want no trouble. I'm willing to go but—

Chorus:

Put him out, put him out. *(Darky Dan frightened, Chorus pushes him towards Slob Coon, he hangs back and makes frantic efforts to get away, Chorus finally gather around Slob Coon and push him out.)*

Man from Chorus:

Well, he's gone, and now let's enjoy ourselves.

Hot Foot Dance

Oh, now, Miss Sally, tek yo' stan',
> T'un roun' an' choose yo' fav'rite man;
Bow to de eas' bow to de wes',
> An' choose de one dat you love bes'.

Chorus:
Now come a prancin' down de flo',
> Back, back de way you came befor',
Now to de center, hyeah's yo' chance
> To show dese coons dat hot-foot dance.

You, dere, Jim Johnson, step up now,
> An' wipe de sweat f'om off yo' brow,

Jes' tek Miss Caline by de han',
　　An' lead huh to de promised lan'.

Oh, Mistah Smif, don' be so slow,
　　A-tekin' Lizy to de flo',
Oh, balance, sashay, prance an' swing,
　　An' now you cut de pigeon wing.
Now, evahbody kill yo' se'f,
　　Jes' lay ol' sorrer on de shelf
Lay down yo' 'ligion by yo' side,
　　An' dance twell you is satisfied.

Darky Dan:
I'm glad that that man has been taken away without any bloodshed. I know
you all perceive how fierce I was growing.

Aunt Chloe:
Oh, yes, we saw, we saw.

Darky Dan:
If you hadn't held me back I'd a paralyzed him.

Aunt Chloe:
Oh, yes, we know, we know.

Man from Chorus:
Now, that's all over, let's have some fun. (*Music Hot Foot Dance. Afterwards,
yell outside. Aunt Chloe rushes to the door and tries to prevent Uncle Ephram
from coming in. Uncle Ephram, drunk, comes in anyhow.*)

Uncle Ephram:
Whoo-oo-ee-ee. Christmas gift, Christmas gift, I'm so happy, I'm so happy.
(*Waves gin jug in the air*) Everybody enjoy yourselves.

Aunt Chloe:
Go 'long out of here Ephram.

Uncle Ephram:

Oh, don't bother me old ooman. Hooray for General Jackson, hooray for General Jackson. I wish I was in Dixie. *(Aunt Chloe pushes him toward bedroom door.)* Old ooman, what's the matter?

Aunt Chloe:

You done gone down town and got drunk.

Uncle Ephram:

I beg your pardon, I'm not drunk, I went down town to argify as to the dislocation of dis world and de other planets.

Aunt Chloe:

(Shaking his arm) I 'low dey ain't a bit of gin in dat jug.

Uncle Ephram:

Old ooman, don't bother me, I don't know you.

Aunt Chloe:

You went out to git some provisions, did you bring some home?

Uncle Ephram:

Yes, I got a possum, I captured dis possum.

Aunt Chloe:

Yes, but you didn't behave yourself.

Uncle Ephram:

Yes, I did. I behaved all right, I got some gin.

Aunt Chloe:

Bet it's all gone.

Uncle Ephram:

All gone? What's de matter with you, dis here possum don't drink gin. Christmas gift everybody. I'm mighty glad fu to see you. *(Staggers up to Parson Jones.)*

Parson Jones:

Ah, my brother, I'm mighty sorry to see you in such a condition.

Uncle Ephram:

Just you let me alone. Just you hold me up and I'll do de rest. I want to be held up.

Aunt Chloe:

Where did you get dat possum?

Uncle Ephram:

Why, I got dis possum, where de possum grows at.

Ephram Jr.:

Pappy, where was de possum first perskivered?

Aunt Chloe:

He wants to know where was de possum first perskivered?

Uncle Ephram:

Now just listen to dat boy, just listen to dat boy. Going to school every day of his life and using such a word. Old ooman, why'nt you rain him better? Don't you know dere's no sich word in de dictionumgary as perskivered?

Aunt Chloe:

Dey is.

Uncle Ephram:

Dey ain't.

Aunt Chloe:

Dey is.

Uncle Ephram:

You know I's got de best edjumingation. I say dey ain't no sich word as perskivered. Reskivered is de most propergumay word. *(Turns to Parson Jones)*

Parson, you's got de most adjummungation of us all. I want you to percide dis question, which is de most propergumay word, reskivered or perskivered?

Parson Jones:
Well, Brother Eph', I'm mighty sorry, but I got to take deception from bofo you and de madam. Neither one of dem words as you renounce 'em is right, but de correct dispression is conskivered.

Uncle Ephram:
I knowed I was right. Now you want to know where de possum was first conskivered? Well, de possum was first conskivered on the whiles of the Isthmus an' de plains of de Massassappi! *(He attempts to emphasize the last word by striking his hand on the table, misses it, and falls to the floor.)*

Aunt Chloe:
Stand up and behave yourself.

Uncle Ephram:
(Rising and making speech. During this the deaf deacon makes unusually frantic efforts to hear.) Now when you go to carve your possum, if you stick de knife dar you will cause a dislocation of de noctorial habitations of the juice of de possum, dereby making the poufligravity in the regions of de— *(Fakes rest, mumbling and mouthing)* Any how is am de consusnoss of opinion dat de possum meat is de best meat after all.

Song:

Possum is De Best Meat After All

Dey was a talkin' an' a squabblin' all erlong de colo'ed line,
Bout dey eatin', bout dey eatin'.
So, says some unsense so many tings dese people t'inks is fine
    Hol' a meetin'. Hol' a meetin'.
But ol' Pahson Brown objected, fu' he said dey didn't need
Fu' to hol' no big convention, leas' ways not de way he seed,
Case dey didn't need to 'semble in de church ner in de hall
Fu' a colored crowd to any de patossum meat is bes' of all.

Chorus
Possum is de bes meat aftah all,
Possum am de meat fu' spring or fall
You kin eat dey hum an' chicken,
An' fur pork chops dey kin squall
But possum is de bes meat aftah all.

But dey held de big convention an de dahkies all turned out,
    To de meetin', to de meetin',
Case dey didn' tend to leave it in de lightest kind o' doubt,
    Bout de eatin', bout de eatin'.
Oh, de cheerman was a colo'ed man o' mos' pu'digious note.
An' he rose to state de question an' to put it to a vote,
But de dahkies had been t'inkin' an' f'om all sides o' de hall
Came de cry, "You needn't put it, possum meat's de bes' o' all."

Evah sence dey been a fu to put some othah t'ngs
    On de table, on de table,
But hit's only to de possum dat de honest nigger clings,
    W'en he's able, w'en he's able.
He kin go into de senate, he kin gain a high degree,
But he allus shous "De possum is de only meat fu me"
Tek yo' ham an' tek yo' chicken, tek yo' lam' an' tek yo' sheep
Tek em all, but Lawsy people, des my possum let me keep.

Uncle Ephram:
Now since we are gathered together, since de pervision is here, it are fair dat de ladies should be apportioned out. Now, since Miss Parthenia am de belle of dis here suspicious occasion, it will be for us to prance and see which one of us shall have her company f'r de week.
    (Cake-walk, cake-walk song. Uncle Ephram wins the prize.)

Uncle Ephram:
Ha, ha, ha, I did win de lady. *(Leads Parthenia forward, Cake walk music.)*

Curtain

Produced Boston Music Hall, December 20, 1899. Text in Library of Congress.

Jes Lak White Fo'ks

A One Act Negro Operetto

Overture

Scene: *At close of overture, voices are heard singing in the distance the refrain;*

"We's a comin
Ole Egypt's people
Am a comin
Comin up on high

Curtain rises at end of refrain and discloses at right of stage Pompous Johnsing's cottage, a two story affair all covered with ivy, rose bushes, etc. two windows, one door and short verandah steps. A sort of revival service is in progress in the house where a number of negroes are congregated. An old negro, Elder Snowball, is leading meeting. As curtain rises he is seen leading and exhorting the people. He sings.

Day am near when Zion
Gwine to lif' its han'
It de book'ram written
Ob ol' Zion's ban
White folks no use tryin'
Fu to do us ha'm
Lord's gwine raise his people
High up in his ahm

> *Refrain:*
> We's a comin'
> Ol' Egypt's people
> Am a comin'
> Comin up on high
> Fum de Valley
> Valley and shadder

Ob de darkness
An' de day am nigh
When he'll call us
Fum out dis wilderness
Ob Trouble
Up into de sky:
Der's a lan' whah possum
Foun' in ebery tree
In de book 'tam written
Jes whah you kin see
Lan' whah milk an' honey
Flowin' fresh an' free
Chicken an de turkey
Waitin' dah fu me
Refrain

All join in chorus of second refrain and following the Elder walk—ecstatically shouting—to center of stage where they finish refrain. Jube Johnson, a boisterous darkey, is so worked up that he does not perceive that all the rest have stopped singing and continues to shout and sing vigorously. In the midst of his singing Pompous Johnsing enters, dragging old Spanish chest full of gold and other articles of value.

Pompous:
I meet a man las' week dat say dey ain' nuttin' in dreams, I say, look heah, man, you crazy, when I dream of a fun'al you know what I do? I go right out an' play dead man row.

Jube Johnson:
Did it come out?

Pompous:
Doan' wander f'um de subject under consideration. Dat ain' de point, I played it. Now las' night I dream de whole sky full of poached eggs. (*Chorus crowd nearer and show great interest.*)

Jube:
No chicken um!

Pompous:
De subject under consid'ation ain't chicken. But to resume, de sky wuz full er poached eggs, but dat doan' do me no good, I ain go no ladder, I ain got no wings. But dey look so fine and dey look so w'am I gaze at em and keep on gazin'? En odd one, one done—drap right—spring down f'om de sky en go th'oo de yearth, en 'en I wake up.

Jube:
What wuz de egg?

Pompous:
De subject und' consid'ation am not eggs. *(Impressive pause)* So-h! It am de gold.

All:
Gold!!

Pompous:
(Beginning to walk back and forth, with an ecstatic sing song enunciations) I wake up en I take my spade en I go en I go en dig right whah dat poached egg fall. I dig so deep an I dig so fas' dat I might nigh come out in wunner dez yer Philipeanut Islands, en way down deep in bottem er de hole, I fin' disher box of gold. *(Beginning to shout)* Spread de news! Spread de news!

All:
Yes, let's go tell evah body. *(All make a movement toward the door.)*

Pompous:
(Continuously) Look hyeah no now, don' be so fas' ain't you got sense enough to know if you do advertise dah gold all ovah town de white fo'ks'l glab it wid a skindicate.

Jube:
What's a skindicate?

Pompous:

(Ominously) You'll know time you get th'ar wid 'em, when wunner dem skindicates gits thar wid you you mighty lucky if you got yo' skin still on. En dat ain't safe ef de sole leathah trust kin use it. Some folks ain't got no mo'sense n'ter walk up to trouble an ask fu' an introduction. All remmine, we won't tell white folks, jes' de colo'ed folks! Dey ain't got no skindicates.

Pompous:

Now I got dis gold I reckon I get down—jes lak white folks.

Song—Spread de News

Spread de news, spread de news
Mistah Johnsing's found de gold
Found de gold dat once was hid.
By de pirate Captain Kidel
Spread de news, spread de news
Let de people all be told
Mistah Johnsing's found de gold
Everybody spread de news.

Chorus exits singing "Spread de News," Pompous pushing them off.

Pompous:

(Impressively) I want you all to und'stand I got a plan in regard to dis gold. I got social aspirations. You know when white men gets rich dem don' stay hyeah wha ezybody knows 'em en knows dey ain' much. Dey go to Europe, an' by 'm' by you readin' de papers en you say: "Huh! Heah Mr. William Vanderbilt Sunflower's daughter married a duke." But I an goin' get no bargain counter duke for my daughter, huh-uh, honey. She is going marry a prince. She done got huh diploma from Vassar, and I has been engaged in diplomatic regotiations wid an A'fican King. Dis will be a ma'iage of convenience. Dats a ve'y insulated term, ve'y consularious. It signify a ve'y convenient ma'ige, wunner dem kin' you don' may till you get suited. I ain' ready yit. I goin' get Mandy a family tree. Dey er so cheap in Europe dey use 'em fer kindlin wood. Mandy she'll have a family tree. Jes lak white folks. *(Pompous walks slowly to door of house dragging chest of gold. As he enters house, chorus enters singing, "Spread de News." Enter Mandy.)*

Mandy:

Girls! Girls! I have a secret. I've just returned from Vassar.

Chorus:

Tell us all about it. *(Song, "Colored girl from Vassar.")*

Mandy:

Have you heard the latest news they tell
It's startling all the nation.

Chorus:

It's startling all the nation.

Mandy:

If you haven't heard the news ah well
Just listen to my song.

Chorus:

Just listen to her song.

Mandy:

There once was a school that was so very rare.

Chorus:

There once was a school that was so very rare.

Mandy:

That a poor dusky maid couldn't breathe its very air.

Chorus:

That a poor dusky maid couldn't breathe its very air.

Mandy:

You couldn't enter in unless you were a millionaire.

Chorus:

You couldn't enter in unless you were a millionaire.

Mandy:

> To be ought but a blue blood or swell you didn't dare.

Chorus:

> To be ought but a swell you didn't dare.

Mandy:

> I am the first dark belle who ever went to Vassar.

Chorus:

> She am the first dark belle who ever went to Vassar.

Mandy:

> I played my part so well I came from Madagascar.

Chorus:

> She played her part so well she came from Madagascar.

Mandy:

> They thought I was a swell and the boys they did adore
> And if I gave a smile they quickly asked for more.

Chorus:

> And if she gave a smile they quickly asked for more.
> They sent bouquets galore to the elegant brunette.

Mandy:

> I've got a stock in store of their billet deux as yet.

Chorus:

> They did not know sufficient to come in from out the wet
> And now they're sore they're sore you bet.

Mandy:

> They had never seen my dark papa
> And I didn't have to show him.

Chorus:

And she didn't have to show him.

Mandy:

Till I bade the others all ta! ta!
Then I didn't mind at all.

Chorus:

Then she didn't mind at all.

Mandy:

Oh the papers howled and said it was a shame.

Chorus:

The papers howled and said it was a shame.

Mandy:

And they really thought that I was to blame.

Chorus:

And they really thought that she was to blame.

Mandy:

They thought that I had played an awful game.

Chorus:

They thought she had played an awful little game.

Mandy:

Tho' they had to own that I got there just the same.
Tho' they had to own I got there just the same.
        Refrain:

Mandy:

And now they're sore.

Chorus:

They're sore you bet.

Mandy:

And now they're sore.

Chorus:

They're sore you bet.

All:

You bet, you bet, you bet they're sore
and now they're sore, they're sore you bet.

(Song, "Lovers Lane"—interpolated. Exit Mandy & Julius. Pompous enters with large tree drawn on a piece of paper.)

Pompous:

Dis is de family tree, heah my father; heah my gran'father, heah me.

Jube:

Roos'n in de branches same coons.

Pompous:

(Taking no notice except to direct a withering glare at Jube) An heah my ancestor. He was a King.

Jube:

What dat wide hole gap in de middle?

Pompous:

Oh dat ain't nut'tn. Dat's a hiatus.

Jube:

A what?

Pompous:

A hiatus. When white comes to about fifty-five yeahs in dey history de don' want know about dis don' hand it up on de family tree to be looked at. Dis tree wuz drafted by, he Herald of de Royal Af'o American Fenian Society of de daughters of de Holland dames an' I told him I wanted it jes lak white fo'ks hiatuses as postrophes an catastrophes en chimpanzers I ain't proud and any how, when you go back to de Jungle evah niggah is a king.

Jube:
Dey ain't no chicken nor possum settin' in tree. I don' believe in no Afro-American tree dat have dem things out.

Pompous:
Huh! What you think dis tree is, a hotel? White folks don't have turkeys en turkey buzzards and squir'ls en shotes roos'n in deir pedigree. I tells you, dis tree is obstructed jes lak white folks. *(Song, Evah niggah is a king.)*

Pompous:
> Dah's a mighty curus circumstance
> Dats a bother in all de nation.
> All de yankees is dissatisfied
> Wid a deir untilled station.
> Dey is huntin' after title
> Wid a golden net to scare em.
> An' dese democratic people
> Dey mos mighty glad to wear em.
> Ho but dey ain't got all de title
> Fu' it is a curus ting.
> When a darky starts to huntin'
> He is sho' to prove a king.

> > *Refrain:*
> > Evah Niggah is a king
> > Royalty is jes' de ting.
> > Ef yo' social life's a bungle
> > Jes you go back to yo' jungle
> > An remember dat yo' daddy was a king.

Chorus repeats:
Once it used to be admitted
Dat the colored man was fervant

When he said dat he was Washington's
Mos' loved and trusted servant.

But you see that little story
Got as stale as soldiers' rations.
So now he builds his perpulation
On his African relations.
An' de very yaller people
Dey don' get into de ring.
An de only blood dats darkey
Dey go native wid a king.
Refrain.
Chorus repeats this twice.

Pompous:
Now ladies and gentleman a few moments the prince JuJu, the Cannibal
King, will be here. He is to marry my daughter, Mandy, then I'll be in high
society. *(Ensemble: "Love Looks Not at Estate.")*

Pompous:
> *(Singing)* To get in high society you need a great reputation
> Don't cultivate sobriety but rather ostentation,
> A million quid laid by in gilt edged stocks
> A few town lots let's a dozen blocks
> A high toned house that builded upon rock
> Then you're in society.

Mandy:
> *(Wait right Shufflefood and chorus)* Then you're in society.

Pompous:
> *(Singing)* To get in get in high society
> I've always had an ambition
> And since I've got the dough now
> We are sure to have position
> A royal prince my little girl shall wed
> For since the day of Lords and Dukes has sped

It takes a prince to place you at the head
Of the best society.

Mandy, W. R. S., and Chorus:
Of the best society.

Mandy:
Father you're only mocking
Such levity is only shocking
Your prince for me would be too far above
A Royal Prince is he I love.

Mandy and Chorus:
A Royal Prince is he I love.

Pompous:
Just to think of a house on 5th Avenue.

Jube:
(Aside) South 5th.

Pompous:
And a Prince who will spend all his time wooing you.

Jube:
(Aside) And your money, too.

Chorus:
Just think of a house on 5th Avenue
And a Prince who would spend all his time wooing you.

Mandy:
Love looks not at estate ah no
T'was folly one should think it so
The beggar maid becomes a queen
Who through her lovers eyes is seen.

Mandy and W. R. S.:

I care not for the world of fools
Love dignifies the soul it rules
The pomp of kings the pride of state
Are naught when love o'er takes the great
The humble cot becomes a throne,
Whose dwelling place love makes her own
So all man's heart and being sing
Love is the king. Love is the king.

All:

The humble cot becomes a throne
Whose dwelling place love makes her own.
So all man's heart and being sing
Love is the king. Love is the king.

(Voices from rear, shouting: "The Prince, The Prince." Prince's introductory music. All cake walk, dance, etc. Sing.)

White folks and black folks all join in the craze
Nothin but cake walks can be seen these days
Dukes' sons and cooks' sons, sons of millionaires
All learn to do cake walking.

The prince enters amid great huzzah, dancing, and general rejoicing. Pompous looks prince over and, finding that he looks rather suspicious, seedy, and generally dilapidated, decides after all that an honest American Negro is a man who will look after his daughter and make a living for her his best. And anyhow he is happier as an ordinary darkey therefore he decides to quit acting just like white folks. All sing "Spread de News."

Finale. [The End]

Produced New York, New York, Cherry Blossom Theater, June 26, 1900. Text in Howard University Moorland-Spingarn Research Center Collection.

Dream Lovers

DRAMATIS PERSONAE:

Torado, A Mulatto Prince from Madagascar	*Baritone.*
Manuel, His Friend	*Tenor.*
Katherine, A Quadroon Lady	*Soprano.*
Martha, Her Sister	*Contralto.*

(Drawing Room. Manuel and Katherine discovered.)

Katherine:

Tell me more about this strange creature whom you are leading into my toils. *(Apart)* Can it be my dream-lover?

Manuel:

There is little to tell. Torado is a mulatto, the son of a traveler and his African wife. He himself was born in Africa, and living there all of his life, has imbibed all the notions and superstitions of the natives themselves. One of his superstitions is that a lady, who appeared to him in a dream years ago, is destined to be his wife, and he has been searching the world over to find her. I have invited him here, thinking that you, fair lady, might well trouble any man's dreams, though leagues might stretch between you.

Katherine:

Am I then so horrid as that?

Manuel:

Horrid, horrid? Listen! *(Sings)*—
> Is the red rose that doth entrap the bee
> At fault for being dangerously sweet?

Katherine:

> *(Sings)* Ah, noble sir, your gracious simile
> Is deftly worded, fairly turned and neat.

Manuel:
Thine eyes would make a poet of a clown.

Katherine:
(Surveying herself complacently) Methinks mine eyes less charming than my gown.

Manuel:
Stars cannot see themselves how bright they are.

Katherine:
(Mockingly) How pretty,—first a flower, then a star!

Manuel:
> 'Tis the bus'ness of a gallant-hearted man,
>> When he is not bearing arms,
>> To extol the ladies' charms—
> That's the bus'ness of a gallant-hearted man.

Katherine:
> 'Tis the bus'ness of a clever-minded maid
>> To let everything she hears
>> In and out her pretty ears—
> That's the bus'ness of a clever-minded maid.

Manuel:
> 'Tis the bus'ness of a gallant-hearted man,
>> When he sees a maiden lone
>> To adore her as his own—
> That's the bus'ness of a gallant-hearted man.

Katherine:
> 'Tis the bus'ness of a clever-minded maid,
>> When she knows a man is nigh,
>> To be just a little shy—
> That's the bus'ness of a clever-minded maid.

Both:

> 'Tis your bus'ness, whether maid or man you be,
>> To keep out a weather eye,
>> For the other sex is sly—
> That's your bus'ness, whether maid or man you be.

(Enter Martha, hurriedly.)

Martha:

Break off, break off, there is such a funny man coming in.

Katherine:

Ah, dear sister, most men are funny. *(Manuel crosses to Martha.)*

Katherine:

> *(Sings)* You may go from bleak Alaska
> To the Isle of Madagascar,
>> But you'll always find some funny, funny men.

Martha:

> I have found this statement truthful,
> When the men are rather youthful,
>> Oh, they're very, very, very funny men.

Manuel:

> Yes! The men are very human,
> And the ones who don't love woman
>> Are the very, very, very funny men.

All:

> My remarks are surely prudent,
> Tho' I say the thing who shouldn't—
>> There are surely in this world some funny men.

Martha:

But now you shall see a really funny man, singing as he goes.

Manuel:

Rather, singing as he comes. Listen!

Torado:

(Singing without)

        Long years ago, within a distant clime,
        Ere love had touched me with his wand sublime,
        I dreamed of one who'd make my life's calm May,
        The panting passion of a summer's day.
        And ever since, in almost sad suspense,
        I have been waiting with a soul intense,
        To greet, and make unto myself the beams,
        Of her, my star, the lady of my dreams.
        Oh, love, still longed and looked for, come to me,
        Be thy far home by mountain, vale, or sea.
        My yearning heart shall never seek to rest,
        Until thou liest rapt upon my breast.

(Enter Torado.)

        The wind may bring its perfume from the south,
        Is it so sweet as breath from thy dear mouth?
        Oh, naught that surely is and naught that seems
        May turn me from the lady of my dreams.

Manuel:

Ah, Torado, mine, you are hard upon my heels; let me present the ladies—the Prince Torado, Miss Katherine, Miss Martha Morton. *(Torado bows, his eyes fastened on Katherine.)*

Katherine:

(Aside) 'Tis he.

Torado:

(Aside) It is the lady of my dreams. *(To Katherine)* Madam, I have seen you before.

Katherine:

And yet, Sir, methinks we have not met before.

Torado:
Not in the flesh, but in the spirit, yes.

Manuel:
(Apart to Martha) Egad, the wight is bold. I myself would hardly have dared that.

Katherine:
In the spirit?

Torado:
Madam, have you never dreamed of me?

Martha:
Oh, I can assure you, Sir, no: she is very careful what she eats at night.

Katherine:
I pray you, sweet sister, give way, and let me speak.

Manuel:
There. *(Talks apart with Martha.)*

Katherine:
Dreamed of you, Sir; pray what is in a dream?

Torado:
I tax you, lady, answer me true.

Manuel:
But think you not, Prince—

Torado:
Pray forbear, at such a time I have eyes and ears but for one.

Martha:
There, we are both sent about our business. *(Talks with Manuel.)*

Torado:

I pray you, answer me as you would answer a priest at high confessional.

Katherine:

(Meditating) Dreamed of you?

(Sings)

> Pray tell me what can dreams avail
> To make love or to mar;
> The child within the cradle rail
> Lies dreaming of the star;
> But is the star by this beguiled
> To leave its place and seek the child?

> The poor plucked rose within the glass
> Still dreameth of the bee;
> But tho' the lonely moments pass,
> Her love she may not see.
> If dreams of child and rose do fail,
> Why should a maiden's dreams prevail?

(Torado and Katherine talk apart.)

Martha:

(Sings)

> If maidens' dreams could e'er avail,
> To dream of this I'd pray,
> That love would fill a hero's sails,
> And bear his bark my way.
> But, ah, my hero seems as far
> As roving bee or flaming star.

> My heart grows weary waiting here
> My lover's kiss to greet;
> I feel half-saddened by the fear
> That we shall never meet.
> If I could dream him to my side,
> My hero soon should call me bride.

Torado:

(Recitative)

'Tis very plainly proper that this maid should hesitate,
She does not know my fortune, and she does not know my state.
If the object of my visit very shortly I would win,
To disclose myself unto her, now I'm sure I'd best begin.

(Sings)

> I'm a wealthy wand'ring wight, I hail from Madagascar,
> I'm a high born man you see.

Manuel, Katherine, and Martha:

> He's a high-born man you see.

Torado:

> Mother's living on the island, if you doubt me go and see her,
> She'll explain my pedigree.

Manuel, Katherine, and Martha:

> She'll explain his pedigree.

Torado:

> I'm a ruler over kings,
> Over counts, and earls, and things,
> And a royal servant brings
> > My cup of tea.

Manuel, Katherine, and Martha:

> He's a ruler over kings,
> Over counts, and earls, and things,
> And a royal servant brings
> > His cup of tea.

Torado:

> I have journeyed all the way, from this Isle of Madagascar.
> Just to see this maiden here.

Manuel, Katherine and Martha:
Just to see this maiden here.

Torado:
My position being sure, I've determined now to ask her.
If she will not be my dear.

Manuel, Katherine and Martha:
If she will not be his dear.

Torado:
She shall never want a gown,
She shall never see me frown,
If she'll only deign to crown
My love sincere.

Manuel, Katherine and Martha:
She shall never want a gown,
She shall never see him frown,
If she'll only deign to crown
His love sincere.

Katherine:
Oh, love, no longer will I tarry.

Torado:
Then we will wed.

Martha:
These two most surely mean to marry.

Manuel:
(Sings) That's what they said,
But listen to me now, I pray,
For I've a little word to say;
There's just a little rule of whist,
To make me clearer, will assist.

To tell the rule I scarcely need,
       For when your partner gives the lead,
              You follow suit, follow suit.
And so in life, if you are free,
       You imitate the best you see.
So, Martha, if you'll take my hand,
       I'll try to be your hero grand;
Since they before our very face
       Have set so elegant a pace—
              We'll follow suit, follow suit.

Martha:

Ah, Manuel, then dreams avail.

(Sings)

       The bee some day shall find the rose,
              The child shall reach the star;
       Nor love that truly, deeply grows,
              E'r roves for aye afar.
       For here's the moral of the tale—
       That dreams avail, ah, dreams avail.

(Quartet repeats verse.)

Torado:

Well, Manuel, you thought my ideas were wild; but see, I have found a bride.

Manuel:

And helped me to find one.

Katherine and Martha:

Nay, we have found you.

Manuel:

It matters not who are found or have been found.

Torado:

We are happy and free from care. Come, Katherine.

Manuel:

Come, Martha. *(The four advance for closing quartet.)*

Quartet:
> Long, long the labor and the grief,
> > But it must end at last.
> And joy and gladness bring relief
> > For all the gloomy past.
> Oh, joy, that I have found thee,
> For cares no more surround me,
> > My *life*, my *love*, my *own!*
> Tho' long the night, the day will break
> > Above the eastern hills,
> And then the larks of love shall wake
> > Their sweet impassioned trills.
> Oh, etc. *(Repeat.)*

This libretto appeared in The Paul Laurence Dunbar Reader (Martin and Hudson, 1975) and was published originally as Dream Lovers: An Operatic Romance (London: Boosey and Co., 1898).

MUSICAL LYRICS
AND FRAGMENTS

From *In Dahomey*

Evah Dahkey Is a King

Dar's mighty curious circumstance
Dat's a botherin' all de nation
All de Yankees is dissatisfied
Wid deir untitled station

Dey is huntin' after titles
Wid a golden net to snare 'em
And de Democratic people
Dey's mos' mighty glad to wear 'em. Ho!

But dey ain't got all de title
Fur it is a 'culiar ting
When a dahkey starts to huntin'
He is sho to prove a King.

> *Chorus:*
> Evah dahkey is a King
> Royalty is jes' de ting
> Ef yo' social life's a bungle
> Jes you go back to yo' jungle
> An remember dat yo' daddy was a King.

Ev'ry dahkey has a lineage
Dat de white folks can't compete wid

And a title such as duke or earl
Why we wouldn't wipe our feet wid

For a kingdom is our station
Am' we's each a rightful ruler
When we's crown'd we don't wear satins
Kase de way we dress is cooler. Ho!

But our power's just as might
Never judge kings by deir clothes
You could never tell a porter
Wid a ring stuck thro' his nose.

      Chorus:
      Evah dahkey is a King
      Royalty is jes' de ting
      Ef yo' social life's a bungle
      Jes you go back to yo' jungle
      An' remember dat yo' daddy was a king.

Scriptures say dat Ham was de first black man
Ham's de father of our nation
All de black fo'ks to dis very day b'longs
Right in de Ham creation

Ham he was a king in ancient days
An' he reigned in all his glory
Den ef we is all de sons of Ham
Nachelly dat tells de story. So!

White fo'ks what's got dahkey servants
An' doan nevah speak insulting
Fer dat coon may be a King.

      Chorus:

1898. Sheet music is in Howard University Moorland-Spingarn Research Center Collection.

Good Evenin'

A walkin' down de street de other evenin' kinder late,
    Jes a thinkin' a to mah se'f
How when it come to runnin' in de race wid old man fate
    Dat I allus a had a been lef'
De hoses I'd been bakin' hadn't nevah seen de wire
    De bones had gone a stray
When I spied a little damsel wid an eye of teasin' fire
    And to huh I did say

    Chorus:
    Good evenin' won't you take a mah ahm?
    Good evenin' I do'n mean no ha'm
    Dat gal she flashed on me huh eye
    An' as she fluttered gaily by
    She waved huh han' an' made reply
    Good evenin', good evenin'

I took it fu' encouragement an' so I went along
    Fu' I sholy a laked a dat chile
I tried to katch huh 'tention wid a little bit o'song
    but she was a runnin wil'
I took mah place beside huh fu I was playin' swell
    I used mah fines' way
I raised mah hat to s'lute huh when dat gal let off a yell
    An' a great big cop did say

    Chorus:
    Good evenin' won't you take a mah 'ahm?
    Good evenin' I do'n mean a no ha'm
    De way he used me was a sin
    An' je' befo' he locked me in
    Sez he: "Next time buy better gin
    Good evenin', good evenin'"

1898. Sheet music is in Howard University Moorland-Spingarn Research Center Collection.

On Emancipation Day

Streets are gay, on de way, all de alleys don turned out
Mistah Giles, wid Miss Liles, make a figure without doubt
Hyeah dey come Lord dat drum in de black band holds de sway
Cept de brass give it sass on Emancipation Day

> *Chorus:*
> On Emancipation Day
> All you white folks clear de way
> Brass ban' playin' several tunes
> Darkies eyes look jes' lak moons
> Marshall of de day a struttin'
> Word he is so gay
> Coons dressed up lak masqueraders
> Porters armed lak rude invaders
> When dey hear dem ragtime tunes
> White folks try to pass fo' coons on Emancipation Day

Heah 'um cry, my oh my, when de 'cession shows its head
Majors brown ridin' down on cart horses decked in red
Teeth lak pearls greet the girls stand there lak dusky storms
Oh! My pet, what a set of owdacious uniforms
Generals stiff as hick'ry sticks
In de dress of sev'nty six

1898. Sheet music is in Howard University Moorland-Spingarn Research Center Collection.

Returned

Empty and So Silent Now the Old Cabin Stands

I heard him murm'ring softly on an old plantation lone,
The mansion house had crumbled and the walls were overgrown,
A Negro aged and hoary sitting there a dreary sight,
No thought of his condition not a murmer of his plight.
His only dream the mem'ry of the days that had gone by,
When master lived and mistress had the sparkle in her eye,
His only dream the sorrow for the land so rent and grey,
His only moan low mumbled for another better day.

> *Chorus:*
> Empty and so silent now the old cabin stands,
> No spot on earth so dreary as these bare wide lands.
> Here the pleasures of my youth spent,
> Here thro' sorrow's first dim path I went,
> Here tho' deserted will I die content.

I rambled north a wand'rer when the old slave days were done,
I worked from early dawning 'til the setting of the sun,
I toiled and prayed and struggled 'till my heart grew sick an sore,
And turned me sad and weary from many cruel door.
And then my heart turned fondly to this dear old homestead here,
Tho' all my friends have left it and all the land is dear,
But now I come back gladly without a plaint or sigh,
No other spot shall hold my dust or see me bend or die.

1898. Sheet music is in Howard University Moorland-Spingarn Research Center Collection.

From *Clorindy, or the Origin of the Cakewalk*

The Hottest Coon in Dixie

When I go out to stroll away,
I wear my rented suit,
Put on my silk plug hat so gay,
My necktie is a beaut',
Put on my gloves and cane in hand,
I wander down the way,
When e'er I meet some merry beaux,
Here's what the darkies say.

Chorus:
Behold the hottest coon,
Your eyes e'er lit on,
Velvet ain't good enough,
For him to sit on,
When he goes down the street,
Folks yell like sixty,
Behold the hottest coon in Dixie.

The reason why I always win,
My manners are complete,
It's not because I've got the tin,
But then I am so sweet,
The ladies cannot pass me by,
I've always got a girl,
And this is just the proper cry,
They give me, with a whirl.

1902. Sheet music is in Howard University Moorland-Spingarn Research Center Collection.

Who Dat Say Chicken in dis Crowd

There was once a great assemblage of the cullud population
All the cullud swells was there
They had got themselves together to discuss the situation
And the rumors in the air.

There were speakers from Georgia and some from Tennessee
Who were makin' feathers fly
When a roostah in a bahn ya'd flew up whah those folks could see
Then those darkies all did cry.

    Chorus:
    Who dat say chicken in dis crowd?
    Speak de word agin' and speak it loud
    Blame de lan' let white folks rule it
    I'se a lookin' for a pullet
    Who dat say chicken in dis crowd?

A famous cullud preacher told his listnin' congregation all about
    de way to ac',
Ef dey want to be respected an become a mighty nation to be
    hones' fu' a fac'.
Dey mus' nebber lie, no nebber, an' mus not be caught a stealin'
    any pullets fum de' lim',
But an aged deacon got up an' his voice it shook wif feelin'
As dese words he said to him.

    Chorus:
    Who dat say chicken in dis crowd
    Speak de work agin' and speak it loud
    What's de use of all dis talkin'
    Let me hyeah a hen a-squawkin'
    Who dat say chicken in dis crowd.

1902. Sheet music is in Howard University Moorland-Spingarn Research Center Collection.

PART TWO

Essays

INTRODUCTION
TO THE ESSAYS

THOUGH DUNBAR'S POETRY and fiction have commanded considerable critical attention, as an essayist and dramatist he remains largely unknown. Further, because he has been read at times as a plantation-school accommodationist, the political dimensions of his essays and stories have often been overlooked. If there is any doubt about Dunbar's true feelings, we need to turn to his essays, where he explored the problems he confronted as an African American writer. In the essays, we find his unrestrained voice, which addressed with force and determination the ills faced by the black community in his time.

The fifteen essays in this volume provide a glimpse of Dunbar in several moods, raising questions he pursued aggressively in journalistic inquiries beginning as early as his high-school days. In "Higher Education" he addresses not only the "moral, social, and industrial" advancement of African-American students, but also the double standard of justice afforded to his people in the criminal justice system. He is also aware of the class divisions emerging from progress ("Negro Society in Washington"); he attacks the "twaddle" of the Negro press when it becomes fixated on "politics to the exclusion of science, art, and literature" ("Of Negro Journals"). Dunbar's polite directness never ceases to fascinate in essays on education, literature, music, and the issues facing turn-of-the century leaders.

NEARLY THIRTY YEARS ago, Gossie Hudson and Jay Martin argued that Dunbar's "work as a journalist" had been neglected because he wrote "from a black point of view" and "for black papers" expressing "allegiance to the black community"(1975, pp. 31–35). *The Paul Laurence Dunbar Reader* provided a generous sampling of what had been overlooked. These newly collected essays provide even more evidence of Dunbar's life-long commitment to the politics, religion, art, and customs of the African American community over a hundred years ago.

Like his poems, short stories, and plays, Dunbar's essays tell stories. His journalistic eye was from the earliest age keenly focused on the details of daily life as well as on the complex nuances of political issues. "Sunshine at Jackson Park" soaks up the feel of the Chicago lakefront during the 1893 Columbian Exposition. His ear was tuned to what DuBois called a few years later "the sorrow songs" of his race when, in "Negro Music" (1899), he paid tribute to the African roots woven deeply into "the heritage of sorrow." In his essays Dunbar acknowledges as well the place of levity and enjoyment alongside the most serious pursuit of advancement. "There are some of us who believe that there are times in the life of a race when a dance is better than a convention, and a hearty laugh more effective than a Philippic" ("Negro Society in Washington").

Undeniably, Dunbar is concerned with the betterment of his people through education and culture. In almost all of his essays, education is of paramount importance. There is no use of humor to project the agenda of his thoughts. The devices used in *Uncle Eph's Christmas* have been set aside; he speaks directly. He demonstrates in "The Tuskegee Meeting" how ineffective education can be when those in positions of power make all the decisions:

> In the first enthusiasm for teaching the newly emancipated negroes, the North, which was largely unacquainted with the material which it had on hand, went to the extreme of making out their curricula. They followed the right principle of offering to black boys and girls, and to black men and women, for pupils ranged in age then from seven to seventy, the opportunity for the broadest culture. But they made the mistake of offering Latin, Greek and the higher mathematics to minds which had as yet no foundation in the commoner branches. Behind this people were no intellectual traditions, and when all this weight of classicity was placed upon them, they became mentally top heavy. There could be but one outcome of all this and it was seen in the pompous, half educated, big-worded negro who came on the stage of active life after the war.

In the dramatic sense of Dunbar's one act we see well the situation he is satirizing. But when he is faced with the devastation caused by the lack of preparation to be educated properly, he attacks the problem head on.

In one sense Dunbar falls nearer to Washington in the argument which split Booker T. Washington and W. E. B. DuBois at the end of the nineteenth century. It is a matter of record that both of these leaders wanted to educate the black citizen, but the quarrel arose over differing goals and methods. Washington was concerned with the masses and DuBois emphasized the "talented tenth." Dunbar seems to suggest that if you do not belong to the "talented tenth" and have not been properly prepared for education, then you are likely to turn into "the pompous, half educated, big-worded negro." Dunbar observes that the African American "began to find that education meant not only knowing but using. He found that broad culture meant not only the use of big words and high sounding phrases, but a capacity for the enjoyment of the highest things in life."

It is at this juncture, Dunbar concludes, that the black man begins to function as citizen of country and world:

> The doctrine of the thinking mind of today is that the negro must work out his own salvation with fear and trembling. No one is doing more to help the work along than Mr. Washington with his school and conferences. Anything that bands black men together for self improvement is an enterprise to be encouraged. Men may disagree with some of Mr. Washington's ideas[,] and some thinkers do, but they cannot withhold their admiration for his energy, industry and singleness of purpose.

In "Higher Education," Dunbar identified problems still with us over a hundred years later:

> No one has the right to base any conclusions about negro criminality upon the number of prisoners in the jails and other places of restraint. Even at the North, the prejudice against the negro reverses the precedents of law, and every one accused is looked upon as guilty until he is proven innocent. In the South it is worse. Taking into account that some of the offenses for which a white boy would be reprimanded and released, would send a negro to the chain gang or the jail, it is easy to see how the percentage of criminals is raised.

In his poems, Dunbar created the irony of the preacher who claims he is "preaching ancient" and not "talking about today" ("An Ante-Bellum Sermon"). In the essays, he dropped the mask and spoke directly.

Dunbar is also aware that with education comes a kind of division of social classes. Clearly the dangers are separation and castigation. For Dunbar, education is the mark of opening up, an enlightenment, an awareness that makes for a stronger social fabric. It is also a mark of civility and this is what Dunbar sees as the most important reason for acquiring knowledge. Through education we become better people, and in the sharing of knowledge we make others better as well. Genuine intellect changes everyone when it is well placed and effectively employed.

Nowhere is this asserted more forcefully and carefully than in the essay "Of Negro Journals," where he suggests that the early "negro newspapers" had a worthy *causa vivendi* and that the more recent "colored newspapers" were the "first shoots of an intellectual growth [in those] who were popularly supposed to be incapable of any such development." Dunbar's eye is extraordinarily accurate in this case:

> The colored newspaper is not literary; it seldom publishes a story or poem, and a review is almost an unknown feature. . . . [The] negro newspaper is nothing if not partisan. The space that might contain some story or poem that would inspire the young reader to do or be something is given over to twaddle. . . . The aspirations of the race are too entirely upon a political line, and that it is so is the fault of the negro press, for it has preached politics to the exclusion of science, art and literature.

Dunbar is fair-minded. If he points to flaws, he will surely let us know the accomplishments as well. The imparting of knowledge is where the news journals have done their best work. In the end, Dunbar argues that the "negro" newspapers

> have taught their people the use and importance of their suffrage, and if they have misguided it, it is because the privilege was so new. They have at every opportunity impressed upon their readers the fact that they were citizens and if they have said more of loyalty to party than of loyalty to country it is because they looked upon the two as synonymous.
>
> They have made mistakes, but they will live to profit by them, for an institution of which a spirit like Douglass' was one of the pioneers cannot fail.

AS AN ESSAYIST, Dunbar saw consistently the way art and social issues informed each other. Published in *High School Times* (April 1890), "Dickens and Thackeray" paid tribute to Dickens's sympathies with "the sorrows of the poor" and his choice of journalism and novels rather than the law. Whether capturing the feel of everyday life or constructing a political argument, Dunbar regularly called for direct action. In the first issue of *The Tattler* (December 13, 1890), he asked for less discussion of "the race problem" in favor of action: "The agitation of *deeds* is tenfold more effectual than the agitation of *words*. For your own sake, for the sake of Heaven and the race, stop saying and go to doing."

Dunbar was a vivid chronicler of everyday life, a perceptive social critic, and an activist on political issues. He used the essay form to build a bridge across the various genres he mastered. His journalistic probing and his expansive exploratory visions in the essays reinforce the abiding concerns of his dialect poems, his ironic songs, and his standard-English plays. A writer accustomed to camouflage and irony, Dunbar set aside indirection in his essays. Consider his observation that "Washington is the city where the big men of little towns come to be disillusioned." Or his retort to an article critiquing "Negro" education: "It might appropriately be called an essay, founded upon observations of the South from a car window." And the forceful but polite: "If he knew very much about this matter, I would fancy him smiling behind his hand, but I give him the benefit of believing he is ignorant of the subject." In the previously uncollected essays which follow, he crafted a persona that was civil, gentle, direct, and forceful.

🥀

Dickens and Thackeray

IN THE LONG LIST of writers of fiction, no name stands higher than Thackeray and Dickens. They were contemporary writers, and humorists to a great degree, but there was a marked difference in their writings.

Thackeray came of a rich family, and had nothing to do but get rid of a large fortune which was left to him, and he succeeded in doing this beyond his most sanguine expectations. He first chose the profession of an artist, but abandoned this for literature, for which the world should be thankful.

On the other hand, Dickens' parents were constantly in straitened circumstances. He was designed for the law, but that genius which is destined to keep the name of Dickens fresh in the memory of English-speaking people for all time, refused to be shut up in a dark office with musty books, whose contents did not agree with the man whom this genius was to lead. He left the office, became a reporter, and soon after began to write sketches. This was his proper sphere, and here he succeeded.

Nowhere is the difference in the lives of the two novelists more plainly shown than in their representative works. While Dickens gives us a glimpse of wealth and high life, Thackeray gives us continual pictures of the homes of the rich and great. Where Dickens sympathizes with the sorrows of the poor, Thackeray satirizes the foibles of the rich. While Dickens partakes of his humble fare with Toby out upon the street, Thackeray dines sumptuously with the Sedleys and Osbornes in their garnished halls. We laugh with Dickens, we sneer with Thackeray, and admire and drink with both.

The noblest character among all of Thackeray's, that I have read, is William Dobbin. We are inclined to love him for his goodness, but always feel like kicking him for his patience. I appeal to anyone who has ever read the greatest of all his works, "Vanity Fair," if he didn't want to see Dobbin married to Amelia long years before he was. We admire the man because he has such a quiet, gentle way of doing his good deeds: they are not done to be seen of men, but are the outbursts of a heart naturally good and charitable. His noble character is brought out more distinctly by being placed side by side with the direct opposite, George Osborne, who loved only one person, and that was George Osborne, and a more selfish, conceited dandy would be hard to imagine. Thackeray very ably illustrates through him the truth, that often things which are easy to attain are not regarded at their proper value. He knew that he had the affection of Amelia Sedley, and so self-assured and self-satisfied was he that he made no effort to keep it; he was continually condescending, and one always has the idea that he considered it a great condescension on his part to allow his betrothed to admire him. We like Osborne better after he is killed, probably because we are glad to get rid of him, or because it is human nature to forget a man's faults after he is dead.

The only character which I have ever encountered which equaled Osborne in selfishness, was Mr. Dombey in Dickens' "Dombey and Son." He seems to have built a wall of gold around him, and then within it, without either light or air, to have literally dried up. His love for his little son was only another kind of selfishness; he loved him only because he should carry the name of

Dombey down, and give the sign over his place of business added dignity with, "and son," suffixed to the "Dombey." Looking at him directly, you do not see a man, only the big glowing letters Mr. Dombey, of the firm of Dombey & Son. Mr. Dombey was a petrifaction, he was a fossil, and we always come out of his presence feeling as if we had been handling an icicle, not to say, though, that anyone handled Mr. Dombey.

Mr. Weller, who has been introduced to us in "Pickwick Papers," is one of Dickens' most amusing characters, even in that day. Mr. Weller saw how the courts of law were degenerating; he saw better than the lawyers for the defendant, that there should have been a writ of "have 'is carcass" in the breach of promise suit of Bardell *vs.* Pickwick. We listen with delight to Mr. Weller, we have the same aversion to writers of poetry, knowing that only coachmen stoop to it, and in closing we say to all mankind, as he said to his son Samivel, "Beware o' the widders."

High School Times 9 no. 8 (April 1890).

December 13, 1890

A GREAT MISTAKE that has been made by editors of the race is that they only discuss one question, the race problem. This no doubt is important, but a quarter of a century of discussion of one question has worn it thread-bare; we may venture to assert without fear of refutation, that no new idea has been presented upon this subject for the last ten years, and yet it is hacked at, and tossed about until one is almost prone to say, that more harm than good is being done. We do not counsel you debaters, writers and fellow editors, to throw away your————on this all important————the contrary———— worthy—const—— the time has come when you should act your opinions out, rather than write them. Your cry is "we must agitate, we must agitate." So you must but bear in mind that the agitation of *deeds* is tenfold more effectual than the agitation of *words*. For your own sake, for the sake of Heaven and the race, stop saying, and go to doing. Find other things than this one question to talk about; the political field teems with abundant material. Give us a variety and cease feeding your weary readers on an unbroken diet of the race problem.

Dayton, Ohio, Henry Romeike news clipping, December 13, 1890, Paul Laurence Dunbar Collection, Reel V, Box 18, OHS.

Of Negro Journals

Special to the Chicago Record.

DAYTON, O., JUNE 22. —For one to dilate upon the important part which journalism has taken in the uplifting of mankind would be an ungrateful, because an unnecessary, task. The power of the press has been too long known and too universally acknowledged for one at this late day to lay upon his shoulders the burden of proving its reality. The freedom of the press has ever been closely allied to the prosperity of the people and a living proof of the statement is in the American nation. From these facts it has come to be an accepted principle to judge the general progress of a people by the character and tone of its press.

If this standard be a true one it may not be amiss to look into negro journalism as a very considerable entity in the discussion of the black man's advancement.

Even a cursory glance over the past history of his journalistic achievements will show that the negro's newspaper, crude and faulty as it may have been, has not merely kept pace with his evolutions, but rather led the way. It was the voice of an oppressed people uplifted through *Freedom's Journal*, the *Ram's Horn* and the *North Star* that awakened pubic opinion and paved —albeit with jagged rocks—the way to emancipation. However feeble the efforts, however incapable the projectors, however brief the existence of many of those ante-bellum journals, they, at least, had a worthy *causa vivendi,* which is more than can be said of some of their successors.

After Uses for These Papers

They were actuated by a stern purpose that was their producer and preserver. They were knights errant arrayed against the dragon Slavery, to whose ferocity many of them were sacrificed. When he was finally laid low, it would have been fair to suppose that this separate and distinct press had no further call for existence, but not so. As soon as the head of Slavery was cut off the negro found that the monster was like Hydra, and that there were a dozen more very aggressive heads newly arisen that needed destroying. In the emergency five papers arose for every head. Subsequently this proposition has been maintained, which accounts for the 250 papers published by colored people in the United States today.

But it has been a question in the minds of some as to whether the colored newspaper has not increased in quantity rather than in quality. Indeed, a few have had the temerity to assert that the old journals were better edited and impressed the reader more deeply than the modern papers. But this is a delusion which the different circumstances surrounding the two publications make natural. The old journals were more impressive, not because they were better edited but because they brimmed with but one purpose, and that a purpose which was alive in the heart of every friendly reader. They discussed but one question, and that a question which was agitating the mind of every unfriendly reader. They called forth more attention because they were rarer. More of the white race read them than read negro journals now, because they were the first shoots of an intellectual growth in a people who were popularly supposed to be incapable of any such development, and as such were novelties.

Papers Read Only by Blacks

It is one of the disadvantages that the negro journal has to encounter in its protest against national wrongs that it is generally read only by the wronged race. It does not reach the people whom it would affect. So confined is its scope that its labors become fruitless. For it is constantly presenting the sad truth to people who already know it and flaunting crimes and outrages in the faces of people who never think of committing them. If a white man takes [i.e. subscribes to] a colored man's paper it is generally, as he expresses it, for the purpose of "helping him along" and he never for an instant supposes that there is or can be anything in it to interest him. But is this true? And if it is true where does the fault rest?

People of intelligent tastes have pleasures in common and there should be no reason why an intelligent, fair-minded white man should not enjoy the same paper that gives pleasure to a black man of like temperament and accomplishments. But the fact of the matter is this: The negro newspaper is too often not a paper designed for general reading. It is too closely a chronicle of unimportant personal facts, unrelieved by the less confined interest of an editorial column. In picking up a strange paper it is to the editorial column that one instinctively turns and if a dearth be found there little hope can be entertained for the rest of the paper. Again, the colored newspaper is not literary; it seldom publishes a story or poem, and a review is almost an unknown feature.

Intelligent colored men read and tolerate these papers because the papers are in closer contact with the people whose doings they chronicle. But what possible interest can the white friend of the race, who pays for a year's subscription, have in the fact that "Miss Peggy Wilson of Plum Tree Center gave a taffy-pull last week"? It is this attention to minute and personal details that precludes any general circulation of the colored man's newspaper.

Partisan Leaning of the Press

Another fault of the colored man's journalism lies in the fact that your negro newspaper is nothing if not partisan. Every petty journal that is started launches out upon the stormy sea of politics—poor, frail craft on a main where so many stauncher vessels are wrecked. Every little sheet, it matters not how insignificant, must needs raise its voice in the affairs of government and throw its featherweight of influence in the scales to help turn the balance one way or the other. The space that might contain some story or poem that would inspire the young reader to do or be something is given over to twaddle about the merits of the candidate for sheriff. The column that might be filled with helpful household hints to the girls whose mothers have so lately come from toiling in the cotton fields, is devoted to exploiting the merits of the man who wants to be county prosecutor. The black race in America is hungry for right, knowledge, and valuable information. And oh, negro editors, they "ask you for bread and you give them a stone." Is it fair to them or best for yourselves?

It is an unfortunate fact that the average colored editor is poor enough to be in the range of temptation. And too often the silver of some candidate, which crosses his palm makes him to prophesy good that never comes and to hide evil that is present.

I do not write as a malicious croaker, but as one deeply interested in the development of the best that is in the negro. And I dare to say that the negro press has not accomplished the best that it could have done; that it has not supplied the wants of its people; that it has given them wrong aspirations and fostered wrong tastes in them.

Men Regarded as Successful

The man who through subserviency to party succeeds in securing a janitorship in a public building is of more weight in the race and more highly respected than he who through constant study and hard labor seeks to put and succeeds in putting himself on an intellectual level with his white brother. The aspirations of the race are too entirely dependent upon a political line, and that it is so is the fault of the negro press, for it has preached politics to the exclusion of science, art and literature.

There is a certain prominent negro journal which supplements its statement of terms with the announcement that all poetical contributions must be accompanied by payment for publication at regular advertising rates. Rare encouragement, indeed, for that proverbially impecunious class, the poets.

"But," some optimistic brother remarks, "look at the training the numerous correspondents of these papers secure." But is this training a fact? Real training consists in having one's faults corrected and one's mistakes set right. But nine-tenths of the negro editors pass the communications of their correspondents without correction and allow them to go forth in cold type with all their imperfections on their head. The correspondent reads it just as he wrote it, and supposes that it must have been right and "the last state of that man is worse than the first."

It is not to be imagined, though, that these papers, faulty as they are, have accomplished no good. Far from it. They have taught their people the use and the importance of their suffrage, and if they have misguided it, it is because the privilege was so new. They have at every opportunity impressed upon their readers the fact that they were citizens and if they have said more of loyalty to party than of loyalty to country it is because they looked upon the two as synonymous.

They have made mistakes, but they will live to profit by them, for an institution of which a spirit like Douglass's was one of the pioneers cannot fail.

God has given them a message to deliver and they will correct their faults and live up to the "high source of their endowment."

Chicago Record, June 22, 1894, Paul Laurence Dunbar Collection, Reel V, Box 18, OHS.

England as Seen by a Black Man

NOTHING COULD BE more significant than the word "impressions," when speaking of England from a Negro's point of view. For "impressed" he is, from the time he sets foot on English soil until he is again upon his native shores. He may not set down the new sensations which he is experiencing as so many separate estimates of a people and a condition, but when he is home again, all that he has seen and heard crystallizes in the changed environment. In so far as he is like other men in his nature and condition, he is similarly affected by what he sees and hears about him. He is astounded by the evidences of age which surround him. He is bewildered by the magnitude of the greatest city in the world. Her temples and her taverns, her homes and her hedges, the places where Romance has blossomed and the spots where History has made her abiding-place—all these stir him to broader views and higher thoughts. But more than by all these, more than is possible to the average man, is he impressed by the new conditions with which he comes into contact.

The Negro who takes a right view of the matter must realize that it is not so much what he has lost in coming home as it is what he has learned in being away, that is of value. To be sure, it is a great thing to have been accepted upon the basis of worth alone; to have found a people who do not assert color as a badge of degradation. But it is more to have learned that an unmistakably great people look upon the black race in America with hope, interest, and admiration. It is a good thing to have been accepted upon terms of equality in excellent English families; but it is of infinitely more importance to have come away from contact with this institution, which has been at the very foundation of British power, with some ideas to inform and elevate Negro family life. This latter seems to me to be a point of especial importance.

The beauty and perfection of a pure family life is one thing which, say what we will, the Negro needs greatly to learn. I must confess that no phase of English social observance struck me more forcibly than this.

It seems to me that we Americans, of whatever caste or complexion, hold too lightly the ties of relationship. More and more are our natures taking on the Gallic character, in which the distinguishing trait is not a love of family. Our whole tendency is to the glorification of the individual. I wish I could have taken some of my black brothers who have come to the North and prospered, and in prosperity forgotten the parental cabin in Kentucky or Virginia or Tennessee, into the heart of a typical middle-class English household. I would want them to see how, with these people, the good of the whole is the primal thing, and how all work together harmoniously for the best ends.

I would have some of those whom I hear exclaiming against marriage and the "bother" of children go into these families and, apart from any ethical consideration, just witness the simple delight of such an association. The father with his sturdy sons grouped about him, the mother in the midst of her healthful, hearty daughters—great, strong, big families; they are kingdoms in themselves.

An incidental point in this same matter which will force itself upon the observer's mind is the manner in which an English boy is trained. I like his reverence for authority, a feeling that is inculcated at the very beginning of his life. He knows how to obey.

Against this view, some one may urge the highhanded violations of which the young English aristocrat has been guilty, their open defiance of law on account of their position; but I do not feel that they are representative either of the whole English people, or of the best English people. I do not believe that a nation is any more fairly represented by her highest than by her lowest. Park Place and Berkeley Square are no more England than is Whitechapel. It is the great middle-class, the bone and sinew of the country, which is the true index of the national tendency; and the way a middle-class boy is trained is a thing to be admired and imitated. The youngster believes that he is a citizen of the greatest country on earth. To him, the world is composed of England, her possessions, and a few other countries. But he looks through all the intervening stages of society up to the one who is the epitome of all the power and glory of his country.

Everywhere he turns he sees the ramifications of this power and glory, which he always refers to the source. So, while he grows up with a pride in his land, with a sturdy independence, yet his strongest emotions are tempered by an earnest and deep-rooted respect for authority.

After considering the boy in his home, I can understand the spirit of the Englishman in the field. The attitude of the youth toward his parents, to me, interprets Balaklava.[1]

I am a little afraid that it is too often taken as an indication of commendable spirit when one of our boys smashes his slate and kicks his governess. It is, without doubt, spirit of a kind. It is true that there are some few geniuses, a necessity of whose being it is that they be a law unto themselves; but it will not do for a whole nation. Indeed, most of us poor mortals need governing. We are clay and must have the potter's hand. On the voyage home I remember being told by a genial Western American that his little son was a perfect aristocrat, and, in support of his statement, he related to me how his young heir would show his extreme contempt for servants and people below his class. He was delighted at the child's early recognition of his own superiority. To my mind, feeling as I do the danger which menaces us from the very feeling of our independence, it was a serious fault that needed speedy correction. The proud father, tho, had the grace to add; "But that boy of mine will

[1]A battle in the Crimean War (1853–56) where the English lost over half of the Light Brigade when they misunderstood an order to charge. The incident is the subject of Tennyson's famous poem "The Charge of the Light Brigade" (1854).

get out of all that before he is through with these American public schools." Perhaps he will.

Here again, in this matter of obedience, of respect for authority and submission to control, the point of view of a black man comes in. I believe that it is Mr. Fortunate who so wisely says that what the Negro needs is not so much leaders as the ability to follow when he is led. This is true, and with a reason. For so long a time he was the sole obeying party that when he did come to have command of his own affairs a violent reaction took place, and he stoutly objected to being led or commanded by anybody. He seemed to think that the highest evidence of a state of freedom was a refusal to obey superiors. He recognized vaguely that the genius of American civilization is the equality of all men; and he reduced the principle to his own ideas and said: "I am as good as anybody else; therefore I will be commanded by nobody. If I cannot lead, I will not follow." To be sure, he held this opinion in common with far too many white citizens; but the black man so deeply needs the centralization of power which would come from following one captain that it is to him especially I would commend the lesson of English obedience.

A not less important thing that is worth deep consideration, if not full imitation, is the British subject's contentment with his lot in life. I have been told that it is not contentment, but the lethargy of despair. But I do not believe it even of the lowest laborers. It is rather, a stolid, common-sense philosophy of life which says: "Let me enjoy whatever of pleasure comes to me and make the best of the inevitable sorrows." It says: "I will love my children and do the best I can to raise them to a better condition; but if I cannot leave them any other heritage, I will not leave them one of discontent and unrest." Our peasantry, if such the laboring blacks may be called, in condition is much like that of England; but in realization and acceptance of their lot, how different. The novel message of freedom has been blown into their ears with such a ringing blast that the din has for the moment confused them. Every man reads his own destiny in the stars, and sees only greatness there. He who preaches the doctrine that "They also serve who only stand and wait" is a heretic.

I know that I shall be accused of applauding, even of recommending, the stifling of honest ambition. But I do not go so far as that. What I mean is, that I prefer peace to popularity, content to a state of constant striving after ideals that cannot for many years be attained by the black race. I mean that

I would have black men, who are vainly beating their heads against the impregnable wall of adverse circumstances, stop and recognize their limitations —learn a lesson of these stolid people and cease to fret away their little lives in unavailing effort. I want this for the blacks because I want them to be happy. I do not want them to continue to imbibe the dangerous draught which has intoxicated their white brothers of this Western world and sent them raving madmen, struggling for life at the expense of their fellows in the stock-markets and the wheat-pits of our great cities. I would not have black men unambitious; but I would not have them disturb the even course of their lives with feverish dreams—dreams from which but one awakening is possible. Few there are who do not know how little it has taken to make these people happy, from how small a flower they have drawn the honey of joy; but because the blossom has developed, I would not have them ravish the plant.

It would be an inestimable blessing if a number of Negroes from every State in the Union could live abroad for a few years, long enough to cool in their blood the fever-heat of strife. Here where there is so much opposition to his development, and, remember, I do not assert that is always conscious and intentional, the black man practices defense until it grows into aggression. Remove him from his surroundings, take away the barrier against which he is constantly pushing, and he will return to the perpendicular—to the upright.

England as the home for Negroes? No, a thousand times, no! Kentucky, Tennessee, Virginia, yes; even New York, Ohio, or Illinois, is better. England has her population. The Negro has a home, one which he loves and reveres. He has tilled its soil; he has felled its forests; he has digged its mines; in bitter times he has wrenched prosperity from reluctant nature; but, like an ignorant boy, I would have him go out into the school of the world and, having learned his lesson, come home and apply it. I would have him go and learn strength from a strong people, and, coming home, use that power, if it be vouchsafed him to use it in no other way, in just living and loving and being quiet.

I would not have the man who fails here go to England to succeed. Because merit is not discouraged there on account of color, neither is it taken for granted because one is black.

The Independent, September 16, 1897.

Our New Madness

WE NEGROES ARE a people who are prone to be taken by sudden enthusiasms. We fly with the swiftness of thought from one extreme to another. We are young, and we have the faults of youth and commit its errors. Age and experience, perhaps bitter, most certainly wholesome, must teach us conservatism.

We are now in the throes of feverish delight over industrial education. It is a good thing, and yet one of which we can easily have too much. There is only one point, hardly large enough, it seems, to make the basis of an article, to which I wish to call attention. It is the danger we court of going to the other extreme of educating the hand to the exclusion of the needs of the head.

The answer naturally comes back: "But industrial education means the equal training of the hand and head." Of course it does; but the danger is that the meaning may be mistaken, and the most easily appearing surface points only seized. That is, that while the high and sublime object of teaching may be to produce an able, thinking carpenter, with the power of enjoying the higher intellectual pleasures of life, is it not likely that what will be produced from this new people will be a carpenter with a steady hand—and I do not decry that—but with a mind out of which is shut all appreciation for the beauty of art, science, and literature.

You say: "But we can't all be doctors and lawyers and preachers." No, to be sure not, but let some of us be; for we cannot all of us be carpenters, tinners, and brick-masons.

There has been here, of late, too great an insistence upon manual training for the negro. He needs it. Any one who has studied his condition, either at the North or the South, cannot but admit that. But that the demands of his heart and mind call also for the most liberal and the broadest culture he can get, the earnest seeker after truth cannot deny.

The statement has been so strongly and so frequently urged that the negro should work with his hands, that the opposite of the proposition has been implied. People are taking it for granted that he ought not to work with his head. And it is so easy for these people among whom we are living to believe this; it flatters and satisfies their self-complacency.

At this late day the negro has no need to prove his manual efficiency.

That was settled fifty years ago, when he was the plantation blacksmith and carpenter and shoemaker. But his intellectual capacity is still in doubt. Any attempt at engaging in pursuits where his mind is employed is met by an attitude that stigmatizes his effort as presumption. Then if the daring one succeeds, he is looked upon as a monster. He is put into the same category with the "two-headed boy" and the "bearded lady." There has not, in the history of the country, risen a single intellectual black man whose pretensions have not been sneered at, laughed at, and then lamely wondered at. If he was fair of complexion, they said that he derived his powers from his white blood. If he was convincingly black, they felt of his bumps, measured his head, and said that it was not negro in conformation. It is his intellectuality that needs substantiating.

Any one who has visited the school at Tuskegee, Alabama, and seen the efficiency of the work being done there, can have no further doubt of the ability and honesty of purpose of its founder and president. But I do fear that this earnest man is not doing either himself or his race full justice in his public utterances. He says we must have industrial training, and the world quotes him (in detached paragraphs) as saying that we must not have anything else.

A young man wants to enter a profession, and he speaks to a white man eminent in that particular work. The reply comes: "Now, what do you want to try a profession for? Why don't you take up a trade of some kind?"

"But I don't want to take a trade," says the young man. "I want to follow my own bent."

"Well, you're all wrong. It's just as your man, Mr. Washington, down there says; you people ought to be content to do manual labor for generations yet. I have always said that the colored people were too ambitious and expected too much."

"But suppose that individual inclinations—"

"You have no right to any individual feeling in the matter. You should consider your race and its especial fitness for certain kinds of work," and so on *ad nauseam*.

Now here I object. I do not believe that the individual should bend his spirit in accordance with ideas, mistaken or otherwise, as to what his race should do. I do not believe that a young man, whose soul is turbulent with a message which should be given to the world through the pulpit or the press, should shut his mouth and shoe horses; nor do I believe that this is what the best advocates of manual training would teach; but it is the interpretation which the great world is putting on their doctrine.

The incident is related that during the late war, just after the fall of a Southern city, an old colored man was seen stealing out of a lawyer's dismantled office with two volumes of Blackstone's "Commentaries" under his arm. To the question "What are you going to do with them, Uncle Ike?" he replied: "Hush, chile! I's gwine to run fu' Cong'ess."

It is just possible that the negro of the present day is not too wise to seize the most palpable tools of a strange system, and miss the deeper meaning of the whole.

I would not counsel a return to the madness of that first enthusiasm for classic and professional learning; but I would urge that the negro temper this newer one with a right idea of the just proportion in life of industry, commerce, art, science, and letters, of materialism and idealism, of utilitarianism and beauty!

The Independent, August 18, 1898.

☙

Negro Music

THE STRANGE, FANTASTIC melody of the old plantation music has always possessed a deep fascination for me. There is an indescribable charm in it—a certain poetic sadness that appeals strongly to the artistic in one's nature.

The idea that art really had anything to do with this quality of negro music I never for a moment entertained. But, question as I might, I could never find out its source until passing through Midway Plaisance[1] some weeks ago

---

[1] Midway Plaisance was the walking street in the center of a group of international pavilions at the World's Columbian Exposition in Chicago in 1893, where an exchange of cultures was on display, and music was heard as those in attendance moved from one exhibit to another.

I heard the Dahomeyans[2] singing. Instantly the idea flashed into my mind: "It is a heritage."

Perhaps this thought has already struck many others, but I must confess that it has just dawned upon me, and I am startled at its suddenness and evident plausibility.

I heard in the Dahomeyans' singing the same rich melody, the same mournful minor cadences, that have touched the heart of the world through negro music. It is the unknown something in the voice that so many people have tried to define and failed.

The Dahomeyan sings the music of his native Africa; the American negro spends this silver heritage of melody, but adds to it the bitter ring of grief for wrongs and adversities which only he has known. The Dahomeyan startles us; the negro American thrills us. The Dahomeyan makes us smile; the negro American makes us weep and smile to weep again.

If my hypothesis be correct, the man who asks where the negro got all those strange tunes of his songs is answered. They have been handed down to him from the matted jungles and sunburned deserts of Africa, from the reed huts of the Nile.

When F. J. Loudin[3] of the Fisk Jubilee Singers told me how the people flocked to hear his troupe sing their simple old plantation songs I wondered. When I heard a college glee club or a white male quartet sing those same songs, with strict attention to every minute detail of time, attack the harmony, I no longer wondered. It is only the negro who can sing these songs with effect. The white professional acts; the negro feels. Here lies the difference. With the black man's heritage of song has come the heritage of sorrow, giving to his song the expression of a sorrowful sweetness which the mere imitator can never attain.

Many of the old plantation hymns, rude and uncouth as they were, improvised by the negroes themselves under the influence of strong religious zeal, are models of melodic beauty. Underlined almost invariably by a strain of sadness, they sometimes burst out into rays of hope, rising above the commonplace and reaching up to the sublime.

[2] "Dahomeyans" is a reference to the people of the former West African Republic called Benin, now part of Nigeria. It is also a reference to one who is a member of the chiefly Ewe-speaking Dahomean people.

[3] F. J. Loudin (1842[43?]–1904) was an Ohioan who joined the Fisk Jubilee Singers (see footnote 3 on page 186) before they toured Great Britain in 1875.

Through them all can be traced the effect of the condition of the people. The years of depression and fear, with their intermittent moments of flickering hope, going out again in despair, and then again brightening into a hope that is almost a surety.

Even at the present day go into some of the small churches of the South and listen to their hymns. The voices of the singers assume a tone that one cannot describe. There is still that wavering minor cadence that cannot be imitated. It is that heritage of expression still there, and through it all one can hear the strain running like the theme of a symphony—the strain a supplication to God for deliverance.

It is said, and generally conceded to be true, that the negro is ashamed of his music. If it be so, it is a shame to be rebuked and one which he must overcome, for he has the most beautiful melodies of any in the world. They are his by inheritance and it is for him to make the best use of his rich legacy. Let black composers—and there are such—weave those melodies into their compositions, and to him who laughs and says that they are only fit to be played upon the banjo let them say that the banjo makes quite as sweet music as the bagpipe.

Foreign critics have said that these plantation songs were the only original music that America has produced. This is a mis-statement, for America has not produced even these; she has only taken what Africa has given her.

If the American negro consults his best interest, he will seize upon these songs, preserve them and make them distinctively his own. It has been recently demonstrated that what he refuses to accept as a gift others will steal. Let him out with false pride and come into the heritage which is his own.

Chicago Record, 1899, Paul Laurence Dunbar Collection, Reel IV, Box 18, OHS.

The Tuskegee Meeting

ABOUT THE NEGRO CONFERENCE,[1] which for the last eight years has been held annually at Booker T. Washington's Tuskegee school, there clings a fine spirit of novelty. The school, itself, is a new departure in the affairs of negro education. Just after the war, when the thirst for knowledge among the black folks was well-nigh insatiable, schools were founded for them, and the best material in the north was sent down to take charge of them. The American Missionary Society,[2] the kindred organizations, took the matter in hand and founded such places of learning as Fisk,[3] Straight[4] and Atlanta[5] Universities. But in the first enthusiasm for teaching the newly emancipated negroes the North, which was largely unacquainted with the material which it had on hand, went to the extreme of making out their curricula. They followed the right principle of offering to black boys and girls, and to black men and women, for pupils ranged in age then from seven to seventy, the opportunity for the broadest culture. But they made the mistake of offering Latin, Greek and the higher mathematics to minds which had as yet no foundation in the commoner branches. Behind this people were no intellectual traditions, and

---

[1] Negro Conference is perhaps a reference to the many gatherings held to discuss the educational needs of the race at Tuskegee.

[2] American Missionary Society (Association) was organized in 1846. It wanted to be a voice of reason which spoke against slavery. Its first schools were elementary but from its inception the organization was interested in normal schools and colleges. It was also an association instrumental in providing relief to poverty stricken freedmen as well as helping to found Straight, Fisk, and Atlanta Universities and Hampton Institute.

[3] Fisk University, a private, co-educational school, was founded in 1866. A year later the Fisk Jubilee Singers formed. In 1870 the university began a critical financial struggle. It was at this point that the group began giving concerts to earn money for the university. By the end of 1880, when they disbanded, they had earned $150,000 for their *alma mater*.

[4] Straight University was founded in 1869. It was later renamed Straight College. In 1930, Straight College and Union Normal School merged to become Dillard University. The school has ties to many Protestant denominations, the Methodist and the Congregationalist in particular.

[5] Atlanta University was founded in Atlanta, Georgia, for the purpose of educating children of slaves. Its first classes were held in a church and a railroad boxcar. Today, Atlanta University consists of four undergraduate colleges: Morehouse, Spelman, Clark, and Morris.

when all this weight of classicity was placed upon them, they became mentally top heavy. There could be but one outcome of all this and it was seen in the pompous, half educated, big-worded negro who came on the stage of active life after the war. He could parse you a Latin noun and could demonstrate a theorem in geometry, he could work out a problem in conic sections, but he could not make a living unless he found some pitiful church in a more pitiful community which he could cling to like an incubus, or found down in the country some school where he could impart his half knowledge to others of his race.

But very soon a gradual change began to take place. The negro began to find that education meant not only knowing but using. He found that broad culture meant not only the use of big words and high sounding phrases, but a capacity for the enjoyment of the highest things in life. He began to teach in the schools that had been organized for him, and began to organize some of his own. The churches of the race came in now, and took up some of the educational work, and their colleges and seminaries aided in sending out men fully equipped for the work of teaching others. But it was out of a school that all those people began to learn, then farm. They compare notes upon the work that has already been done, upon the improvements that have already been made, and each year shows the good results of the suggestions of last year's conference. Old men, who have been plodding on in their own ignorant way, year after year, wrenching from the reluctant earth a bare livelihood, after attending one or two perhaps, of these meetings, come back to report new methods of labor, better success with crops, and money saved. The bane of the black farmer's life has been the mortgage of his crops before they are planted, and the rental of his land paid in its best products. The former kept him ever in debt, the latter left him with only the scantiest remnants of what he had grown, when the land owner was paid. But eight years of planning together, eight years of intelligent attention to the ways and means of managing his affairs, has changed all this in the region about Tuskegee. Many of them own their own land, and the money from the products which at the end of the year once went into the owner's treasury, now goes to fill their own.

Taking as his text that the home is the foundation of all society, Mr. Washington has constantly preached in these meetings the importance of the home life. The one room log cabin where neither health——especial good plan for making——does not require a paper on scientific principles of

————making———tells her sisters how she does it; and Mr. Washington re-
wards this part, the cooking, as a very———I do not know that he has———
one———nevertheless true, that it is necessary to keep his stomach quite as
condition as to keep his soul———God knows that it is a hard thing for a
man, white or black, to be upright, industrious and honest on heavy bread
and sodden meat.

Perhaps the highest tribute to the wisdom of the Tuskegee conference is
the fact that they gain in interest year by year. More and more people come
to attend it, and the district from which its numbers are drawn grows wider
and wider. It teaches the people what they have never yet known, how to enjoy
home life. It comes as a revelation to men who have known no higher pleasures
than in the gin jug and the frequent fight. It has shown that there is some relief
from labor, or other indulgence in vice and rowdyism. It has taught them con-
fidence in themselves and in each other, and given the impetus to mutual aid.

The doctrine of the thinking mind of today is that the negro must work
out his own salvation with fear and trembling. No one is doing more to help
the work along than Mr. Washington with his school and his conferences.
Anything that bands black men together for self improvement is an enter-
prise to be encouraged. Men may disagree with some of Mr. Washington's
ideas and some thinkers do, but they can not withhold their admiration for
his energy, industry, and singleness of purpose.

Providence, R. I. *Telegram* news clipping, February 19, 1899, Paul Laurence Dunbar
Collection, Reel IV, Box 16, OHS.

Negro Life in Washington

WASHINGTON IS THE CITY where the big men of little towns come to be
disillusioned. Whether black or white, the little great soon seek their level
here. It matters not whether it is Ezekiel Corncray of Podunk Center, Ver-
mont, or Isaac Johnson of the Alabama black belt—in Washington he is apt
to come to a realization of his true worth to the world.

In a city of such diverse characteristics it is natural that the life of any portion of its people should be interesting. But when it is considered that here the experiment of sudden freedom has been tried most earnestly, and, I may say, most successfully, upon a large percentage of the population, it is to the lives of these people that one instinctively turns for color, picturesqueness, and striking contrast.

It is the delicately blended or boldly differentiated light and shade effects of Washington negro life that are the despair of him who tries truthfully to picture it.

It is the middle-class negro who has imbibed enough of white civilization to make him work to be prosperous. But he has not partaken of civilization so deeply that he has become drunk and has forgotten his own identity. The church to him is still the centre of his social life, and his preacher a great man. He has not—and I am not wholly sorry that he has not—learned the repression of his emotions, which is the mark of a high and dry civilization. He is impulsive, intense, fervid, and—himself. He has retained some of his primitive ingenuousness. When he goes to a party he goes to enjoy himself and not to pose. If there be onlookers outside his own circle, and he be tempted to pose, he does it with such childlike innocence and good humor that no one is for a moment anything but amused, and he is forgiven his little deception.

Possibly in even the lower walks of life a warmer racial color is discoverable. For instance, no other race can quite show the counterpart of the old gentleman who passes me on Sunday on his way to church. An ancient silk hat adorns a head which I know instinctively is bald and black and shiny on top; but the edges are fringed with a growth of crisp white hair, like a frame around the mild old face. The broadcloth coat which is buttoned tightly around the spare form is threadbare, and has faded from black to gray green; but although bent a little with the weight of his years, his glance is alert, and he moves briskly along, like a character suddenly dropped out of one of Page's stories. He waves his hand in salute, and I have a vision of Virginia of fifty years ago.

A real bit of the old South, though, as one sees it in Washington, is the old black mammy who trundles to and fro a little baby-carriage with its load of laundry-work, but who tells you, with manifest pride, "Yes, suh. I has nussed off 'n on, mo'n a dozen chillun of de X fambly, an' some of de men dat's ginuls now er in Cong'ess was jes nachully raised up off'n me." But she, like so many others, came to Washington when it was indeed the Mecca for colored people, where lay all their hopes of protection, of freedom, and of advancement. Perhaps in the old days when labor brought better rewards, she saved something and laid it by in the ill-fated Freedman's Savings Bank. But the story of that is known; so the old woman walks the streets to-day, penniless, trundling her baby-carriage, a historic but pathetic figure.

Some such relic of the past, but more prosperous withal, is the old lady who leans over the counter of a tiny and dingy restaurant on Capitol Hill and dispenses coffee and rolls and fried pork to her colored customers. She wears upon her head the inevitable turban or handkerchief in which artists delight to paint the old mammies of the South. She keeps unwavering the deep religious instinct of her race and is mighty in her activities on behalf of one or the other of the colored churches. Under her little counter she always has a contribution-book, and not a customer, white or black, high or low, who is not levied upon to "he'p de chu'ch outen hits stress." But one who has sat and listened to her, as leaning chin on hand, she recounted one of her weird superstitious stories of the night-doctors and their doings, or the "awful jedgement on a sinnah man," is not unwilling to be put at some expense for his pleasure.

The old lady and her stories are of a different cast from that part of the Washington life which is the pride of her proudest people. It is a far cry from the smoky little restaurant on the Hill, with its genial and loquacious old owner, to the great business block on Fourteenth Street and its wealthy, shrewd, and cultivated proprietor.

Colored men have made money here, and some of them have known how to keep it. There are several of them on the Board of trade—five, I think —and they are regarded by their fellows as solid, responsible, and capable businessmen. The present assessment law was drafted by a colored member of the board, and approved by them before it was submitted to Congress.

As for the professions, there are so many engaged in them that it would keep one busy counting or attempting to count the dark-skinned lawyers and doctors one meets in a day.

The cause of this is not far to seek. Young men come here to work in the departments. Their evenings are to a certain extent free. It is the most natural thing in the world that they should improve their time by useful study. But why such a preponderance in favor of the professions, you say. Are there not other useful pursuits—arts and handicrafts? To be sure there are. But then your new people dearly love a title, and Lawyer Jones sounds well, Dr. Brown has an infinitely more dignified ring, and as for Professor—well, that is the acme of titular excellence, and there are more dark professors in Washington than one could find in a day's walk through a European college town.

However, it is well that these department clerks should carry something away with them when they leave Washington, for their condition is seldom financially improved by their sojourn here. This, though, is perhaps apart from the aim of the present article, for it is no more true of the negro clerks than of their white confreres. Both generally live up to the limit of their salaries.

The clerk has much leisure, and is in consequence a society man. He must dress well and smoke as good a cigar as an Eastern congressman. It all costs money, and it is not unnatural that at the end of the year he is a little long on unreceipted bills and short on gold. The tendency of the school teachers, now, seems to be entirely different. There are a great many of them here, and on the average they receive less than the government employees. But perhaps the discipline which they are compelled to impart to their pupils has its salutary effect upon their own minds and impulses. However that may be, it is true that the banks and building associations receive each month a part of the salaries of a large proportion of these instructors. The colored people themselves have a flourishing building association and a well-conducted bank, which do part—I am sorry I cannot say the major part—of their race's business.

The influence which the success of a few men will have upon a whole community is indicated in the spirit of venture which actuates the rising generation of this city. A few years ago, if a man secured a political position, he was never willing or fit to do anything else afterward. But now the younger men, with the example of some of their successful elders before them, are beginning to see that an easy berth in one of the departments is not the best thing in life, and they are getting brave enough to do other things. Some of these ventures have proven failures, even disasters, but it has not daunted the few, nor crushed the spirit of effort in them.

It has been said, and not without some foundation in fact, that a colored man who came to Washington never left the place. Indeed, the city has great powers of attracting and holding its colored population for, belong to whatever class or condition they may, they are always sure to find enough of that same class or condition to make their residence pleasant and congenial. But this very spirit of enterprise of which I have spoken is destroying the force of this dictum, and men of color are even going so far as to resign government positions to go away and strike out for themselves. I have in mind now two young men who are Washingtonians of the Washingtonians, and who have been in office here for years. But the fever has taken them, and they have voluntarily given up their places to go and try their fortunes in the newer and less crowded West.

Such things as these are small in themselves, but they point to a condition of affairs in which the men who have received the training and polish which only Washington can give to a colored man can go forth among their fellows and act as leaveners to the crudity of their race far and wide.

That the pleasure and importance of negro life in Washington are overrated by the colored people themselves is as true as that it is underrated and misunderstood by the whites. To the former the social aspect of this life is a very dignified and serious drama. To the latter it is nothing but a most amusing and inconsequential farce. But both are wrong; it is neither the one thing nor the other. It is a comedy of the period played out by earnest actors, who have learned their parts well, but who on that very account are disposed to mouth and strut a little and watch the gallery.

Upon both races the truth and significance of the commercial life among the negroes have taken a firmer hold, because the sight of their banks, their offices, and places of business are evidences which cannot be overlooked or ignored.

As for the intellectual life, a university set on a hill cannot be hid, and the fact that about this university and about this excellent high-school clusters a community in which people, unlike many of the educational fakirs which abound, have taken their degrees from Cambridge, Oxford, Edinburgh, Harvard, Yale, Cornell, Wellesley, and a score of minor colleges, demands the recognition of a higher standard of culture among people of color than obtains in another city.

But, taking it all in all and after all, negro life in Washington is a promise rather than a fulfillment. But it is worthy of note for the really excellent things which are promised.

Baltimore News, January 13, 1900, Paul Laurence Dunbar Collection, Reel IV, Box 18, OHS.

Higher Education

It is a matter of some surprise to me that the article by Mr. Charles Dudley Warner on the education of the negro should have attracted so much attention, for it is so evidently the work of one who speaks without authority. It might appropriately be called an essay, founded upon observations of the South from a car window.

It is a somewhat new view of the case to note the negro considered as one of the less "sensitive" races. Heretofore we have been told, and believed, not without reason, that his character was decidedly the opposite—malleable, yielding, sensitive to impression, good or bad. The argument has been made so frequently that it has almost become axiomatic that this was the cause of so many of his faults—even of the imitativeness that made him ape the vices and the foibles of the white race.

Passing, this, however, as a minor matter, another statement made by the writer that the higher education applied to the negro in his present development has operated against his value as a worker and producer, is not borne out by the facts. Every graduate from a negro college, it is true, does not become a Moses in the community where he is settled, but, on the other hand, in every section where a negro college is located, and where there are negro graduates, it is proven beyond dispute, whatever detractors may say to the contrary, that the moral, social, and industrial tone of the people has been raised. They have gone into districts where the people did not even know how to live, and by their own example taught the benighted the art of life, which they have learned in the schools for higher education. They have made their own homes attractive, and if by no other power than that of envy, which is prevalent in my own race, they have drawn the people about them somewhat up to their own level.

I believe I know my own people pretty thoroughly. I know them in all classes, the high and the low, and I have yet to see any young man or young woman who had the spirit of work in them before, driven from labor by a college education.

Mr. Warner makes his greatest mistake in citing New Orleans as an example. In the first place, in all but one of the schools there for higher education for the negro, the moral training of the black race is in the hands of the whites as he recommends. And in all of them the industrial idea is insisted upon strongly and constantly. If he believes that the condition of these negroes is lower than it was before I am at a loss to know how he can reconcile the growth of industry, the widening out of their charitable organizations, and the larger and purer social life which is being instituted among the colored people there.

Within the last four years there have been opened two new drug stores, patronized by both races; a hospital and training school for nurses has been started by the unaided efforts of the negro people, a free kindergarten has been set going for the black children of the city who are shut out from such advantages as the whites are blessed with.

One more point that Mr. Warner cites is easily set aside. He brings statistics to prove the increase of negro criminality. If he knew very much about this matter, I would fancy him smiling behind his hand, but I give him the benefit of believing that he is ignorant of the subject. Statistics may prove anything, but in this case, especially, they are very inadequate. No one has the right to base any conclusions about negro criminality upon the number of prisoners in the jails and other places of restraint. Even at the North, the prejudice against the negro reverses the precedents of law, and everyone accused is looked upon as guilty until he is proven innocent. In the South it is worse. Taking into account that some of the offenses for which a white boy would be reprimanded and released, would send a negro to the chain gang or the jail, it is easy to see how the percentage of criminals is raised. A fight upon the street, picking up coal, with the accusation of throwing it off the cars, brawling generally, that with white boys would be called children's fights, land the black boy in jail, and so the percentage of criminals increases, and the Northern friend of the negro holds up his hands in dismay at the awful thing he sees before him.

Mr. Warner's ill-advised article has done the negro, who has looked to him as a friend, unutterable harm, more harm really than he knows. It is a pitiful thing altogether. He has observed badly or been misinformed, and until he is able to strike more closely at the heart of things, it were better for him to return to his easy chair.

St. Louis, Mo. *Dispatch,* June 3, 1900, Paul Laurence Dunbar Collection, Reel V, Box 18, OHS.

Negro Society in Washington

IN SPITE OF all the profound problems which the serious people of the world are propounding to us for solution, we must eventually come around to the idea that a good portion of humanity's time is taken up with enjoying itself. The wiser part of the world has calmly accepted the adage that "All work and no play makes Jack a dull boy," and has decided not to be dull. It seems to be the commonly accepted belief, though, that the colored people of the country have not fallen into this view of matters since emancipation, but have gone around being busy and looking serious. It may be heresy to say it, but it is not the truth.

The people who had the capacity for great and genuine enjoyment before emancipation have not suddenly grown into grave and reverend philosophers. There are some of us who believe that there are times in the life of a race when a dance is better than a convention, and a hearty laugh more effective than a Philippic. Indeed, as a race, we have never been a people to let the pleasures of the moment pass. Any one who believes that all of our time is taken up with dealing with knotty problems, or forever bearing around heavy mission, is doomed to disappointment. Even to many of those who think and feel most deeply the needs of their people is given the gift of joy without folly and gayety without frivolity.

Nowhere is this more clearly exemplified than in the social doings of the Negro in Washington, the city where this aspect of the colored man's life has reached its highest development. Here exists a society which is sufficient unto itself—a society which is satisfied with its own condition, and which is not asking for social intercourse with whites. Here are homes finely, beautifully, and tastefully furnished. Here comes together the flower of colored citizenship from all parts of the country. The breeziness of the West here meets the refinement of the East, the warmth and grace of the South, the culture and fine reserve of the North. Quite like all other people, the men who have made money come to the capital to spend it in those social diversions which are not open to them in smaller and more provincial towns. With her sister city, Baltimore, just next door, the Negro in Washington forms and carries on a social life which no longer can be laughed at or caricatured under the name "Colored Sassiety." The term is still funny, but now it has lost its pertinence.

Society Sufficient to Itself

The opportunities for enjoyment are very numerous. Here we are at the very gate of the South, in fact we have begun to feel that we are about in the centre of everything, and that nobody can go to any place or come from any place without passing among us. When the soldiers came home from the Philippines last summer, naturally they came here, and great were the times that Washington saw during their stay. At a dinner given in honor of the officers, two Harvard graduates met, and, after embracing each other, stood by the table and gave to their astonished hearers the Harvard yell at the top of their voices. One was a captain of volunteers, and the other, well, he is a very dignified personage, and now holds a high office.

And just here it might not be amiss to say that in the social life in Washington nearly every prominent college in the country is represented by its graduates. Harvard, Yale, Princeton, Cornell, Amherst, Pennsylvania, with women from Smith, Wellesley, Cornell, Oberlin, and a number of others of less prominence.

The very fact of our being so in the way of traffic has brought about some very amusing complications. For instance, and this is a family secret, do any of you uninitiated know that there were three inaugural balls? The whites could only afford one, but we, happy-go-lucky, pleasure-loving people, had to have two, and on the same night. There were people coming here from everywhere, and their friends in the city naturally wanted to show them certain courtesies, which was right and proper. But there are cliques, and more cliques, as everywhere else, and these cliques differed strenuously. Finally, they separated into factions: one secured the armory, and, the other securing another large hall, each gave its party. And just because each tried to outdo the other, both were tremendous successes, though the visitors, who, like the dying man, had friends in both places, had to even up matters by going first to one and then the other, so that during the whole of that snowy March night there was a good-natured shifting of guests from one ballroom to the other. Sometimes the young man who happened to be on the reception committee at one place and the floor committee at the other got somewhat puzzled as to the boutonniere which was his insignia of office, and too often hapless ones found themselves standing in this midst of one association with the flower of the other like a badge upon his lapel.

Each faction had tried the other's mettle, and the whole incident closed amicably.

The War of the Social Cliques

One of the beauties and one of the defects of Washington life among us is this very business of forming into cliques. It is beautiful in that one may draw about him just the circle of friends that he wants, who appeal to him, and from whom he can get what he wants; but on the other hand, when some large and more general affair is to be given which comprises Washington not as a home city, but rather as the capital of the nation, it is difficult to get these little coteries to disintegrate. The only man who is perfectly safe is the one who cries, "The world is my clique!" and plunges boldly into them all.

Of course, there are some sets which could never come together here. And we are, in this, perhaps imitators; or is it the natural evolution of human impulse that there should be placed over against each other a smart set? — yes, a smart set, don't smile — and a severe high and mighty intellectual set, one which takes itself with eminent seriousness and looks down on all the people who are not studying something, or graduating, or reading papers, or delivering lectures, as frivolous. But somehow, in spite of this attitude toward them, the smart young and even the smart old people go on having dances, teas, and card parties and talking small talk, quite oblivious of the fact that they are under the ban.

Washington has been card crazy this year, and for the first time on record the games did not end with the first coming of summer, but continued night after night as long as there was anybody in town to play them. For be it known that we also put up our shutters and go to the mountains or seashore, where we lie on the sands or in the open air and get tanned, if our complexions are amenable to the process, and some of them are.

There are to my knowledge six very delightful card clubs, and I know one couple who for twenty-five years have had their friends in for cards on every Thursday night in the autumn and winter. If the charitable impulse overtakes us there is a run on the department stores of the city for bright new decks of cards and bisque ornaments, the latter to be used as prizes in the contests to which the outside world is invited to come and look on.

Even after the shutters are put up, when our Negro lawyers lay aside their documents, and our doctors put their summer practice on some later sojourner in town, the fever for the game follows the people to their summer resorts, and the old Chesapeake sees many a game of whist or euchre under the trees in the daytime or out on the lantern-lighted porches at night.

But let no one think that this diversion has been able to shake from its popularity the dances. And how we dance and dance, summer and winter, upon all occasions, whenever and wherever we can. Even when, as this year, we have not been compelled by the inauguration of a President to give something "socially official," there is enough of this form of amusement to keep going the most earnest devotee. There are two leading dancing clubs formed of men and one which occasionally gives a dance, but mostly holds itself to itself, formed of women. The two first vie with each other winter after winter in the brilliancy of their affairs, one giving its own especial welcome dance with four assemblies; the other confining itself to one or two balls each year.

Not the Comic Balls We Know

Do not think that these are the affairs which the comic papers and cartoonists have made you familiar with; the waiters' and coachmen's balls of which you know. They are good enough in their way, just as are your butchers' picnics and your Red Men's dances, but *these* are not of the same ilk. It is no "You pays your money and you takes your choice" business. The invitations are not sent to those outside of one particular circle. One from beyond the city limits would be no more able to secure admission or recognition without a perfect knowledge of his social standing in his own community than would Mrs. Bradley-Martin's butler to come to an Astor ball. These two extremes are not so far apart, but the lines are as strictly drawn. The people who come there to dance together are people of similar education, training, and habits of thought. But, says some one, the colored people have not yet either the time or the money for these diversions, and yet without a minute's thought there come to my mind four men who are always foremost in these matters, whose fortunes easily aggregate a million dollars. All of them are educated men with college-bred children. Have these men not earned the right to their enjoyments and the leisure for them? There are others too numerous to mention who are making five or six thousand a year out of their professions or investments. Surely these may have a little time to dance?

There is a long distance between the waiter at a summer hotel and the man who goes down to a summer resort to rest after a hard year as superintendent of an institution which pays him several thousand a year. In this connection it afforded me a great deal of amusement some time ago to read from the pen of a good friend of mine his solemn comment upon the Negro's lack of dramatic ability. Why? Because he had seen the waiters and other servants at his summer hotel produce a play. Is it out of place for me to smile at the idea of any Harriet[1] of any race doing The Second Mrs. Tanqueray?[2]

View us at any time, but make sure that you view the right sort, and I believe you will not find any particular racial stamp upon our pleasure-making. Last year one of the musical societies gave an opera here, not perhaps with distinction, but brightly, pleasantly, and as well as any amateur organization could expect to give it. Each year they also give an oratorio which is well done. And, believe me, it is an erroneous idea that all our musical organizations are bound up either in a scientific or any other sort of study of rag-time. Of course, rag-time is pleasant, and often there are moments when there are gathered together perhaps ten or twelve of us, and one who can hammer a catchy tune, rag-time or not, on the piano is a blessed aid to his companions who want to two-step. But there, this is dancing again, and we dare not dance always.

Indeed, sometimes we grow strongly to feel our importance and to feel the weight of our own knowledge of art and art matters. We are going to be very much in this way this winter, and we shall possibly have some studio teas as well as some very delightful at-homes which will recall the reign, a few years ago, of a bright woman who had a wealth of social tact and grace, and at whose Fridays one met every one worth meeting resident here and from the outside. The brightest talkers met there and the best singers. You had tea

[1] Harriet reference is unknown.
[2] The Second Mrs. Tanqueray is a social drama written by the British playwright Sr. Arthur Wing Pinero (1855-1934).

and biscuit, talk and music. Mostly your tea got cold and you forgot to munch your biscuit because better things were calling you. This woman is dead now. Her memory is not sad, but very sweet, and it will take several women to fill her place.

A Season of Literature, Music, and Art

There are going to be some pleasant times, though different in scope, in the studio of a clever little woman artist here. She is essentially a miniature painter, but has done some other charming and beautiful things; but above all that, and what the young people are possibly going to enjoy especially, she is a society woman with all that means, and will let them come, drink tea in her studio, flirt behind her canvases, and talk art as they know it, more or less. Her apartments are beautiful and inspiring. The gatherings here, though, will be decidedly for the few. These will be supplemented, however, later in the year by one of the musical clubs which is intending to entertain S. Coleridge Taylor,[3] who is coming over from London to conduct his cantata, "Hiawatha." Mr. Taylor is a favorite here, and his works have been studied for some time by this musical club. It is expected that he will be shown a great many social courtesies.

An article on Negro social life in Washington, perhaps ought almost to be too light to speak of the numerous literary organizations here, the reading clubs which hold forth; but, really, the getting together of congenial people, which is, after all, the fundamental idea of social life, has been so apparent in these that they must at least have this passing notice.

In the light of all this, it is hardly to be wondered at that some of us wince a wee bit when we are all thrown into the lump as the peasant or serving class. In aims and hopes for our race, it is true, we are all at one, but it must be understood, when we come to consider the social life, that the girls who cook in your kitchens and the men who serve in your dining-rooms do not dance in our parlors.

To illustrate how many there are of the best class of colored people who

[3] Samuel Coleridge Taylor (1875-1912) was an African British composer. He is celebrated for his setting of Henry Wadsworth Longfellow's *Hiawatha*. He collaborated with Dunbar on several works, principally *African Romances* and *Dream Lovers*.

can be brought thus together, a story is told of a newcomer who was invited to a big reception. A Washingtonian, one who was initiated into the mysteries of the life here, stood beside him and in an aside called off the names of the guests as they entered. "This is Doctor So-and-So," as some one entered the room, "Surgeon-in-Chief of Blank Hospital." The stranger looked on in silence. "The man coming in now is Judge Somebody Else, of the District." This time the stranger raised his eyebrows. "Those two men entering are consuls to Such-and-Such a place." The newcomer sniffed a little bit. "And ah!" his friend started forward, "that is the United States Minister to Any-Place-You-Please." The man who was being initiated into the titles of his fellow-guests said nothing until another visitor entered the doorway; then he turned to his friend, and in a tone of disbelief and disgust remarked, "Well, now, who under the heavens is that? The Prime Minister of England or the King himself?"

Last summer was the gayest that Washington has seen in many a year. It is true that there are hotels and boarding-houses at many summer resorts and that some of our people gather there to enjoy themselves, but for the first time there was a general flocking to one place taken up entirely and almost owned by ourselves. The place, a stretch of beach nearly two miles long with good bathing facilities, and with a forest behind it, has been made and built up entirely by Negro capital. Two men, at least, have made fortunes out of the sale and improvement of their property, and they, along with many others, are the owners of their own summer homes and cottages at Arundel-on-the-Bay and Highland Beach, Maryland. Here the very best of three cities gathered this last summer. Annapolis and Baltimore sent their quota and our capital city did the rest. It was such a gathering of this race as few outside of our own great family circle have ever seen.

There is, perhaps, an exaltation about any body of men and women who gather to enjoy the fruits of their own labor upon the very ground which their labors have secured to them. There was, at any rate, a special exaltation about these people, and whatever was done went off with éclat. There was a dance at least once a week at one or another of the cottages, and the beauty of it was that anyone who was spending the summer there needed to look for no invitations. He was sure of one by the very fact of being there at all, a member of so close a corporation. The athletes did their turns for the delectation of their admirers, and there were some long-distance swimming contests that would have done credit to the boys in the best of our colleges. There were others who took their bathing more complacently, and still others who followed the injunction of the old rhyme, "Hang your clothes on a hickory limb, but don't go near the water." Cards, music, and sailing parties helped to pass the time, which went all too swiftly, and the Isaak Waltons of the place were always up at five o'clock in the morning and away to some point where they strove for bluefish and rocks, and came home with spots. The talk was bright and the intercourse easy and pleasant. There was no straining, no pomposity, no posing for the gallery. When September came we began to hear the piping of the quail in the woods away from the beach, and our trigger-fingers tingled with anticipation. But the time was not yet ripe. And so the seal is to be set this winter upon our Maryland home by a house party, where men will go to eat, smoke, and shoot, and the women to read, dance, and — well — women gossip everywhere.

This is but a passing glimpse of that intimate life among our own people which we dignify by the name of society.

Saturday Evening Post, December 14, 1901, Paul Laurence Dunbar Collection, Reel IV, Box 12, OHS.

Dunbar Did Not Plagiarize

EDITOR POST: Through the kindness of a friend I have just come across the gleeful accusation of plagiarism made by Mrs. Anna H. Southworth, I have no plea to make. In the first place, the thought is entirely different. I see the wind, the harpist sitting beside the great strings of the rain and playing upon them, while Alexander Smith finds them "smiling his thunder harp of the pines." There were not any pines in Chicago where the poem was written, and I shall be glad to give you the incident that called it into being. It was an Illinois summer rainstorm, and we were sitting, a few friends and I, in an inner room of the house, when an elderly lady came in, and looking through the window said:

"Why, the rain looks just like harp strings."

"Why, Mrs. Letcher," said I. "That deserves a poem," and I sat down to write. In a little while I read to a friend, Herbert L. May, my "Rain Songs." Then I called her in, and she insisted on taking half the honors, which I was perfectly willing to grant. There were present at the time Herbert L. May, 109 Bank Street, Dayton, Ohio; Mrs. Meta Murphy, 5747 Lafayette Avenue; Mrs. Priscilla Letcher, 5747 Lafayette Avenue, and myself.

I must temper Mrs. Southworth's unholy joy in having found a culprit by telling her that I am not a reader of almost forgotten poetry.

At the same time I must make the humble and very unliterary confession that I have never read a line of Alexander Smith's and haven't the least idea on earth who he is or was.

I am sorry if a chuckle stops in the throat of the dear old lady who found the nest.

Washington Post, March 20, 1905, Paul Laurence Dunbar Collection, Reel IV, Box 15, OHS.

ᗝ

The Leader of His Race

WHEN BOOKER T. WASHINGTON went from the Virginia plantation, where he was born about 1857 or 1858, to the mines of West Virginia, he took the first step in a career which has done as much as that of any other man for the uplifting of a race. His first idea comprehended only the care of his mother and the rest of the family about her. To him, freedom meant the opportunity to work and to earn, and the weekly pittance that the salt-owners gave the boy was the tangible evidence of his free state. But suddenly a brighter gleam illumined his consciousness. After four or five years of severe and poorly paid labor he heard of General Armstrong's school at Hampton, and with a little money in his pocket, saved from his own earnings, and eked out from his mother's scanty store, he started thither.

Hardly knowing where Hampton was, he yet set out with sublime faith, and Hampton drew the boy toward itself as Canada did the fleeing slaves of old. At last he found himself in Richmond; penniless, but with a brave heart, strong hands, and a sturdy will, he was prepared to do the thing that was nearest to him. This happened to be to help in unloading pig-iron from a vessel, and at the unwelcome task he worked all day. At night, homeless and without friends, he crept to the protection of a levee.

Starting Life on Fifty Cents

To every one who has followed Mr. Washington's later career there is apparent in these early struggles the same spirit that has characterized his subsequent achievements. His cry has ever been, "Let down your buckets where you are!" and it has come not only from the tip of his tongue but from his heart of hearts. It was what he did when finally he reached Hampton, and with fifty cents in his pocket sought out General Armstrong. They put a broom into his hands, and he took it, and did the best he could with it.

It was what he did when leaving Hampton, instead of coming North to exploit his newly acquired knowledge. Instead of tagging at the heels of some influential man and burying himself in one of the Government offices, he went into the black belt of Alabama among the most degraded and ignorant of his race, and there let down his buckets. The shanty church, with its thirty pupils, has grown into a school where over a thousand young men and women are taught, and whose fame is as wide as the continent.

But apart from his character as an orator, an educator, and a man of affairs, Mr. Washington displays a most charming, personal side. When one has grown sufficiently used to him to overlook his frequent lapses into preoccupation, one enjoys the childlike simplicity of his nature, and the utter lack of self-consciousness in his manner.

The Little Washingtons

His diffidence is well known, and the following story which will be vouched for by a certain distinguished New York clergyman, illustrates this side of his character, as well as another—his love for his family. Mr. Washington's two boys, Davidson and Baker, are a pair of as vivacious, mischief-loving youngsters as can be found in the State of Alabama. They adore their father and it has been his habit to go to them every night at bedtime and hear their prayers. As a general thing, nothing prevents this busy man from fulfilling this duty when he is at home. It happened one night during the visit of the aforementioned divine that Mr. Washington and his friends had gathered on the lawn, and, being held by his obligations as host, Mr. Washington was unable to get away. Time and time again he cast furtive glances at the house, but still he was held. At last he gave up, looked at his watch for the last time, and resigned himself to the disappointment. "Of course," thought he, "Dave and Baker are in bed and asleep by this time." But he had reckoned without his host. All of a sudden, two night-gowned forms dashed down from the porch and across the lawn, and to the dismay of the guests plumped themselves down at the host's feet, and began pattering off their prayers. Mr. Washington stood ashamed and helpless until they were through, and then led them into the house.

Saturday Evening Post, November 9, 1901, Paul Laurence Dunbar Collection, Reel IV, Box 14, OHS.

Negro in Literature

THE ENTERTAINMENT GIVEN yesterday at the Waldorf-Astoria for the benefit of the Hampton Institute was slow in beginning, audience and principals being alike held back by the storm. One by one came in the cheerful black faces of Hampton students,[1] members of the quartet, who were down to sing spirituals and folk-songs; then Henry T. Burleigh,[2] the soloist; Paul Lawrence [sic] Dunbar, the author of a book of poems, *Lyrics of Lowly Life,*

[1] Hampton Institute was founded in 1889 by General Samuel Chapman Armstrong. He "taught his students that labor was a spiritual force, that physical work not only increased wage earning capacity but promoted fidelity, accuracy, honesty, persistence, and intelligence." The School was often thought of as "the patron saint of industrial education."

[2] H. T. Burleigh (1866-1949) was a distinguished baritone, arranger, composer, and music editor. He was for many years a soloist for St. George Episcopal Church and the choir in Temple Emanu-El in New York City.

who was to give an author's reading; and Charles W. Wood of Tuskegee,[3] who was to read selected pieces.

As this interesting group of men of the negro race, standing by one of the windows where all outside showed white with flying snow, fell to talking, the reporter joined it. He felt that there were many questions to be asked, much that these men might say if they would. And the reporter plunged right into the middle of a subject, turning to Mr. Dunbar with this question:

"In the poetry written by negroes, which is the quality that will most appear, something native and African and in every way different from the verse of Anglo-Saxons, or something that is not unlike what is written by white people?"

"My dear sir," replied the poet, "the predominating power of the African race is lyric. In that I should expect the writers of my people to excel. But, broadly speaking, their poetry will not be exotic or differ much from that of the whites."

"But surely, the tremendous facts of race and origin—"

"You forget that for two hundred and fifty years the environment of the negro has been American, in every respect the same as that of all other Americans."

The reporter still objected: "Isn't there a certain tropic warmth, a cast of temperament that belongs of right to the African race, and should not that element make its lyric expression, if it is to be genuine, a thing apart?"

"Ah, what you speak of is going to be a loss. It is inevitable. We must write like the white men. I do not mean imitate them; but our life is now the same." Then the speaker added: "I hope you are not one of those who would hold the negro down to a certain kind of poetry—dialect and concerning only scenes on plantations in the south?" This appeared to be a sore point, and the questioner at once truthfully denied having any such desire.

"There are great questions in my mind regarding the forms of poetry," continued Mr. Dunbar. "Do you think it is possible now to invent a new form? Have the old ones completely exhausted the possible supply? Then, I wonder if the negro will ever reach dramatic poetry."

"Edwin Booth once said to me," remarked Mr. Wood, "that he considered that the negro should make the greatest actor in the world—because he had the most soul."

"I don't think that," said Mr. Dunbar. "The black man's soul is lyric, not

[3] Charles Winter Woods was on the faculty of Tuskegee and avid orator of poetry.

dramatic. We may expect songs from the soul of the negro, but hardly much dramatic power, either in writing or in acting."

"Is there a large school of negro poets?"

"Haven't you read McClellan?[4] Then there's Moore,[5] Carruthers,[6] Whitman,[7] who has just finished an epic called *The Rape of Florida*. It appears to me, also, that that is not negro poetry only which is written by negroes, but all that is written by whites who have received their inspiration from negro life. The races have acted and reacted on each other. The white man who, as a child, was suckled at the breast of a black mammy has received the strongest influence of his life, perhaps, from the African race. Why, the white people in the south talk like us—they have imported many of our words into the language—and you know they act like us."

"Which one of the current writers of negro stories best represents the race?"

"Joel Chandler Harris[8] shows the most intimate sympathy—Mrs. Stuart,[9] too."

"You omit the one who is perhaps most popular."

"You mean Paige?[10] Yes, I left him out with intention. His attitude is condescending, always."

Interview of Dunbar, *New York Commercial*, 1898, no by-line. Paul Laurence Dunbar Collection, Reel IV, Box 16, OHS.

[4] George Marion McClellan (1860-1934) was a poet. He refused to write in dialect.
[5] Possibly John Hebron Moore, author of *Simon Gray, Riverman: A Slave Who Was Almost Free*.
[6] James D. Carruthers (1869-1917) was a clergyman and poet. He was both encouraged and inspired by the work of Dunbar and proceeded to publish poems in newspapers and magazines. His *Selected Poems* appeared in 1907 and *The Dream and The Song* was published in 1914.
[7] Alberry Whitman (1851-1902) is not to be confused with the better known Walt Whitman (1819-1892). Born in slavery, he was thought to be the best dialect writer before Dunbar. He authored six volumes of poems. *Rape of Florida* is written in Spenserian stanzas.
[8] Joel Chandler Harris (1848–1908), humorist, storyteller, and editor, was the creator of the famous Uncle Remus tales. He authored two novels: *Sister Jane* and *Gabriel Tolliver*.
[9] Ruth McEnery Stuart (1849(52?)–1917). There is some argument about the date of her birth. She was born in Louisiana. She authored some twenty books in her lifetime. It is said that she exploited an extra ordinary knowledge of Southern types including Creoles, plantation Negroes, and "poor whites," by using them in her stories.
[10] Thomas Nelson Paige (1853–1922) was a short story writer and essayist. He is particularly noted for his dialect stories. He is thought of as one of the foremost genre writers of the south who helped to revive regionalism. Today much of his work has been forgotten.

Booker T. Washington

It is a very pleasant duty which devolves upon me to say a few words in tribute to the worth of Mr. Washington's work. In the swift march of events since the issuance of the Proclamation of Emancipation, the Negro has developed but few heroes. But those who have come forward to raise the name of the race to an honored place in the records of the world, have been what the age now demands, the heroes of peace. Our history has been fraught with struggles, with hardships and with disappointments. We have been despised and abused. We have been misjudged and hated; but in spite of all, there has been a steady upward trend from the very time that the words which made a man of the chattel were written and published to the world by Illinois' immortal son. To-day if we are more envied, it is because we are more prosperous. If we are more hated, it is because we are more formidable. If we are more opposed, it is because we are more worthy of opposition; and our brothers of the other race fight nothing that is not worthy of their mettle.

For a long time, we have heard of this man of Tuskegee, and for a long time we have been told great things of the work he has done away down there in the Black Belt of the South, where our own people, our brothers and sisters and their children have so little opportunity for development along the best lines. But hear what we may, from whatever source we may, we can know nothing of the great work that is being done there, until we have been and seen for ourselves. Then our cry will be that of the Queen of Chubby in coming to the court of Solomon, "The half has never been told."

I can never forget my first visit to Tuskegee. I went there a skeptic; I came away, a convert. I went there questioning; I came away wondering. Before me there lay no longer a theory, but facts in the case; facts in broad acres, wide fields, bricks and stone, and a thousand bright advancing young men and women, who said indeed, what that boy years ago had said in words, "We are rising."

The history of that institution reads like romance. About twenty years ago, a little school of thirty pupils conducted in a log cabin; to-day a great institution, world-wide in renown, building upon building, a large corps of teachers, and an ever-increasing number of pupils, who are studying to make for the betterment of our race. That this is the work of one man, seems almost incredible, but that Mr. Washington's untiring energy, perseverance in so short a time against so great odds, must ever redound to his honor and glory.

So new a people are we that we have not yet learned greatly to honor those who are doing and having done the pioneer work of our advancement. We have been very prone to carp at them, and to watch their every movement with hyper-critical eyes. But it seems that now the time has come when it seems that our own enlightenment will compel us to give honor to whom honor is due. And tonight, I know no one to whom more honor is due than the distinguished gentleman here with us, Mr. Booker T. Washington.

Through dark and dismal valleys our way has laid. Up arduous steeps and by rugged ways we have traveled. It has been through the storm and through the night and through the flash of lightning and the thunder's roar. But ever ahead have we seen the one light that led us on and on.

By rugged ways, etc.

Typescript, undated, Paul Laurence Dunbar Collection, Reel IV, Box 12, OHS.

✑

Sunshine at Jackson Park

AFTER A LONG period of cold, cloud, and rain, the sun is shining again over Jackson Park[1] and a consequent increase in attendance is plainly noticeable. To any one who attended only on the opening day and then comes back now, it may seem like an untruth to speak of the attendance here as increasing. But the fact of the matter is that, since the great opening day when half a million people were on the grounds, there has been but a comparatively small attendance at the fair.

---

[1] Jackson Park is located on Lake Michigan in Chicago and was the site of the 1893 Columbian Exposition. Dunbar was hired to work at this time by Frederick Douglass. The article focuses on activities at the exposition.

On Monday night the announcement that there would be a grand electrical display brought an unusually large crowd to the grounds, and no one went away disappointed. The center and chief object of the electrical display was the handsome administration building in the eastern part of the grounds. The building is surmounted by a high and imposing dome which was set with incandescent lights until it glittered like a magnificent coronet of fiery gems. Beads of lights were strung from the crown down to the first ledge of the dome, where a circle of stars entirely surrounded it. The glowing spectacle could be seen for miles around and the white statuary looked more magnificently white than ever beneath the strong electric glare.

Within the building there was no less magnificent a spectacle to be seen. The terraces were decorated with bouquets of light and every available space was made the recipient of some artistic design in illumination.

The administration building beautiful as it was at night is not an object of admiration under the light of day. Elevators are plying constantly from the ground floor up to the dome and terraces. And from the highest terrace, about 220 feet above the ground, you have a grand view of the eastern portion of the place.

The most inspiring view I believe is looking eastward toward Lake Michigan, a misty bank of gray and green in the distance. The massive statue of the Republic, which stands at the eastern head of the lagoon, is facing you. Round about you the roofs of half a score of buildings tower white in the sun. Yes, they tower, and yet you are above them towering higher still. You look over there to the northwest, and there stretches the dazzling expanse of the Manufacturer's Building,[2] the largest building in the world, covering an extent of thirty-six acres. Attendants claim to be able to show the record of an enormous number of men killed in the construction of this building, but the number stated is such an impossible one that I have not taken the trouble to investigate, where the falsity of the thing is so evident. Though looking at its great curving glass roof, one can see how many men might, day after day, making a slight misstep roll down its swift incline into eternity. But I don't like to think of these things especially standing where I am, looking down a sheer descent of 200 feet. Some hot day when you are here at the Fair, I want you to try walking around the outside of the Manufacturer's Building. When you are through you will be able to appreciate its

[2] The Manufacturer's Building was the largest building at the Chicago World's Columbian Exposition in 1893.

size. Then climb, don't take an elevator, but climb to the administration building terrace and I think you will be equally able to appreciate its height.

There is a pleasurably inspiring feeling comes over one standing away up here above the world, when the breeze brings to one's ears the familiar notes of "The Last Rose of Summer"[3] and then "Home Sweet Home,"[4] why, even the German workmen, who are still busy about the dome, join in and begin humming that. But when the band in the pavilion far below you switches off and begins playing "America" with a dozen or more ultra-skillful flourishes and variations, and one looks at the flags about over these evidences of America's greatness and genius—why, an attack of rapture is just inevitable, and—"There, now, sir, don't stand so near to the edge."

It is the voice of the Columbian Guard.[5] This adjunct to the exposition is autocratic. He is always a young man, and he hasn't been a guard very long, a few weeks at the longest, and he often grows dizzy at the startling height of his own greatness and makes a consummate donkey of himself. But when he has gotten more used to it, when the summer's sun has wilted some of the starch of his regalia, when the spruce, turkey-cock stride has degenerated to weary step, then, maybe, he will come down and act like an ordinary man.

The Columbian Guard is, as a generality, not as nice a set of fellows as the guides and chair rollers, who are mostly college boys, students at Chicago University. If the fair does no other good, it will have, at least, this act recorded to its merit, of having helped many an impecunious student through his college course by means of this employment. For seventy-five cents an hour you can be rolled in one of these comfortable chairs all over the grounds, with a learned dissertation on every sight you see, by a courteous freshman or sophomore. It is a standing joke with Chicago girls now that they go to Jackson Park for the sole purpose of hiring "a rolling chair with student attachment."

Some one, well not some one, but every one has been kicking about the prices in Chicago. Now it is true that nothing is given away out here, but it is equally true that a person with common sense and ordinary economy need not spend a fortune to see the World's Fair.

There are plenty of places where if you are a common person you can get a good common meal for twenty-five cents, or if you are above common

[3] The melody for "The Last Rose of Summer" was composed by Thomas Moore (1779—1852).
[4] "Home Sweet Home" was a popular Civil War song with the words written by Henry R. Bishop (1786—1855) and the music by John H. Payne (1791—1852).
[5] The Columbian Guards were hired to protect pavilions as well as patrons.

feeding, you can get a meal according to your pocket from fifty cents up to fifty dollars. There is no place on the grounds that can be said to be really "cheap." But there are many restaurants where you can eat your fill at a reasonable price. There will be places you will strike where they will ask you twenty cents for a sandwich, ten cents for a cup of coffee, five cents more if you put cream in it and ten cents for a small glass of beer; you will be perfectly justified in asking the prices in such a place and then leaving it immediately. It is extortion and neither the Chicago press nor people approve it.

The lagoon is a popular sporting place for visitors these bright days as it has been all along even when the winds were sharper and the sun less warm. There could be no more striking comment upon the differences of old and new world ways than the difference between the two sorts of craft that frequent this lagoon. One stands upon the bridge looking down and here comes gliding dreamily by a gaily decked gondola, with golden fringe trailing in the water, its passengers reclining upon cushions of many colored velvet. There are two gondoliers, bright ribbons, stripes, knickerbockers, and colored hose till you can't rest. One is stationed in the bow and one in the stern of the graceful boat and they move together, stroke after stroke, with the perfection and precision of automation. Their rowing is both pretty and graceful. There is first the forward stroke that sends the boat gliding ahead like a swan and then a pause and poise upon the toes before the recoil and repetition of the forward stroke. The passengers loll on their luxuriant cushions and the gondola goes gliding on. This is the poetry of locomotion.

Then one hears the scream of a whistle, and gondolas, ducks, sea gulls, and all look out, for here comes the electric boat. A little brown craft that fairly skims over the water. Two blue-coated and blue-capped men have charge, one is conductor and one is pilot. A turn of the wheel starts her, another turn changes its course and a reverse checks her speed. The passengers sit on seats of brown leather. No velvet cushions here, nor oars, nor velvet fringe; this is the practical prose of locomotion. One is of the old and the other of the new world. One is the embodiment of old fashioned dreamy indolence, the other, of bright vivacious thought and inventive genius. Each is a fit emblem of the thought of its native land. One labors and plods, the other shoots.

The Palladium, undated news clipping, Paul Laurence Dunbar Collection, Reel IV, Box 16, OHS.

PART THREE

Short Stories

INTRODUCTION TO
THE SHORT STORIES

DUNBAR WAS ALREADY well-known as a poet when he began publishing novels and short stories. Between 1898 and 1904, four volumes of stories appeared. Many other selections appeared in newspapers and magazines, which makes them difficult to find a century later. *The Paul Laurence Dunbar Reader* collected twenty-three of these stories, and this volume adds seven more.

Critical commentary on Dunbar's fiction has been conflicted. His novels and stories have been read within both the romantic and naturalistic traditions, and it is not surprising to find critics linking the lyricism of his poems to his fictional style. Kenny J. Williams has noted that Dunbar "masks" his social protest in conventional forms in order to gain acceptance while expressing his views behind the veil. Williams sees Dunbar joining other African American novelists in being the "conscience of the American experience" because his protest writing still believed in the possibility of change (1975, p. 204). Others have read his fiction as a satire on the plantation tradition and a forerunner to the work of Wright, Ellison, and Baldwin (Rodgers 1992), or as narrative that uses lyricism to go beyond the constraints of conventional forms of the time (Bender 1975). He is also credited with being a skillful maneuverer "within the narrow confines of decorum" who won "marginal victories" by combining conformity and protest (Wakefield 1977). In fact, Wakefield may best sum up Dunbar's ways of working with the short story as a genre: "Only by an almost scrupulous adherence to decorum could he save himself from falling prey to public opinion" (1977, p. 50). In his short stories, therefore, as well as in his plays and poems, Dunbar worked within conventional patterns in order to construct his own distinctive artistic vision. The seven previously unpublished or uncollected stories presented here add to that body of Dunbar's work to be counted as a victory of conscience and irony.

Dunbar's short stories demonstrate his mastery of a variety of dialects, his grasp of short-fiction conventions of his time, and his ironic commentary on slavery as well as the hypocrisy of much "charitable" activity in a society where class divisions remained sharply drawn. Several of these stories create extended analogies or parables addressing his deepest feelings on slavery and its aftermath. "Ole Conju'in Joe,"—published here for the first time—displays a mastery of the conventions of the horror tale presented through local color in the aftermath of the Civil War and builds to an ironic commentary on tricksterism gone awry. Joe Haskins lives in and is represented by a gruesome shanty which "Negroes young and old dreaded to pass." Joe and his house had long "fallen into disrepute" though—Dunbar adds with a large dose of formality—circumstances "had not always been thus." Joe had been a fiddler of great reputation: "Time was when the whole countryside rang with his praises, when the white aristocracy favored him and the black belles adored him." He earned enough with his artistry to purchase his freedom, though he did continue to experience "the prejudice exercised in those days against free negroes." He soon built a cabin and planned a wedding with a former slave whose freedom he had bought. But suddenly "a great change" befell him, the cause of which no one could determine. Locking himself up in his house, Joe refused to play at functions, and rumors abounded that he had learned to be a conjurer and was striking up deals with the devil. When people heard singing coming from the house, indignation meetings were scheduled "to protest against the toleration" of the nuisance he had become. The parson preached that Joe should be asked to leave his home, and a "notification committee" was selected to make haste the eviction. "Never did men walk with more dignity, and less courage," than did those pillars of the community as they strode up to inform him of his fate.

When Joe finally welcomed the "solemn, silent, and scared" committee members, they were "transfixed" to find the corpse of Sam, a slave who had died naturally after Joe had harbored him for ten years. In Joe's words, death made Sam "past bein' tuk back into slabery." In hiding for several long years, Joe had not heard of the Civil War and the freeing of the slaves. "He wanted freedom, dat's why I shet up my cabin, dat's why I quit fiddlin' ha, ha, ha, I've cheated his master out ob one good niggah." Dunbar underscores the irony that Joe harbored Sam not knowing that "de white people's done had a wah, a wah, and wese all free." He emphasizes even more the futility of a situation in which Sam can't now wake up into his freedom or recover the time lost in hiding out. "Sam, Sam, wake up, don't be dead," Joe cries out: "why, chile, youse free, arter a waitin' all dese yeahs de Lawd hab come to yo' deliberance." Sam's stolen years and his senseless death are symbolic of the lost and wasted aspirations of countless slaves over time. In this powerful story of indirection —lost for nearly a hundred years—Dunbar creates at once a tale of Joe's trick-sterism that boomerangs and a parable about all the time and talent that slavery snatched away from an entire people. "Ole Conju'in Joe" combines standard English and dialect and masters the storytelling conventions of the time in order to craft them into a moving enactment of the pain of loss and of courage in the face of long-standing adversity.

"The Emancipation of Evalina Jones" is another parable of a life ren-dered dormant through restraint and suffocation. The story once again por-trays a form of slavery and at the same time places Dunbar in a tradition of late nineteenth-century women authors who created liberated heroines. In the midst of life and color in the celebration of emancipation, only Evalina Jones is "stolid" in her slavish marriage, which had "killed all the brightness in her." Abused and ignored, Evalina nonetheless feels the stirring of a spirit in her "that had lain dead for the five years that she had been Jim's wife." When "all her youthful lightness" seems to return, Evalina turns the tables on her husband who lapses into grieving and self pity. Typical of the rebel-lious conversion stories of the time, the liberated wife tells her husband she "don't care nothin'" about him—all the while assuring him she will make din-ner so long as he talks better to her and is careful to "walk straight."

In the approximately one hundred short stories Dunbar wrote in his ac-celerated career, he was more concerned with character and irony than plot, and he overcame regionalist niches to develop what commentators have called his "sense of community" and his ability to make "connections between so-cial groups in America" (Martin and Hudson 1975, p. 64). The seven stories collected in this volume find him embracing certain conventions in order to use their popularity and to modify their patterns to create ironies not possi-ble otherwise. In Dunbar's hands, the formula story turns back upon itself as he creates parables of liberation and pointed attacks on hypocrisy and com-placency. Just as alleged conjurer Joe's signifying goes awry, Evalina's eman-cipation is as much about the powerful feeling of time lost and energy wasted as it is about achieving pain-bought freedom.

In several other stories collected here, Dunbar reproduces formulaic pat-terns in order to introduce often very slight modifications that drive home a point. In "Little Billy," the unexpected horse thief brings his crime back home to ruin his nurturing, forward-looking single dad. In "A Prophecy of Fate," the horror is worthy of Edgar Allan Poe or Alfred Hitchcock until the haunted narrator's forebodings actually turn out to save his life. In another of his series of "tenderfoot" stories, the predictable once again doesn't quite happen as the city slicker winds up saving the child in distress. In "His Bride of the Tomb"—a story Dunbar wrote while in high school—the nuances of romance are formulaic, the bride is assertive ("no man shall ever have the power to command me"), and the plot is just predictable enough to usher in the obligatory coincidence that saves the day. In this volume's additions to the Dunbar short story canon, his conventionality never disappoints. Each story in its own way works through predictable patterns in order to create an ironic twist forceful enough to clear a path but subtle enough to gain acceptance.

"Jimmy Weedon's Contretempts" merges conventionality and ironic rupture with great success. There may not be a likeable person to be found in this satire on do-gooders who engage in "slumming" and richly enjoy "the novel sight of the poor amusing themselves." Jimmy Weedon himself was one of those privileged folk who had the resources and time to be wild, a following of rare folks who considered themselves above ordinary mortals, and a fiancée (Helen) who didn't understand him. Jimmy's "predilection for low life" gets him in trouble with everyone, though—in contrast with the do-gooders in the story—he was at least "honest in his motives for slumming." Enter Mrs. Carrington who assembles a contingent of "righteous accomplishment" who attend a "slum dinner" where they dress down for the crowd and select "but two wines" out of "self-denial." After discourses on the "brotherhood of man" and an assortment of opportunities for doing good, the "peregrinations of the Carrington Party" wind down—but not before Jimmy forgets himself after thirteen highballs and joins the "spirit of things." Thus Jimmy's pursuit of genuine—if decadent—fun of the fast and furious kinds runs smack into Helen and the other aristocrats "huddled together" in a display of the "complacent dissipation of charity." Helen returns Jimmy's ring and all go off to separate but equally unpleasant parties "to which none but the elect" may come. The story is vintage Dunbar anger, akin to his novel *The Sport of the Gods* or the short story "Mr. Cornelius Johnson, Office Seeker." Even the word *contretempts*—so formal and so bitter—reflects the conventionality Dunbar works through to achieve his ironic effects.

The short story will never be considered Dunbar's strongest genre. He mastered the conventions of the form well, however, and stretched the nuances of character, plot, and language for ironic effect. As in his poems and plays, he often masked his indignation or disappointment in conventionality, humor, or irony. His modest but significant achievements in this genre find additional support in the seven stories which follow.

Ole Conju'in Joe

IF THERE WAS any house in all the "black creek district" which more than another, the negroes young and old dreaded to pass, it was the little hut of old Joe Haskins, "Old Conju'in Joe," they called him; and not a one of them but would walk a half mile out of his way to avoid passing the proscribed shanty.

It was indeed a gruesome looking place and it was no wonder that it had fallen into disrepute. The house itself was slowly rotting away; the roof was battered and rough looking minus half its shingles, and the shutters, which were always kept tightly closed, were fastened to the framework of the house by strips of old leather in lieu of the hinges which had long since rusted away. The gate had dropped from its place and the fence sagged away from the perpendicular as if the rails and posts were sadly inebriated. The yard was choked up with many years' growth of rank weeds, save in one spot where a little kitchen garden struggled for life. The whole scene was anything but an inviting one, and it might well have been the abode of a devotee of the black art.

And yet, Joe Haskins had not always been thus, an avoided and dreaded outcast from his kind. Time was when the whole countryside rang with his praises, when the white aristocracy favored him and the black belles adored him. When never a dance was complete without Joe Haskins to lead the music, for the fame of his skill as a fiddler—that skill which was at the same time, the envy and delight of all who knew him, had gone forth among all the community. His earnings were such that after awhile he was enabled to purchase his freedom and begin work for himself. In spite of the prejudice exercised in those days against free negroes, his success suffered no falling off on account of his liberated condition, and he was soon able to build himself a little cabin on his own ground, for Joe, be it said, was both industrious and frugal. His cabin was adorned with that luxury unheard of among negro huts, of a shingled roof. You can imagine that all this prosperity had the effect of making Joe more popular among the belles of his race.

For a long time, he seemed to be impervious to Cupid's shafts; but after awhile, the attentions he began paying to Almarnia, one of old Jack Venable's slave girls, gave evidence sufficient that he had succumbed to the skill of the blind archer. The trend of his intentions became conclusive when he began negotiating with Almarnia's master for the purpose of buying her freedom. The bargain was made, and Joe began his task. Never did man labor so cheerily as did Joe, working all day, and fiddling all night to earn money enough to pay off the sum that kept his bride from him. And at last it was accomplished. Almarnia was paid for and her "free papers" signed; Joe's bliss was at its height, for the wedding was to be celebrated in two weeks; the preparations had been made and even the preacher spoken to, when a great change occurred in the prospective bridegroom.

No one knew what caused it. The first intimation which anyone received indicating all was not right with Joe, came through his refusal to play for the great dance up to Colonel Dare's. Through all his life, there had been no better friend to Joe than his old master's favorite cousin, Harrison Dare, and for him to refuse to play for this man, especially at a function where the black fiddler knew all the "quality" of the county would be present, was a wonderful surprise. But the messenger who returned several times could get no answer from him other than the stubbornly repeated statement, "I'se too po'ly to play fo' Mas' Harry, too po'ly." And even this answer came through a door opened only about three inches.

From this time, Joe left off playing and was rarely seen. The negroes, prone to give everything they did not understand a supernatural bearing, said that he was having intercourse with Satan, "a learnin' to conju'" and they began to avoid him. The poor whites inclined to the same idea, while the better classes merely decided that he had become mentally deranged and left him to himself.

Then came the stormy days of the rebellion, when the peace and pleasure of southern homes were blighted and destroyed forever. The hurried answer of the call to arms; the parting from loved ones, sons, lovers, and brothers, and the return of the wounded and dead; the four years of fiery struggle, of blood and tears, and then peace and reconstruction.

But in the rushing times of war and the subsequent changes that took place in the conditions of both blacks and whites, Joe was forgotten. Unmolested, he had lived his life; year after year, the weeds had grown up about his shanty, and the house itself had fallen into decay all unnoticed.

It was long after the close of the war that an unusual incident called attention to the place and renewed some of the old interest in him who had once been its occupant. Someone passing within unaccustomed proximity to the house, heard sounds as of someone singing. It was so unusual coming from the long silent place that the matter was instantly reported, and all the tongues of the town began to wag. The old idea about Joe was renewed and someone said that he was singing songs of propitiation to the Devil. Several others now ventured near enough to hear or imagine they heard his weird incantations, and the old cry of "Joe, Joe conju'in' Joe" was taken up on again.

It was very evident that he was doing quite serious work, so many of them said, "fur dat showed f'um his goin's on, as plain as day," and when Uncle Frog Martin's barn burned down, everyone knew just where to lay the blame. The old women sighed and said "Lawd, Lawd, how long," and the old men said, "Look a hyeah, chillun, whut's dis world a comin' to, any how!" The Baptist preacher said in his Sunday sermon that "de Lawd was a lettin' loose his almighty wrat' upon de people a, an' de debbil was unchained a an' a going' about a lak a rabenin' lion a seekin' who he mought devour a." And everyone knew he referred to Joe.

So, when Jabes Harlem, the most public-spirited citizen in the whole place, went around trying to organize an indignation meeting to protest against the toleration of such a nuisance in their midst, public opinion was worked up to such a pitch that all the community readily agreed with him and the meeting was held. It was opened by the parson with an address emphatic in expression and powerful in influence.

"Bruddahs an' Sistahs," said he, "I ain't got nothin' again' no man, and I wouldn't by wud, ner deed harm nuther chick nor child, but I jes' rises to ax dis one question, what is we gwine to, whar is we gwine to? You 'member in bible days, conju's an' sich things was bu'ned, but sine de Lawd hab come,

He hab taught a new lesson an' in dese days ob humility, we ain't got no oddah way but to vanish all such wo'kers ob iniquity f'um ouah midst. De man whut tries to hindah his feller man is a walkin' in de shades ob da'kness and de Lawd ain't agwine countenance no such doin's, so I moves you, Mistah Cha'man, if so be's I kin git a second, dat it be de consensus ob dis meetin' dat a sut'n pusson—no name, no blame—dat a sut'n pusson libin' in dat old to' down shanty at de end ob town, be notified to leab de place, an' dat a c'mittee be appointed to dat effec'."

After the parson's influential speech, there was nothing further to be said, save to second, put and carry the motion. On the notification committee, the chairman appointed first, the Reverend Ebenezer Clay and then the injured Frog Martin, with sage Uncle Silas Marplot as a sapient third.

Never did men walk with more dignity, and less courage, than did the members of the "committee" as they strode up the door of "Conju'in' Joe." They knocked. No answer. They knocked again. Still no answer. And again with the same result. Then the Reverend Ebenezer Clay swallowed something in his throat and said: "Conju'in' Joe, we is de c'mittee, open de do'!" The door opened a few inches, and a trembling voice said, "Is yo' cullud?"

"We is," said Parson Clay, "the Lawd had made us so agin' ouah will."

Back swung the door. "Den come in," said Joe, bravely.

The "c'mittee" stalked in, solemn, silent, and scared. The importance of their mission shone in their faces. The Parson was spokesman, and they waited for him to begin. But in vain. With his finger pointing straight before him, he was standing transfixed. They followed his gaze and their tongues froze in their mouths. For upon the unkempt bed lay a corpse, seemingly but just dead. As their eyes fell upon it and they stood rooted to the spot with terror, Joe gave a half triumphant, half simple laugh and spoke.

"He's done past yo' reckenin' now, po' runaway niggah, he come to me a huntin' fo' freedom, an' I couldn't tu'n him away, you kin had me whupped and bu'ned, but Sam, po' Sam has enjoyed him freedom and he's past bein' tuk back into slabery. He wanted freedom, dat's why I shet up my cabin, dat's why I quit fiddlin' ha, ha, ha, I've cheated his master out ob one good niggah; tell him, he can hab him now fo' he caint hyeah him cuss ner feel his whup. Po' Sam, po' Sam, jes' befo' he died I sung fo' him. 'I want to be a sojer in de army ob de Lawd,' praise de Lawd, he's gone to be a sojer now!"

The committee stood speechless for a minute. Then Parson Clay said "Joe, ain't yo' heard about de wah?"

"De wah?" said Joe.

"Joe, de white people's done had a wah, a wah, and wese all free."

A blank expression came over the face of the ex-slave and he rubbed his head wildly as if to waken himself. "Free, free" he murmured, and then the dawn of comprehension seemed to break through his benighted mind, and he clasped his arms, crying "Free, free."

"Yes, free," said the preacher.

"You ain't afoolin' me, is yo'," said Joe, "you know yo' caint bring him back now."

"It's true," said the parson.

Joe fell on his knees beside the bed and the room shook with his convulsive sobs.

"We hab be'n free dese ten yeahs," the preacher added.

"Ten yeahs, ten yeahs," moaned Joe, "oh, praise de Lawd, praise de Lawd, an' me a hidin' po' Sam all dis time, too, you ain't a foolin' me, is you? Free, free, niggahs free, why, Lawd A'mighty, youse be'n on ea'th, sho' 'nough, don't fool me, you won't fool me, will yo'. Free, free, no, yes, ha, ha, ha, praise de Lawd! Sam, Sam, wake up, don't be dead, why, chile, youse free, arter a waitin' all dese yeahs de Lawd hab come to yo' deliberance. Come out in de light, Sam, come out an' show yo'se'f, nobody cain't hu't yo' fo' youse free now, ha, ha. Tell me, is your mastahs all slabes? No, well praise de Lawd, anyhow, ha, ha, ha; free, Sam, free." He seized the corpse's hand, his head sunk down upon the dead man's breast, "We don't need to hide now, Sam, we'se free, free," he murmured.

The committee tenderly lifted him up and laid him beside his dead comrade. He did not speak. They felt his heart, it had ceased to beat; for "Ole Conju'in Joe" had passed to that land where all are free indeed.

Undated manuscript, University of Dayton Rare Books Collection.

His Bride of the Tomb

"YOU MIGHT CONSENT to spend one day with me Violet, knowing that I have so little time to be with you," he said. "You may just as well lay aside your foolish prejudices and go with, Philip, for I am determined upon going," replied Violet Harcourt; she was speaking to her betrothed husband Philip Trevelyn. The gay party with whom she was spending a week or two in a quaint little out-of-the-way village, had in an overflow of thoughtless mischief determined upon picnicking in an old and long unused grave-yard; after dinner they were to amuse themselves by reading the rude epitaphs and visiting the gray old tombs, where "the rude forefathers of the hamlet sleep."

"I can't see," said Trevelyn, "what pleasure people can find in scampering over graves or picnicking among them, it shows very scant respect for the dead, to say the least." "Well every one doesn't choose to look at it in that way, Philip, you oughtn't to expect the whole world to think as you do, although you are Philip Trevelyn, Esquire, a rising young lawyer," she replied with almost a sneer. "There are some opinions in the world besides your own, although you don't seem to think so," she went on with rising anger.

"I am doing what I believe to be right, Violet, and you will acknowledge it some day"; he said coolly.

"Oh, of course you're always in the right, no one is ever right but you; well, at any rate I shall go tomorrow whether you choose to go or not."

"Violet, let me ask you, nay, nag you not to go; you will not enjoy it"; but with averted face she answered, "I shall go."

"Go," he replied flushing with anger, "Violet Harcourt, I command you as my betrothed wife not to go." She was hasty and willful, and, turning on him with a defiant look, she murmured, rather than spoke, "I shall disobey; no man shall ever have the power to command me; I am my own mistress; if you want me for your slave, take back your ring"; slipping the glittering band off her finger she held it out to him. For a moment he stood as though dazed, and then taking the ring, he placed it in his pocket and slowly turned away, just as Fred Tracy sauntered up saying, "It is our dance, Miss Harcourt." She placed her hand in his arm and entered the house, where the music of Strauss' "Merry Waltz" was filling the air with its beautiful rhythm.

It was an informal party which the young people were giving in the parlors of the one hotel which the village afforded, and the rooms were full of light and merriment. But Violet Harcourt's heart was heavy. Her companion's conversation became odious to her, and she began to think what abominable music that city orchestra was making.

She was a beautiful girl, dark haired, with rich complexion slightly dark, that betrayed the Spanish blood in her veins, though even had that been less indicative, her great lustrous black eyes must have told upon her; her mother was a Spaniard and from her she had inherited all the fire and ardent passions of that race. For nearly a year she had been the betrothed wife of Philip Trevelyn, and she loved him with her whole soul. But he was proud and she was proud and they quarreled often, though never before had they come to such a point.

Violet was a divine dancer, but tonight she could not dance; the music seemed to drag; she was angry and sick at heart; no gaiety could dispel the gloom that was gathering over her. "Are you ill?" asked her companion. "I am not!" she answered angrily. He should have been warned and not pursued the subject further but, Tracy unconscious that he was walking on forbidden ground remarked, "You do not seem to be in your accustomed spirits this evening." She deigned no reply, but the deadly look she gave him made the young man tremble.

When he left her, Philip Trevelyn walked rapidly trying to make his feet keep pace with his thoughts, cursing his fate and gnawing his cigar as though it had been the author of all his trouble. A man in this state is always likely to be more or less unjust. So there being no one else present, he cursed himself for ever coming to the village, he let his cigar go out, and then cursed the cigar for going out. Before he got through his cursing he had reached the little grave-yard which had been the innocent cause of all his pain, so, to end it all, he cursed the ring in his pocket, and taking it out, threw it as far into the grave-yard as he could, and turned his steps homeward; a light rain began to fall as he went along. "Humph," he muttered, "it isn't enough for me to be scorned but even the heavens are conspiring against me. This rain will just make it cool and pleasant for those frivolous picnickers tomorrow, and I had hoped that they would be scorched by a blazing sun while they were scampering among the graves and laughing at my foolish notions."

And as he went on the rain fell more heavily and he distinctly heard the ominous sighing of the weeping willows in the grave-yard, sighing that sounded like the half suppressed groan of a spirit damned.

The morning dawned in great beauty, the air was cool and fresh, the trees full of birds, singing thankfulness for the little shower. Philip Trevelyn did not rise early; he had passed a sleepless night, so when, at nine o'clock, the picnic party started away he was not up to see them go.

A very similar night Violet Harcourt had spent, weeping and chiding herself. For awhile she was determined to go to Philip and confess herself in the wrong, but the demon Pride rose and quenched the desire; it was with very red and swollen eyes that she left her bed to dress for the picnic, half-doubting that the affair of last night was real, that it had not all been a troublous dream; but the sight of her bare finger, where had sparkled Philip Trevelyn's ring was conclusive evidence that it was not all a dream. With heavy heart she donned her hat, as she heard Fred Tracy's voice at the door asking, "Are you ready?" "In a moment," she answered, and her voice sounded unnatural even to her own ears. She was bewitchingly beautiful in dead white and as she stepped out, Tracy glanced at her with a smile of pleasure, saying, "You are rivaling the morning in beauty"; and then he walked down the little corridor by her side singing cheerily,

"My love she's a beauty, but oh she's proud.
And many a quarrel have we."

"Where did you get that abominable song, Mr. Tracy?" said Violet. "It's perfectly harrowing."

"Well," he laughed in reply, "you're not very complimentary to my composition. I confess that the song is my own and I was foolish enough to think that it had quite a sweet melody."

"Tastes differ greatly," she said.

"De gustibus non disputandum," he replied, "but if you do not like my song it shall never be heard again, although I had hoped great things for it."

"Oh," said Violet, indifferently, "my opinion of it can have no influence over what others may think." By this time they had reached the street; she quietly entered the vehicle which waited to take them to the solemn seat of their gaiety, and as one person cannot keep up a conversation, the short ride was a very silent one. The little cemetery was gloomy but beautiful even in its gloom, the weeping willows, nature's ever constant mourners, hung over the sunken graves caressingly, and their drooping branches swept the green carpet of the ground. But notwithstanding the beauties of nature, the day was not what the picnickers expected it to be, and so, soon after dinner they by common consent decided to return, they were to walk home and were far upon the way when some one remarked the absence of Violet Harcourt. "Oh," said Tracy, "she's been in a bad humor all day, so I suppose she went home some time ago and left me to my fate." At this there was a general laugh as they walked home without her.

Just before they had started for home, Violet noticed a gray stone tomb with a heavy iron door which stood open; anxious to explore it and fearless, she entered and looked around for awhile at the dark caskets that seemed to frown at her boldness. But without a moment's warning the heavy door swung to and she heard the bolt outside as it fell into place. At first she was almost unable to realize her position, but as it dawned upon her that she was imprisoned with the dead, she raised her voice in a frantic cry for help. But the walls only seemed to hurl back the sound with redoubled force to her own ears, and then, when there seemed no help, she fell upon the floor in a dead faint. How long she lay there she did not know, but when she opened her eyes on the dense darkness again, she knew that her only escape lay in a continual cry for help, which might attract some passer's attention. As cry after cry went up, she suddenly heard a step and the latch was lifted, the door swung open, and she staggered out into Philip Trevelyn's arms. The past was forgotten, "Oh, Philip, my savior," she cried. He laughed for joy and pressed her to his heart saying, "There was a providence in our quarrel last night; if I had not quarreled with you and forbidden your coming I would not have been here now to save you. I was looking for the ring you returned and which, in my anger, I threw into this grave-yard, will you help me find it, darling?" "Yes," she murmured, "but oh, Philip, can you forgive me?" He caught her to his arms again crying, "There is nothing to forgive, my bride of the tomb!"

Dayton Tattler, December 13, 1890, Paul Laurence Dunbar Collection, Reel III, Box 9, OHS.

The Tenderfoot

BACK IN THE '50s, we old miners didn't hev much respect fur them weak-kneed, white-handed chaps, thet you call "dudes" now. They was rank pisen to us an' one of 'em never struck our camp without hevin' so many tricks played on him thet arter awhile he was glad enough to git away.

We thought that a "dude," "tenderfoot" we called him, didn't hev no rights which a miner was bound to respect, an' we treated him accordin'ly. Even in them days we had the barroom bummer who didn't do nothin' all day long but hang aroun' the tavern doin' odd jobs fur his meals an' watchin' fur the stage to come jest as anxious as if he was waitin' fur friends.

Sich sort o' chap was Jerry Malcolm, he was the most shiftless sort o' cuss I ever seen. He wouldn't work under no circumstances, exceptin' jest enough to feed him.

Jerry would stand at thet tavern winder all afternoon, waitin' fur the stage to come in, with no reason in the world fur doin' so, thet is, as anybody could see. The boys used to rig him a goo' deal about it, but he never seemed to care much—took it all good natured as you please.

He wasn't a bad sort o' fellow, drunkard nor nothin' o' thet kind; but jest natchelly shiftless and don't-care-like.

One day, jest arter time fur the stage to come in, a half a dozen or so us fellows was su'prized clean out o' our wits to see Jerry Malcolm come a tearin' down the trail leadin' to the mine whar we was a workin', both hands throwed up and his feet goin' like wings.

"Wonder what's the matter with Jerry?" said Dan McCoy, shadin' his eyes with his hand and lookin' up the trail.

"Somethin' mighty pertickler's goin' on to make Jerry lift them feet o' hisn thet away."

"Mebbe Mulligan's gang has struck the camp again," said Tom Haydon, laying his hand on the butt of his revolver as he spoke. Every other man in-stinctively made the same movement as the thought flashed across their minds; for another visit from Tim Mulligan's dare-devils wasn't a very pleasant out-look.

So in silence we waited till Jerry come up out o' breath, puffin' and blowin' like a steam engine. "Boys," says he, "what d'you think?"

"We ain't thinkin' a tall," said Haydon, gruffly. "We're waitin' to hear, so spit it out as quick as you kin."

"Thar's a tenderfoot just landed from the stage," gasped Jerry, between puffs.

"A tenderfoot!"

We was a good deal relieved, but we didn't let on t' each other, an' each fellow laughed an' he went back to his work an' began to hatch some divilment in his mind agin' that pore "tenderfoot."

Well, work jest flew along thet arternoon, fur we wanted to git done and go down to the tavern. When quittin' time come, you never seen men drop their tools an' make fur camp quicker in your life. We couldn't git to the tavern quick enough; but even when we did git there, we was disappointed, fur there wasn't a sign of a "tenderfoot" in sight. They said he had shelled out of his store clothes and gone out in the hills prospectin'. It was a hard strain on us but we had to sit down to supper without seein' him.

When the meal was about half over, Jerry Malcolm came a tiptoein' in like he was afraid he'd wake hisself, an' said kind o' low like; "He's a comin', fellers." Every eye turned toward the door. It opened sort o' quick like an' in stepped our man. Wall, we'd all been kind o' holden' our breath, an' all of a sudden we let it go with a gasp. Man alive! There was six foot of as good a man in that tenderfoot's clothes as ever I seen.

He was togged out in a rough workin' suit, but his hands give him away, fur they looked soft an' tender an' there wasn't nothin' like sunburn on 'em to spoil their whiteness. He didn't look like a very likely feller to fool with, an' I guess all the boys must a thought the same, fur none of them said anything to him.

Like as not, nothin' wouldn't ever hev bin said if it hadn't bin fur thet devil, Tom Haydon, who spoke up and says, "Wall, stranger, you've cast in your lot amongst us; you might as well git acquainted. Who are you and what's your business?"

"I'm an assayer, an' my name's Fred Bender," the young feller answered; very polite.

But Tom wasn't satisfied; he wanted to take the feller down, so he said, with a kind of sneer: "Oh, you're one of them college-taught miners, are you, a' squintin' around the rocks with a lead pencil an' microscope."

The young feller didn't make no answer, but I saw his eyes kind o' gleam in a way thet would 'a' warned most men. But Haydon went on: "What'd you expect to find here anyhow, gold or brass?" laughin' an' winkin' at the other fellers.

"If I'd ben lookin' fur brass," said the stranger, lookin' Haydon straight in the eyes, "I wouldn't have had to go far to find it after meetin' you."

Haydon was a good deal took back but he laughed with the rest of us an' nothin' more was said thet evenin'.

But anyone thet knowed him could 'a' told thet he wasn't satisfied; fur he was one o' these kind o' fellers thet hold a grudge agin' you if you git a little ahead of 'em even in fun.

Fur two months, things moved along smooth enough. The tenderfoot was still amongst us and he'd begun to grow into consid'able favor, fur we found thet he was a plain sort o' unassumin' man thet knowed his business an' tended to it. He was friendly, but not familiar, an' so we all kind o' took a likin' to him.

It was a rainin' like blazes one mornin' when we got up, an' the boys thought it was too wet to do much work; so we all got together in the big bare barroom of the tavern to amuse ourselves the best we could. One of the fellows had a banjo an' played an' sung whilst some of the others danced jigs an' breakdowns in their rough fashion. Fred Bender had joined us an' seemed to be enjoyin' the fun as much as anybody.

At last some one proposed havin' a wrasslin' match.

Now anyone thet ever knowed a camp o' miners knows thet's jes the thing fur 'em; so we hailed the idee with a shout an' cleared space fur a ring.

Haydon was the champion strong man of the camp, so he was put up agin' all comers. Dan McCoy first faced him, an' in five minutes was on his back on the floor. Then Barney O'Shea, a jolly young Irishman, tackled the champion and went down the same way.

He hed throwed his fourth man, the whole crowd was hoarse with hollerin', an' he was tickled to death with his victory, when some one ups and says: "What's the matter with you tryin' him, Bender? You're about one size."

Bender kind o' hesitated an' I guess would hev refused, if Haydon hadn't o' sneered out: "Wall, I reckon I kin lay a tenderfoot in about half the reg'lar time."

At this the young feller got up and said he guessed he'd try his muscle anyhow. They was so nigh one size thet the fellers like to 'a' went crazy jest anticipatin' what a match it 'ud be.

Wall, sir, they grappled an' went to work in earnest, twistin' and strainin' like two big sarpents. The crowd kept gettin more an' more excited; those on the outside of the ring craned their necks an' pressed for'ard; those on the inside laid back an' hollered: "Give 'em room; give 'em a show."

But it wasn't no use they jest pressed up until they was packed together like a lot o' sardines.

In the ring the struggle was growin' fiercer an' fiercer; the fighters acted like they was in earnest, their faces was red, their [eyes] they was goin' to bust, an' the sawdust flying from under their feet in a perfec' cloud.

Then, I don't know how it happened, it was done so quick, but one of them went down. Fur a few minutes, in the confusion and dust, no one could tell who it was. But as the men began to git up the crowd saw his face an' a rousin' cheer went up. It was Haydon.

There was a very unpleasant look on his face as he turned an' left the room without a word.

Bender took his vict'ry in a very quiet way, an' the men hed soon furgot the matter turnin' their attention to cards an' dice. 'Bout three o'clock Haydon come in agin, an' begun a loadin' up purty heavy with sperrits. We all begun to expec' mischief, but he laid our fears to rest by goin' out agin without trouble.

"Them's strange actions fur Tom Haydon," says Dan McCoy; an' they was, too.

About sunset we heard a terrible clatter outo' doors an' every man rushed to the door to see what it was.

An' thar, down the road, came Tom Haydon on one o' them devilish little mustangs, brandishin' a gun, right an' left above his head. He'd made his plans well, an' it all flashed on our minds in a second. He knowed that the noise 'ud bring us all out, an' then he would pick out his man easy enough.

We knowed who the doomed man was an' so we didn't take the trouble to git out o' the way fur Tom Haydon was a sure shot an' wouldn't fail to hit the right one.

All of a sudden somethin' mes our gaze, right in the path o' the gallopin' critter; it was Tom Haydon's little gal Bess, only four years old. Right in the path air, an' that pony almost layin' flat in his mad gallop. Every man seemed froze with fear; we give one shout, Tom was blind and deaf to all but one thing. He hed his eyes fixed on Fred Bender, the tenderfoot, never movin' 'em as he bore down on his own child. I would a hid my eyes from the sight but somehow I couldn't. I was jest kind o' fascinated.

Then like a flash we saw a streak o' blue shirt right across the pony's path, a child flyin' away off to one side, a man down under the horse's feet, an' an instant later, *"ping,"* went a bullet from Tom Haydon's revolver right into the door post whar Bender had been standin'.

All was confusion fur a minute or so an' then the men went out an' picked pore Bender up. He was hurt purty bad an' a gaspin' hard.

Wall, I never seen a man sober up as Haydon did in all my life. As soon as he could stop the pony, he jumped off an' come a runnin' back. He'd seen what had happened jest at the last moment. "My God!" said he, "he saved my child, my little Bess, an' me a tryin' to kill him." An' then, pushin' the men aside, he took Bender up in his arms as tender as a mother liftin' her sick baby.

He carried him into his own cabin, which was right across the street from the tavern, an' then leavin' his wife to make the pore feller easy, jumped on the pony an' went tearin' away after a doctor.

The first thing the tenderfoot gasped when he opened his eyes was: "Is the kid all right?"

Wall, sir, fur four months Tom Haydon an' his wife nussed that tenderfoot like their own brother an' he furgive Tom jest as if nothin' had happened an' didn't put on no airs 'bout his sacrifice.

The miners purty nigh worshiped him. He stopped his business o' jest assayin' and went to minin' fur all that's out, and to-day you can't git inside the border o' Californy without hearin' o' Fred Bender, president o' the Bender-Haydon Minin' Company. An' it's him that was the tenderfoot.

Sold to A. N. Kellogg Syndicate, December 19, 1891, Paul Laurence Dunbar Collection, Reel IV, Box 15, OHS.

Little Billy

WHEN CONSUMPTION TOOK ol' Mis' Sanders off she left a pore, little, sickly baby boy, not more'n two year ol' fur her husband to raise. It was a turrible trial to a man workin' like Bill Sanders had to work, to hev a puny, cryin' baby on his hands. Ef it had a be'n one o' these great big strappin' childern thet kin knock about anywheres, it wouldn't a' be'n so bad; but it look purty hard to be hampered with one thet needed tender nussin' all the time.

To a' looked at Bill Sanders, you'd'a thought thet he couldn't be tender enough to nuss a sick elephant. He was a great big rough-lookin' feller with a voice like a foghorn an' hands as hard an' horny as a weather-beaten rock.

But somewhere, away down under all the rough shell, he had a heart brimful o' gentleness and kindness. He didn't take no great flarin' way o' showin' it, but you didn't hev to know him long to find it out.

There's some men thet hev to do big things to show how much heart they've got, but he didn't; a body jest naturally seemed to feel it. Fur two or three days arter his mother's death, the little boy didn't do nothun' but holler an' cry all the time, until you'd 'a thought Bill's soul was almost worried out o' him.

When the fun'l was over an' pore Sally Sanders laid away forever, the women folks gathered to decide which of 'em should take the boy. Wall, you know how women are when there is any good act to be done, they all want to be the one to do it. An' so there was several willin' to take the child. They couldn't decide which of 'em was to hev him, an' so it was agreed thet the offer should be made to Sanders fur all of 'em an' left for him to choose between 'em.

Bill was touched by their kindness, but shook his head in answer to the offer. "No," says he, "Sally told me allus to keep little Bill with me 'cause he was sickly, an' I promised I would; I couldn't break a promise made to my dead wife fur no reason in the world."

"But you can't give the pore little feller the care he orter hev," said Tim Hodge's wife, who hed be'n sent to do the talkin'.

"I'll do the best I kin," answered Bill, "an' thet's all anybody could do."

It wasn't no use to try to shake his determination; what he said he meant an' stuck to. He made the child a little cart in which, wrapped up warm, he hauled him to the mines every day, an' then, stowing him in a safe place he would go on to work, runnin' back every little while to see thet he was gettin' 'long all right.

In spite of all the toys an' things thet Bill raked up, it couldn't help but be lonesome an' tiresome fur the child; but the litter feller seemed to know thet his father was doin' the best he could fur him an' he didn't make much trouble.

At first it was a kind o' funny sight to see the great big man going to his work every mornin' draggin' the cart with thet little peaked baby in it. People said that a man wouldn't stand anything like thet very long an' prophesied thet it wouldn't last.

But it did, an' big Bill haulin' the little Bill to work growed to be a common sight. An' how the women went on about him, holdin' him up as a model to their husbands an' pointin' him out as the only true man thet ever lived.

Wall, the air must 'a' done the child good, fur it commenced to grow stronger lookin'. It was wonderful, how it filled out, an' Bill got as proud of him as a peacock of his tail. He hed allus be'n kind an' gentle to him, but he hedn't be'n so powerful affectionate.

With his sole care of the child, it hed kinder growed around his heart. His eyes would take on the softest look an' his voice would sink so low an' lovin' when he talked to little Billy thet every action showed how he was bound up in him.

When the boy was seven or eight years ol' a thing turned up thet showed thet Sanders's feelins hedn't changed a bit. A gang o' youngsters broke into the tool house, an' stole a lot o' the men's tools. They wasn't found for a long time, but arter awhile some boys was traced into a cave which was dug in the side of the hill. Two or three men followed an' raided the place, an' there was the tools, everyone of 'em, an' about a dozen young shavers layin' around.

Among 'em was little Billy, big as anybody.

Wall, they bagged every one of 'em an' marched 'em into camp, pretendin' they was a goin' to try 'em. They was as bad skeered a set o' boys as ever you seed 'cause they knowed what happened to thieves when they was ketched 'round there. They was most all a snivelin' an' pleadin' 'cept little Billy. He was game an' went along with his mouth shet as tight as wax.

They hed to come right up past a place where a lot o' the men was standin', laughin' at the sight. In the crowd was Bill Sanders; as his eyes fell on little Billy he jumped for'ard, sayin': "What's the meanin' o' this?"

"Oh, these are the fellers what stole them tools from the tool house an' we're a goin' to make 'em up an' try 'em," says Hank Simms.

"Didn't steal no tools, dad," little Billy bawled out.

His father went up to him and takin' his arm drawed him away from the crowd. Turnin' to Hank he says, in a low, dry voice: "I don't want no such darned foolishness with my boy. He didn't help steal them tools; he says so, an' I'd believe his word again' any of you; there ain't a drop o' lyin' or stealin' blood in his veins."

"Why, it's only fun, Bill," said Hank.

"Fun or what not, I don't like it," and Sanders took little Billy an' went home.

Mebbe Sanders was a little too particular, but every hen knows best how to cover her own chickens.

Boys in them days struck out soon fur themselves, an' when little Billy was about sixteen he left the camp an' went somewheres where he thought he could do better an' make more money. For a time Sanders heerd from him reg'lar an' he was allus a gettin' along well; but by 'n' by the letters commenced fallin' off. An' as he got further an' further away from the ol' man, they got slacker an' slacker until they quit entirely.

Not a word could be heerd from him; nobody even knowed where he was. But Sanders didn't worry or take on as you might 'a' expected he would. He was allus calm, for he said he knowed wherever little Billy was he was safe an' doin' well, 'cause he was honest an' willin' to work an' he hed hed good raisin'.

I tell you he hed lots o' faith in thet boy, a good deal more than anybody else hed, fur there was several times when he was in camp thet purty mean tricks was laid at his door, an' thet upon good proof, too; but he always managed to get out of it somehow or other, an' knowin' how his father doted on him, most everybody hated to press a thing against him. There's be'n more boys than one saved trouble thet way. But arter while, little Billy was furgot an' even Sanders himself hed stopped tellin' every listener the good points "o' thet boy Billy." Fact is we hed to furget everything in them rushin' times. The minin' camp hed growed into a town with reg'lar gov'nment an' a court an' jedge thet got in his work on offenders whenever his flourishin' an' expeditions rival Jedge Lynch giv him a chance.

An' there was plenty of work for both of 'em, 'cause every kind of thief under the sun was layin' 'round, waitin' fur a chance to nab the dust o' some unsuspectin' miner. An' now, hoss thieves, had be'n added to the list. Several valuable animals belongin' to different folks in the town hed walked off in a very mysterious manner.

Now, you know, thet is our sore point—hoss thieves!

We hate 'em worse 'n murderers, 'cause they're sneakin'er about their work. Wall, this yere thief was about the cutest one that ever laid fingurs on hoss flesh; didn't leave no tracks, seemed to jest pick the animals up an' fly away with 'em.

We come to the conclusion thet it wasn't no gang, but jest one powerful slick man by hisself. No gang could 'a' moved so quiet an' mysterious an' be'n quick at the same time. We tried every way to ketch him, but he was too slick fur me. But at last we got desp'rate an' vowed we'd ketch thet feller ef it took every bit o' dust we hed an' our lives to boot. We studied an' studied to think how we could fix it, an' at last Bill Sanders hisself hit on a plan which we all agreed to.

So the next night seen in his own stable the finest hoss thet a heavy collection taken up amongst us could buy, an' a score o' determined men hid 'round in the dark. Now a really fine hoss draws a hoss thief like a magnet does steel, an' we knowed thet we hed the chap dead sure.

Wall, not a leaf stirred the first night an' we was considerable disappointed, so durin' the follerin' day the horse was driv' around the town to show him off to any watchers thet might be lurkin' about, an' we watched thet night in hopes, but it was like the first, no go. Fur ten solid days we watched without success an' then the men began to drop off, ontil the guard hed be'n entirely broken up.

We believed thet the hoss thief hed left us an' for good too. But I reckon thet chap was even slicker then we thought; fur one night arter we'd growed keerless, Sanders, who was a mite more keerful then the rest of us, heerd the hoss whinny. He was out to the stable in a minute. There was a man beside the hoss; at the sight of him, Sanders darted in but the feller vaulted into the saddle an' lettin' drive a shot thet took Bill in the shoulder, dashed out o' the back door.

Furgittin' the pain of his wound, Sanders was on a mustang an' arter him like a flash, alarmin' the town as he passed through, cryin', "Hoss thief, hoss thief, hoss thief!" Them thet looked out seen two hosses gallopin' past, but heard only one. The first hoss must 'a' hed his hoofs padded heavy.

It wasn't long before about twenty-five or thirty men hed jined the chase an' wen' gallopin' arter the sound o' the second hoss. But the thief hed a purty good start ahead, an' it was two good hours before even Sanders was sighted. In another hour the crowd overtook him. His face showed pale in the moonlight an' he looked like he could hardly keep his saddle an' his hoss was purty nigh wore out; but there was a sullen determination in the way he urged the pore beast on. Away off in the front a shadow could be seen movin' whenever the foremost rider passed between the moon an' a cluster o' rocks an' now an' then the sound of a hoof strikin' the stony ground could be heard. The hoss hed wore through or throwed off one of his pads.

The sight o' the prey made the men more eager 'n ever an' they spared neither lash nor spur. The hosses staggered an' stumbled under the strain, but thet wasn't the time fur pityin' brutes with a subject fur lynchin' a mile ahead.

So clatter an' dash over short spaces o' level land an' longer tracts o' hilly road, we went; up an' down over the bowlders that blocked our way an' gainin' not more 'n an inch in a hundred feet. When day broke, we was still a-goin'. Steady, steady. A foot at every hundred. Two feet. Three. But our hosses was gone up; they began to slow down. We would lose the gained ground, but we were in shootin' distance. Bill Sanders, who is still in the lead, raises his gun. It is our only chance, so a number follow suit. A report: twelve bullets fly on their mission. The man in advance throws up his arms an' falls back out of his saddle an' the hoss droops away riderless.

We ride up to where the body lay, face upward.

Bill Sanders glances at it an' then gives sech a cry as I never heerd before, an' God grant may never hear again.

"My God!" he screams. "My son; my little Billy!" and flingin' himself from his hoss he drops down beside the body.

How, in one glance, he ever recognized his son Billy in thet bronzed, scarred man, I can't see. I reckon mebbe there's sympathetic chords in the hearts o' parents an' children thet throb when they're brought together.

Like a brute thet laps the wounds of the injured young one, so Sanders fondled the body of his dead son, callin' him by name an' kissin' the bearded face. But the eyes were fast glazin' an' the lips were closed in the last silence.

We would a' taken the body up, but, springin' up, he stood over it like a

tiger at bay. "Go 'way, go 'way, leave me alone with the son I hev murdered."
An' we hed to obey.

We stood to one side as alone he strapped the sad load to the back o' the
stolen hoss, then, mountin' his own an' leadin' the other, silent he led the way
to town.

Sold to A. N. Kellogg Syndicate (ca. 1893), Paul Laurence Dunbar Collection, Reel IV,
Box 15, OHS.

Jimmy Weedon's Contretempts

HAD YOU ASKED any one in his set, he would have told you with a polite
uplifting of the brows, "Oh, yes, Jimmy Weedon is a little wild, but then—"
You would not have asked, though. First off, because if you had belonged to
his set you would have known all that his friends knew, and if you happened
to be one of those ordinary mortals outside of that rare sphere, you would
never have dared to approach one of the elect.

Jimmy was wild, though, and rather more so than Mama or Papa Weedon
knew, or any of his world suspected. He was sowing his wild oats, and hered-
ity was strong. So, like his father in his commercial enterprises, Jimmy chose
a wide field of action. As far as people knew, he was not so bad as young men
go, and they rather winked at the rumors of his little escapades, for he was
such a favorite in his particular set, and then he was only to have his freedom
for a little while longer, because under parental persuasion, aided by threats
as to the non-payment of certain debts, he had finally agreed to propose to
Helen Greville, and had been accepted.

Now did young Weedon groan in spirit. Until the last, he had hoped
against hope that Helen would refuse him. Not that Helen was not a nice
girl. On the contrary, she was very nice. And even putting aside the snug for-
tune that was hers, she was much too good for Jimmy, and moreover, Jimmy
knew it.

It is all very well, this marrying a woman who is one, a superior, if, as the
writers say, after the wedding she will stand still and let the man equal and

then surpass her, but it is possible that he may continue to come out second in the race to the end of his days, and then—well, a man needs to do a deal of thinking before he consents to be the husband of somebody.

Two people were never more unlike than Jimmy and Helen. He was a good looking chap, fleshly and easy-going who excused his own faults and evaded responsibility with a calm that would have been startling to moralists. On the other hand, Helen was a serious girl, who looked everything, her faults, virtues, duties, everything except her prejudices, in fact, squarely in the face. She had not a saving grace of humor, and there were those who even accused her of being straitlaced. On the score of dignity she had disapproved of Jimmy's taking part in a cake walk, and was not sure it was nice for him to want to do so. She accepted him because he was thoroughly likable, and no one had moved her more than he, but she did not understand him. How could she? The vague rumors about him disturbed her. If he did do awful things, she thought that when they were married, her influence would change —she would not say, "reform"—him. This was all very foolish, had Helen only known it, because there was no common ground where she could meet her fiancé to analyze his doings. She had never met a temptation and Jimmy had never resisted one. Just now, he was finding particular pleasure in certain excursions down into the shady districts of New York, where he could have a good time, be a prince of good fellows, and at the same time, be under none of the galling restrictions that hampered him in his own world.

Be it said, however, that Jimmy's predilection for low life had been of short duration, and was usually emphasized after the earlier part of the evening had been spent in pursuit of higher game. Then when his head was ringing, his cheeks flushed, and he felt in his heart the joy of possessing the whole world, he would hie himself to his favorite cabman and go down to inspect the lower half of his domain. There was one thing about Jimmy, though, a thing that will please men. He never deceived himself as to why he sought out these lowly companions and their abodes. Never for an instant did he soothe his conscience or excuse his tastes, by thinking that he was searching for types or studying conditions. The life of these people so far from his own amused him and he went among them without moralizing about it. He cared nothing about their types or conditions except as they appealed to his humor. He was as honest in his motives for slumming as was Helen, who went in for charity—spiced.

Charity hideth a multitude of curiosities. Also the pursuit hath in it much of that variety of life which is supposed to put ginger into existence. Virtue is its own reward, of course, and a certain joy comes from the very doing of a good deed, but when this same righteous accomplishment is accompanied by the sight of various zest-giving things that could not otherwise come within the range of one's experience, the pleasure is measurably increased. Not one of the companions of Helen who poked about with her among the tenements and dives of the poor and depraved would have confessed that he or she was actuated by any save the highest motives. They must see and diagnose the disease ere they could provide a remedy for it, and any suggestion of curiosity as a main spring of action or morbid pleasure in the unusual would have been met with indignant denial.

Mrs. Carrington was one of those who indulged in the complacent dissipation of charity. She was also original, and so her friends were glad to accept her invitation to a slum dinner with a mysterious entertainment afterward. It was to be a very simple affair as befitted the motive behind it. They were not to dress for the occasion and they were to have but two wines. What great proof of sincerity could there be in this self denial?

When the simple dinner was over, Mrs. Carrington made a politely hesitating little speech: "I, ah—felt," she said, "that—ah—the special need of us, ah—who have the well being of the poor at heart to—ah—be—a closer— that is, a—, more intimate insight into their needs and their disabilities. What we want fully to realize is—ah—the—ah—real brotherhood of man, and so I have asked you to this simple little—ah—. I can hardly call it a dinner," a deprecating little laugh, "in order to show our sympathy with the people who are on the underside. I did not tell you—ah—what we should do afterward because I wanted it to come—ah—in the nature of a surprise. Officer Mulligan of the oth precinct has—ah—consented to come and go with us through some of the dwellings and—ah—amusement places of the poorer classes in order that—ah—we may see for ourselves just the types and ah— ah—conditions that obtain there."

There was a buzzing murmur of applause that brought the roses of pleasure to the face of the hostess.

"Isn't it sweet of her?" said a little lady in Helen's ear, "and how clever, we don't have to dress."

"It is noble of her," said Helen, "and what an opportunity she gives us for seeing just where and how we can do good."

After the necessary mutterings attending upon any feminine movement, Detective Mulligan in plain clothes and a state of contempt, with the nervous young rector of St. Asaphs, led them out to their carriages, which by the way, were to await them at a convenient distance from their place of research, so as not to give the lowly brother any aggressive idea of luxury.

By some fortuitous circumstance, it happened to be Jimmy Weedon's off night, and he had decided to go slumming on his own account without a detective or a charitable motive. This was bad for Jimmy. One hour after the lowly peregrinations of the Carrington party had begun, he bade Teddy Van Guysen good bye over their thirteenth high ball, went airily down the steps of the club and gave a whispered direction to his confidential cabman. Now if Jimmy had only stopped with his twelfth high ball, this story might never have been told, but he didn't. He took one more, and thirteen is an unlucky number. He was the most inconsequently happy man that New York held that night. He hummed gaily as he rolled along, and tried, unsuccessfully, to be sure, to twirl his stick in the cab. He had the cabman stop at several glittering places along the way, where he added others to the thirteen, and one would have thought that it would have broken the "hoodoo,"[1] but it didn't. The "thirteen" had gotten in its work.

When he was within the radius which for the evening he intended to grace with his presence, Jimmy leaped from the cab and dropped into a little chop house that he knew. Here people of rather a different cast from himself hailed him joyously as a man and brother, for there were always good times for the less fortunate when gay young Weedon was doing the town. Moreover, Jimmy was one of the few of his class who could so utterly merge his personality in his surroundings as never to invite suspicion and resentment. He was never superior. When one accepted a treat from him it was really by way of doing him a favor.

"Say," said one of his confidential friends, "dey's a big time over to Reddy Blake's dance-hall to-night. Don't you want to go? He's givin' a free blow-out, an' dey'll be lots o' de goils an' boys down?"

"Don't care if I do, if they don't throw me out."

"T'row you out? All, gwan. De guys won't do nuttin' to yer because dey knows yer."

[1] *Hoodoo* is the African American term for the West Indian *voodoo*.

"All right."

A short time later, Mr. Weedon with his friend, who went under the simple name of Mike, rolled luxuriously up to the door of Reddy Blake's dance hall. Blake welcomed Jimmy as if he had been an alderman, while Mike, in the moments when he was not his companion's shadow, got around among those of his set who were inclined to be offish, and "copped off" his protégé as "dead game, an' a all roun' swell guy."

Jimmy entered at once into the spirit of things and as the night wore on apace, the fun grew fast and furious. He was somewhat of a speiler, and the way he swung those girls around was a matter of disgust or admiration according to whether his critic were jealous or generous.

"And now," said Mrs. Carrington, "we have seen a great deal, and I know you must all be tired. We will go to just one more place, a dance hall." Up at Reddy Blake's Jimmy's good angel neglected him, but he danced on. One can judge the needs of the masses by the way they amuse themselves as well as by the way they live.

"This is practical work," said the little rector of St. Asaphs.

"How instructive," murmured Helen, and under the guidance of Mr. Mulligan, they made their way to Reddy Blake's.

The floor was very full when they entered, but their embarrassing presence caused some of the dancers to withdraw leaving the dancing place less crowded.

The aristocrats huddled together and looked on at the novel sight of the poor amusing themselves.

They seem to be having a good time," whispered Mrs. Carrington, "but it is all—ah—so different from us."

"Quite different, quite," murmured Helen, "not only temperamentally, but—ah—every way."

"One couldn't conceive of a person in our class enjoying this however," said the rector.

"There is one good dancer if only he weren't so wild, there, that young man with the slender girl, coming this way."

Jimmy was waltzing wildly down the floor to the closing strains of the music. The playing stopped, and laughing and flushed he paused directly in front of the group. There was a gasp in concert, and looking up, he met Helen's horrified eyes. He gazed dumbfounded. Then he grinned, and there is no telling what other sort of fool he might have made of himself, had not Mrs. Carrington saved the day by hustling Helen away with a brisk, "Come, we've had enough of this, now to supper."

She cast only one backward glance at Jimmy, that destroyer of complacent theories and then swept out. The rector or St. Asaph's coughed and looked unhappy.

Helen went white at first and then red as she tugged at the ring under her glove. The women were subdued. The few men who lagged indifferently with the party, smiled behind their hands, and conversation languished. The supper was not a success.

As for Jimmy, with the philosophical reflection that one had as well die for an old sheep as for a lamb, he went on dancing.

It was the next morning when he received a cold note from Helen accompanied by his ring. His head was aching, and there were dark lines under his eyes. But he smiled as he read the curt note: "After what has happened, etc., etc." He put the towel to his head again. "It's an ill wind," he murmured cheerily.

And that night there was a supper at Reddy Blake's over which Jimmy presided and to which none but the elect of that quarter came.

Typescript (ca. 1895), Paul Laurence Dunbar Collection, Reel IV, Box 12, OHS.

The Emancipation of Evalina Jones

DOUGLASS STREET WAS alive with people, and astir from one dirty end to the other. Flags were flying from houses, and everything was gay with life and color. Every denizen of Little Africa was out in the street. That is, every one except Evalina Jones, and even she came as far as the corner, when with banners flying, and the sound of the colored band playing "'Rastus on Parade," the "Hod-Carriers' Union," bright in their gorgeous scarlet uniforms, came marching down. It was a great day for Little Africa, the twenty-second of

September, and they were celebrating the emancipation of their race. The crowning affair of the day was to be this picnic of the "Hod-Carriers' Union," at the fair grounds where there was to be a balloon ascension, dancing, feasting, and fireworks, with a speech by the Rev. Mr. Barnett, from Green County, a very famous orator, who had been in the legislature, and now aspired to be a Bishop.

Evalina looked on with eyes that sparkled with the life of the scene, until the last of the pageant had passed, and then the light died out of her face and she hurried back to her home as she saw a man coming toward her up the street. She was bending over her wash-tub when he came into the house.

"Got any money, Evalina?" he asked, leering at her.

"I got fifty cents, Jim, but what do you want with that?" she replied.

"Nevah you mind what I want with it, give it to me."

"But Jim, that's all I got to go to the picnic with, an' I been hu'yin' thoo so I could git sta'ted."

"Picnic," he said. "Picnic, I'll picnic you. You ain't goin' a step f'om this house. What's the mattah with you, ain't you got that washin' to finish?"

"Yes, but I kin get throo in time, an' I want to go Jim, I want to go. You made me stay home last yeah, an' yeah befo', and I'm jes' the same ez a slave, I am."

"You gi' me that money," he said menacingly. Evalina's hand went down into the pocket of her calico dress, and reluctantly drew forth a pitiful half dollar.

"Umph," said her worse half. "This is a pretty looking sum fu' you to have, pu'tendin' to wo'k all the time," and he lurched out of the door.

Evalina stopped only long enough to wipe a few tears from her eyes, and then she went stolidly on with her washing. She had been married to Jim for five years, and for that length of time he had bullied her, and made her his slave. She had been a bright, bustling woman, but he had killed all the brightness in her and changed her bustling activity into mere stolid slavishness. Cheerfully she bore it at first, for a little child had come to bless her life. But when, after two pain-ridden years, the little one had passed away, she took up her burden sullenly, and without relief. People knew that Jim abused her, but she never complained to them; she was close-mouthed and patient. The very firmness with which she set her mouth when things went particularly hard, indicated that she might have beat her husband at his own game, had she tried. But somehow she never tried. There was a remarkable reserve force about the woman, but it needed something strong, something thrilling, to stir it into action.

Now and again, as she bent over the tub, her tears fell and mingled with the suds. They fell faster as the image of the little grave, which she had worked so hard to have digged outside the confines of Potter's Field, would arise in her mind. Then a tap came at her door.

"Come in," she said. A woman entered, bright in an array of cheap finery.

"Howdy, Evalina," she said.

"Howdy, yo'se'f, Ca'line," was the response.

"Oh, I middlin'. Ain't you goin' to the picnic?"

"No, I reckon I ain't. I got my work to do. I ain't got no time fu' picnics."

"Why, La, chile, this ain't no day fu' wo'k—Celebration Day! Why, evah-body's goin'; I even see ol' Aunt Maria Green hobblin' out wid huh cane, an' ol' Uncle Jimmy Hunter."

"I reckon they got time," said Evalina; "I ain't."

She looked the woman over with an unfriendly eye. She knew that this creature who made of life so light and easy a thing, stood between her and any joy that she might have found in her bare existence. She knew that Jim liked Caroline Wilson, and compared his wife unfavorably with her. She looked at the flashy ribbons, and the brilliant hat, and then involuntarily glanced down at her own shabby gown, torn and faded and suds-splashed, and an anger, the heat of which she had never known before, came into her heart. Her throat grew dry and throbbed, but she said huskily,

"'Taint fu' me to go to picnics, it's fu' nice ladies what live easy, an' dress fine. I mus' wo'k an' dig an' scrub."

"Humph," said the other, "of co'se there's a diffunce in people."

"Well, that's one thng I kin thank Gawd fu'," said Evalina, with grim humor.

Caroline Wilson bridled. "I hope you ain't th'owin' out no slurs at me, Evalina Jones, cause I wants you to know I's a lady, myse'f."

"I ain't th'owin' out no slurs at nobody," said Evalina, slowly. "But all I kin say is thet ef that shoe fits you, put it on and waih it."

Her visitor was angry, and she showed it. She stood up, and the spirit of battle was strong in her. But she gave a glance first at her finery, and then at the strong arms which her hostess had placed akimbo as she looked at her, and she decided not to bring matters to an issue.

"Well, of co'se," temporized Caroline, "I'd like to see you go, but it ain't none o' my business. I allus got along wid my po' hu'ban' w'en he was livin'."

"Oh, I ain't 'sputin' that, I ain't 'sputin' that. They ain't no woman that knows you goin' 'ny you got wunnerful pow'rs fu' handlin' men."

"Well, I does know how to keep what I has."

"Yes, an' you knows how to git what you hasn't." The light was growing greatly in Evalina's eyes, and Caroline saw it. She wasn't a coward, not she. But she looked at her finery again. It did look so flimsy and delicate to her eyes; then she said, "I mus' be goin', goo'bye."

"Goo'bye. Well, ef I didn't have a min' to frail that 'ooman, I ain't hyeah," and Evalina went back to her work with a shaking head and a new spirit.

Some instinct drew her to the door, and feeling that she might at least avail herself of a little breathing space, she walked as far as the corner of the now entirely deserted street. It was good that she had come, for the sight that she saw there aroused the life in her that had lain dead for the five years that she had been Jim's wife. She stood at the corner, and gazed down at the street that ran at right angles. Her arms unconsciously went akimbo, and she grinned a half-mouthed grin, showing the white gleam of her upper teeth like a dog when someone has robbed him of his precious bone.

"Oom-hoomph, Ca'line," she said, "oom-humph, Jim, I caught you." There was no shade of the anger she felt in her heart expressed in her tones. They were dry, hard and even, but she grinned that dog-like grin which boded no good to Jim and Caroline, who, all unconscious of it, walked on down the street towards the Fair Grounds.

She was done by eleven o'clock. Then she put on the best dress she had, and even that best was shabby, for Jim "needed" most of her money, and went up town to see Mrs. Wharton, for whom she worked. Mrs. Wharton was a little woman, with a very large spirit.

"Why, Evalina," she said, when she saw the black woman, "why on earth aren't you at the picnic?"

"That's jes' what I come hyeah to talk to you about," was the reply.

"Well, do let me hear! If you didn't have the money, why didn't you come to me? That's just what I say about you, you never open your mouth when you need anything. You know I'd have helped you out," rushed on the little lady.

"'Taint that, 'taint that," replied Evalina, "I'd a spoke to you this week. 'Taint the money, Mis' Wharton, it's Jim."

"Jim, Jim, what's that great hulking lazybones got to do with your going to the picnic?"

"He say I ain't to go."

"Ain't to go! Well, we'll show him whether you're to go or not."

At this sign of encouragement, Evalina brightened up. "Mis' Wharton," she burst out, "you don't know what I been bearin' f'om that man, an' I ain't nevah said nothin', but I cain't hol' in any longer. I ain't got a decent thing to wear, an' this very day, Jim tuk my las' cent o' money, an' walked off to the Fair Grounds wid another ooman."

"Come into the sewing-room, Evalina," said Mrs. Wharton with sudden energy. "You'll go to that picnic, and if that brute interferes with you, I'll put him where the rain won't touch him."

In the sewing-room, where Mrs. Wharton led the bewildered and de-lighted Evalina, there was wonderful letting out of seams, piecing of short skirts, and stretching over of scanty folds. But the washer-woman came out from there smiling and happy, well dressed and spirited. Say not that clothes have nothing to do with the feeling of the average human being. She felt that she could meet a dozen Jims and out-face them all. The day of her awaken-ing had come, and it had been like the awakening of a young giantess.

Jim was enjoying himself in a quadrille with Caroline when Evalina reached the dancing hall. He was just in the midst of a dashing farandole, much to the delight of the crowd, when he caught a glimpse of his wife ar-rayed in all her glory; he suddenly stopped. The people about thought he had paused for applause, and they gave it to him generously, but he failed to re-peat his antics. He was surprised out of a desire for their approval. He gazed at his slave, and she, his slave no longer, gazed back at him calmly. For the rest of that quadrille he proved a most spiritless partner, and at its close Caroline, with a toss of her head, yielded herself to some more desirable companion. Then, with a surprise which he could not suppress, struggling for expression on his lowering brow, Jim went over to Evalina.

"What you doin' out hyeah?" he said roughly.

"Enjoyin' myse'f, like you is," replied Evalina.

"Didn't I tell you not to come?"

"What diffunce do yo' tellin' make?"

"I show you what diffunce my tellin' make," he said threateningly.

"You ain't goin' to show me not a pleg-goned thing," was the reply which started him out of his senses, as Evalina started away on the arm of a partner, who had come to claim her for the next dance. Jim leaned up against a post to get his breath. He had expected Evalina to be scared, and she was not. There was some mistake, surely. This was not the Evalina whom he had known and married. Suddenly all of his traditions had been destroyed, and his mind reached out for something to grasp and hold to, and found only empty air. Meanwhile his wife, all her youthful lightness seeming to have come back to her, was whirling away in the mazes of the dance, stepping out as he had seen her step, when she had charmed him years ago. He stood and looked at her dully. He hadn't even energy enough to seek another partner and so show his resentment.

When the dance was over, Jim went up to Evalina and said shamefacedly, "Well, sence you're out hyeah, folks are goin' to 'spec' us to dance togethah, I reckon?"

"Don't you min' folks," she said, "you jes' disapp'int 'em. Thaih's Ca'line ovah thaih waitin' fu' you," and she bowed graciously to a robust hod-carrier, who was on the other side asking "fu' de pleasure."

Jim could stand it no longer. He wandered out of the dance hall, and walked down by the horse stables alone, thinking of the change that had come to Evalina. He felt grieved, and a great wave of self-pity surged over him. His wife wasn't treating him right. He was a very much ill-used man.

Then it was time for the speaking, and he went back to the stand, to find his recreant wife the center of a number of women-folk, drawn about her by the unaccustomed fineness of her quiet gown. She was chatting, as he remembered she had chatted before he had discouraged all lightness of talk in her. When the speaker began there was no applause readier than her own. The Rev. Mr. Barnett was a very witty man. In fact, it was his wit, rather than his brains or his morals, that had sent him to the legislature; and when he scored a good point, Jim heard her laugh ring out, clear, high, and musical. He could not help but wonder. It dazed him. Evalina had not laughed before since her little one had died, and when the speaking was over she was on the floor again, without a glance for him.

"That's the way with women," he told himself. "Hyeah I is, walkin' 'roun' hyeah all alone, an' she don't pay no mo' 'tention to me then if I was a dog." So he wandered over to the place where they were selling drinks, but they would not give him credit there, and feeling worse abused than ever, he went back to stand a silent witness of his wife's pleasure.

Evalina did not approve of remaining until after dark at the Fair Grounds, when the rougher element began to come, so she left before Jim. She had finished her supper, and was sitting at the door when he came home. He passed her sullenly and went into the house, where he dropped into a chair. She was humming a light tune and paid no attention to him. Finally he said:

"You treated me nice to-day, didn't you? Dancin' 'roun' without payin' no 'tention to me, an' you my own lawful wife!"

This was too much for Evalina, it was too unjust. She got up and faced him, "Yo' own lawful wife," she said, "I don't reckon you thought o' that this morning' when you tuk my las' cent, an' went out thaih wid Ca'line Wilson. Yo' lawful wife! You been treatin' me lak a wife, ain't you? This is the fust 'Mancipation Day I've had since I ma'ied you, but I want you to know I'se stood all I'se goin' to stan' f'om you, an' evah day's goin' to be 'Mancipation Day aftah this."

Jim was aghast. Rebellion cowed him. He wanted to be ugly, but he was crushed.

"I don't care nothin' 'bout Ca'line Wilson," he said.

"An' I don' care nothin' 'bout you," she retorted.

Jim's voice trembled. This was going too far. "That's all right, Evalina," he said, "that's all right. Mebbe I ain't no angel, but that ain't no way to talk to me; I's yo' husban'." He was on the verge of maudlin tears. Somewhere he had found credit, and his conquered condition softened Evalina.

"You ain't been very keerful how you talk to me," she said in an easier tone. "But thaih's one thing suttain, aftah this you got to walk straight,—you hyeah me! Want some supper?"

"Yes," said Jim humbly.

The People's Monthly 1, no. 2 (April, 1900), Paul Laurence Dunbar Collection, Reel V, Box 18, OHS.

☙

A Prophesy of Fate

I WAS HALF DROWSING over my cup of strong coffee that morning; supping it slowly, meditatively. There must have been that far-away look in my eyes, which writers always ascribe to the optics of people in deep thought.

Through the haze of the years which have intervened, it all comes back to me so plainly now. The gray dreariness of the time, the heavy oppressive stillness; the very objects in the room seeming to take on an aspect corresponding to my mood.

I was feeling mean that morning—yes that comes nearer expressing it than anything else—mean, decidedly mean.

There had been nothing yet in the course of the day to ruffle me. It was but nine o'clock. And yet I was possessed by that half sad, half angry, and utterly vague feeling, which I can only denominate, mean.

Now I am not a superstitious person by any means. I should not hesitate to allow a cat to cross my path, without the remedy of taking nine steps backward; I would willingly break a looking-glass, if some one else would pay the expense; ghosts and night have no terrors for me; and, call it foolhardy if you will, I am even prone to disregard the prophetic howling of a dog.

But I must confess that at this time a sense of peculiar creepiness had attacked me, in reference to a dream of the preceding night.

I had gone to bed under auspices, which one would adjudge unfavorable to vivid dreams. I had eaten but a light supper and it was early when I retired. There had been no heavy mental labor to weary my mind, for leisure was then my *sine qua non*. But yet I had dreamed and the vivid events clung with startling distinctness in my mind.

I was a somewhat active member of a club, called "The Diners Out," which every now and then, gave entertainments of a more or less pretentious sort to their male acquaintances.

Editors' note: The several bracketed interpolations in this story represent an attempt to restore portions of the manuscript which have decayed.

I dreamed that it was at one of these gatherings, I sat among the fellows drinking in deep draughts of pleasure, with more moderate sips of champagne; the toasts were bright, and the laughter boisterous. The time was never so merry. How the room shook with the bursts of mirth; and with what smiling approbation, the crowd of flushed, merry faces looked up into mine, as I responded to the time-worn toast of "Wine, Wit, and Women"; for I was one of the club's crack speakers, and it was their bounden duty to laugh and applaud me, whether I said anything worth it or not. As I was closing my remarks the lights seemed suddenly to darken and swim about me. While weaving itself among the merry final words of my toast, seeming to struggle for utterance, the ill-foreboding phrase, "the last time," obtruded itself.

I could not tell what it meant. But when I sat down, I was more fully possessed by the terrible fancy. A voice seemed to whisper in my ear, "This is the last time you will sit among them, the last time." I tried to disregard it and shake off the feeling, but it only grew more and more upon me as the feast progressed. I retained presence of mind enough to laugh and appear merry, but all within, my heart was burning with a strange sadness.

Often I wished to break out and tell the assembled company how I felt, but I feared that my speaking of the prophesy would dispel the half doubt which I felt in regard to it. And I looked forward to the time when people would say with shaking heads; "Poor fellow, he foresaw his own death and spoke of it there that last night." And I tried to avert the impending calamity by keeping silent regarding it. Never was mortal man so beridden by dread; even now I shudder as I think of it.

At last I could bear it no longer, and, excusing myself on a plea of sudden illness, left the company.

It is strange with what regular, natural sequence, events follow each other in that unconscious life which we call dreaming.

The walk home only continued the former feelings, and I moved with the consciousness that I was going home to die. I tried to doubt it. I could not. It was a stern fact. I turned my mind and looked the startling situation in the face, but my vague, indefinite dread was not quieted.

I reached home. The dark shadows hung about my door like mourning draperies, and just as I ascended the steps and entered,—a dog howled. Another time, I would not have noticed such a thing, but this was the very signal bell of my doom.

The fire in my room was low, the embers were just dying to ashes, anon a spark sprang up trying to revive the former brightness, but sank down again overwhelmed by the surrounding gloom.

I sat down before the grate and pondered. My thoughts went back over all my past life; I could hide nothing in my soul from my soul's eye. The relentless light of consci[entious] sun was turned upon my every deed good or bad. Oh, the menace in the faces of the stern procession which passed before my eyes. I raised my hands to my head. It was burning with fever. I felt of my lips, they were parched.

The blood coursing through my veins was hot and cold by turns. My hands trembled. The sound known as the death bell began ringing in my ears.

The clock struck twelve. The dog howled again. I was ill unto death and I could not shut out the truth from myself. My breath came in gasps; my blood seemed to clot.

My God! Was I dying thus alone; I could not speak or cry out, and though I strained as though I should burst my heart I could not move a finger. Thank heaven great agonies are not long-lived!

With one last gasp, I fell backward from my chair. A horror of icy gloom fell about me. In my last throes, I burst the terrible bonds of silence and cried aloud! "Is this death?" The sound of my own voice awoke me, trembling and perspiring.

[I] dreamed.

And that morning the dark mantle of my vivid vision still hung about me, touching me with its cold, damp, clammy folds, making me shudder even while I reproached myself for my weakness. I will think no more about it. I began to muse; "What fools, we can . . ."

"Ding," goes the door-bell. I hear the door open—and then shut. Then Robert, my valet, brings me a note. It is from Tom Hilliard, president of the Diners Out. It runs:

Dear Vesey:

Be sure and be around to the club tonight; a few of the boys have conceived the idea of giving an informal banquet to young Danvers, of Chicago, who is in town.

Yours etc.

Tom Hilliard

The note made me uneasy; it seemed to be a kind of, "by-the-way-apropos-of-your-dream," affair. I sat dangling it in my hand asking myself, Should I go?

Why not? Those dream fantasies might be reason enough to cause some superstitious fools to remain at home; but what effect should they have on a man of enlightened mind? I would go.

It was not without many misgivings that I went about my few duties during the day. And when night came, my excitement was in no manner abated. It seemed as I dressed for the banquet, that I was going to test a prophesy of fate, and I trembled for the result.

It was not a good night for the banquet, the sky was murky and a cold drizzling autumn rain was falling. A good strong cocktail taken on the road set me nearer right. I felt better and as I approached the club house and saw the friendly lights shining out into the streets, my spirits rose.

Once within, the bright happy surroundings made me forget my gloom, I laughed and joked with the rest. Not a shadow was there of my former distress to oppress me. Nor did I even think of it until some one proposed the toast "Wine, Wit, and Women" and I was asked to respond. The coincidence struck me, but I was in too happy a frame of mind to pay any particular attention to it then.

You know the effect of anything upon a man is always according to his mood. I spoke and spoke as I felt, the laughter became infectious, for there's nothing so contagious as joy,—unless, perchance, it is fear. But suddenly, even as in my dream, the lights began to darken around me and the sickening prophetic dread, felt before in my dream, to seize me. I struggled against it and talked on more wildly, recklessly. I was confident that it was but the effect of my dream and would soon wear away. But still, the laughter with which my words were greeted began to sound harshly in my ears; the chink of the glasses, and the twinkle of the lights seemed far away, while like an echo from the grave, those dismal dream words came darting through my mind,—"the last time."

But what need to repeat it all; detail after detail was the precise counterpart of what it had been in the dream. Even to leaving on the pretense of illness; the walk home; the shadows over my door; the dying fire. As I sat before the grate, the long low howl of a dog [came] through the open window. As I rose to close it, shutting myself [away] from all outside sounds, I said to myself "It is fate, there is no [reason to] fight it; my destiny is sealed and has been shown to me."

Turning out the gas, I sat down again wrapped in gloom and depression. So far I had followed, without deviation each event of my dream and now some power seemed to be forcing me to still follow in its ways by going into that retrospection of my life which had not been satisfactory even to my sleep ridden brain. Thus I sat thinking and thinking until, as a result of entire mental exhaustion, a heavy drowsiness came over me. I closed my eyes and I knew this was not death, for I could not feel the flutter of the dark wings.

How long I drowsed—it was not sleep—I do not know; but I was at last awakened by a difficulty in breathing. My head ached in a dull way and every breath came with a gasp. I knew that I was reenacting the last scene of the dream, that I was dying. And it was with a kind of grim satisfaction that I gasped out, "At last!"

Breathing became more difficult; the air about me seemed to grow denser and denser; all terror had left me and I calmly waited for the end, for it was fate.

A knock at the door partially aroused me, and I could hear a voice, far off it seemed,—saying, "Let me in Vesey, I want to spend the night with you, it's so late I'm locked out and I hate to disturb the old folks."

I felt perfectly helpless, but the thought that I would not have to die alone, seemed to pierce through the dull chaos of my mind and give me strength. With one final effort, I rose, tottered across the room and unlocked the door. It opened, a great rush of air came in, I turned to reach my chair again but fell prostrate.

And then the far off voice exclaimed, "Thunderations, man, the room's full of gas!" A window was thrown up and I knew no more until I found myself next morning lying upon my bed, with a physician and my friend Jack over me.

"He's coming around all right now," said the former as I opened my eyes.

"Well, it was a pretty close shave," replied the other.

"How could it have happened?" asked the Doctor.

"Why, it seems that he had turned the gas out, but not entirely off, and the room, being close, soon filled with it. It's a blamed good thing that I didn't want to disturb the old folks last night and so sought lodging with him."

"It was very fortunate," answered the doctor gravely.

When I was well enough to explain, I told Jack that after I turned out the gas, I went to sleep and so did not notice its presence.

But I did not admit to him what was really the truth, that my nose was so busy hunting out my destiny from foolish dreams, and my mind so deep in morbid thought, that I couldn't tell the smell of gas from the hand of fate. *[Here Dunbar's manuscript has deteriorated so the final five lines cannot be deciphered.]*

Undated manuscript, Paul Laurence Dunbar Collection, Reel IV, Box 12, OHS.

PART FOUR

Poems

INTRODUCTION
TO THE POEMS

WILLIAM DEAN HOWELLS introduced Dunbar's poetry to the American reading public first in his review of *Majors and Minors* in 1896 and then in his introduction the same year to *Lyrics of Lowly Life*. Howells's appraisal contributed particularly to the popularity of Dunbar's dialect poems:

> The contents of this book are wholly his own choosing, and I do not know how much or little he may have preferred the poems in literary English. Some of these I thought very good, and even more than very good, but not distinctively his contribution to the body of American poetry. What I mean is that several people might have written them; but I do not know anyone else who could have written the dialect pieces. These are divinations and reports of what passes in the hearts and minds of a lowly people whose poetry had hitherto been inarticulately expressed in music, but now finds for the first time in our tongue, literary interpretation of a very artistic completeness. (1896, p. ix)

Dunbar appreciated Howells's judgment, and he wrote to thank him in a letter dated July 13, 1896:

> Now from the depths of my heart I want to thank you. You yourself do not know what you have done for me. I feel much as a poor, insignificant, helpless boy would feel to suddenly find himself knighted. I can tell you nothing about myself because there is nothing to tell. My whole life has been simple, obscure, and uneventful. I have written my little pieces and sometimes recited them, but it seemed hardly by my volition. The kindly praise you have accorded me will be an incentive to more careful work. My greatest fear is that you may have been more kind to me than just.

Dunbar did not have to worry. While Howells's statement contributed greatly to Dunbar's fame and reputation, it also, inadvertently, created stereotypical expectations of Dunbar. Howells suggested that the standard English poems were good, and in some cases very good, however this part of his endorsement went unnoticed by the editors who were willing to publish this poet of African descent. They were for the safer part more willing to concentrate on Howells's assertion about the energy, power, and force in the tone and character of the dialect poems.

There is truth in the numerous critical observations concerning the authenticity of voice in Dunbar's work. A special humanity emanates from the dialect poems especially, and when we admit this point, we must also quickly point out that no one—including Dunbar—believes for an instant that African Americans were the perpetual happy dancers and singers while they suffered the yoke of slavery. The institution took much and gave sparingly in return. There is no doubt that Dunbar is cognizant of this fact in numerous poems and essays, as well as in his dramatic and fictional works. Within this context it is reasonable to assume that Dunbar was not an accommodationist but rather a clever maneuverer who walked that fine line between acceptance of the *status quo* and condemnation as a firebrand radical. Dunbar became a tightrope walker who managed to steer his career with expert forthrightness between the radical writer and the one who chose to work within the system. He was rational and firm in his observations, where many a writer before and since would have taken flight or been forced into silent exile. Just how much maneuvering Dunbar had to do is suggested by Henry Louis Gates Jr.'s assessment:

> We tend to read Dunbar backwards, as it were, through the poetry of Sterling A. Brown and the early Langston Hughes, and through the often unfortunate poetic efforts of Dunbar's less talented imitators, and we tend to forget how startling was Dunbar's use of black dialect as the basis of a poetic diction. After all, by 1865, dialect had come to connote black innate mental inferiority, the linguistic sign both of human bondage (as origin) and the continued failure of "improvability" or "progress," two turn-of-the-century key words. (1988, p. 176)

In addition to the influence of the oral tradition, Dunbar's poetry was shaped by two literary traditions which enjoyed popularity in the mid- to late nineteenth century. On the one hand, a romantic view of life influenced his portrait of African American customs, beliefs, and daily activities. At the same time, the minstrel tradition led to caricature and stereotyping of many aspects of daily life. Dunbar went beyond the ordinary in both the romantic and minstrel traditions by creating portraits of sadness and cynicism. The romanticism and the realism found in his poems can be traced more to the influence of his parents than to the literary traditions which might have contained him but for his remarkable talent. While there are surely elements of minstrelsy in his dialect poems, his romantic views of slave life are due more to the expressions of his mother. Matilda Dunbar, a former slave, lived a quiet life. She apparently knew the worth of a good education. She took in washing and ironing and encouraged her son to get a high-school education. Joshua Dunbar, Paul's father, was more realistic about the opportunities offered blacks. He had escaped slavery, made his way to Canada, and returned to join the 55th regiment of the Union army. Perhaps if we view Dunbar's literary output from a romantic or realistic perspective we may, once and for all, free him from the assertion that he aspired to be an accommodationist. His themes and his deft handling of them demonstrate a writer trapped between stating the truth and succumbing to a lynch mob. Dunbar was caught between the action of those who believed whites could do no wrong and the professed beliefs of Christianity.

In an influential essay he wrote nearly thirty years ago, Darwin T. Turner set out to dispel a series of myths which he felt were preventing the recognition of Dunbar's strengths and weaknesses as a poet. Foremost among these misconceptions he called the "myth of the natural versifier," which obscured examination of his technical achievements as well as the diction and tone of his poems. (This myth of "naturally talented" minorities persists into our own time and contributes to the denial of acclaim for their hard-won achievements.) Turner concludes as well that Dunbar was an artist "for the folk—not just for black people but for all common people . . . who love and laugh among friends and who pursue the simple pleasures of hunting, fishing, eating, telling stories to children, and napping by a fire" (1975, p. 73). Dunbar was at his best, Turner maintains, when he placed his characters in their homes, by the hearthside. He created a variety of dialects which he used mainly to craft "homely appraisals of life." Here is Southern white dialect in "The Spellin'-Bee":

> But Lawyer Jones of all gone men did shorely look the gonest,
> When he found out that he'd furgot to put the "h" in "honest."
> An' Parson Brown, whose sermons were too long fur toleration,
> Caused lots o' smiles by missin' when they give out "condensation."
> (Braxton 1993, p. 45).

Here is Dunbar's use of German dialect in "Lager Beer":

> I lafs und sings, and shumps aroundt.
> Und somedimes acd so queer.
> You ask me vot der matter ish?
> I'm filled mit lager peer. (Braxton 1993, p. 295),

Here is how Dunbar uses Irish dialect in "Circumstances Alter Cases":

> They say the gossoon is indecent and dirty,
> O chone!
> In spite of his dressin' so.
> O chone!
> Let him dress up ez foine ez a king or a queen,
> Let him put on more wrinkles than ever was seen,
> You'll be sure he's no match for my little colleen,
> O chone! (Braxton 1993, p. 261).

DUNBAR'S POETRY HAS been much better known and appreciated since the two Centennial celebrations in 1972. Before that exciting time of rediscovery, he was acclaimed mostly for dialect poems, with a considerable body of his work suffering neglect. *The Paul Laurence Dunbar Reader* (Martin and Hudson 1975) made available in one place a large number of poems that had been difficult to locate, and in 1993 the University Press of Virginia published *The Collected Poetry of Paul Laurence Dunbar,* with masterful editing and commentary by Joanne M. Braxton.

This volume presents forty-one previously unpublished or uncollected poems that add to the range and significance of Dunbar's canon. The poems included here display the variety of tone and rhythm and the nuance of characterization we have come to expect in performances of Dunbar's work. They also augment the stature of his dramatic achievement and support connections to issues he raises in his letters, essays, and dramatic pieces.

The poems brought together for the first time in this volume do not present a "new Dunbar" (as Hudson and Martin had rightly claimed for their work). These previously uncollected poems draw attention to Dunbar's mastery of technical form in his very earliest apprentice works; to the subtle beauty of his ballads, lullabies, and love songs; and to the themes of social protest that link his poetry to his essays and novels.

Poems from his high school days demonstrate his early mastery of conventional forms and genres. "Sing, heavenly muse, in accents tender" he invokes, and then with adolescent fervor and reckless mock-epic splendor proclaims a "bright romance of a local fruit-vendor." The joys are fleeting, the rhymes come hard, the salesmanship is "smooth-tongued" and "slick." This seventeen-year-old epic bard concludes: "Lament, oh muse, the wiles of men! / Farewell, ye dimes, we'll ne'er see again." A similar ceremonial work, "Remembered," incants, "Chant ye no dirges for the dead to-day" or for the brave who "rest in Glory's laurel-mantled shrine."

The everyday event poems in this collection are impressively simple. "Lullaby (II)" sings of "the Land of Sleep / Where the tired children go." "The Farm House by the River" is a sad ballad of unfulfilled love. "The Valse" orchestrates "sweet music" for when "my lady is dancing"—and it becomes slow and sad and gray at the brink of their parting. "The Making Up" is a childlike storybook portrait of little Miss Margaret and her Dolly who are in a pout after having a falling out. They try anger, tears, and silence before concluding: "Let's don't play and cry, it's too much like true, / Let's make up Dolly I ain't mad is you?"

The social protest poems presented here reinforce the irony and anger we see in his essays, stories, and plays. Somewhat innocently, Dunbar mocks lawyers who proclaim with abandon how they "love to lie." In "The Song of the Gatherer," we read of a parade of plutocrats, farmers, and misers who make great plans only to find in the end it is the lawyer who "gathereth all." In "After the Struggle," flowers to sweeten the world will loom out of the "conflict fraternal" and boundless love can be born of strife. "Our Hopes and Home" anticipates the Civil Rights Movement: "Tramp, tramp, tramp, the negro's marching, / Onward, onward, to the goal / So then foreman, clear the track, for you cannot keep him back, / He has got the fire of freedom in his soul." That fiery freedom is here in these poems, whether in the gently parodic experimentation with form, the celebration of ordinariness in songs about every day, or the passionate proclamations of political fervor. Again, these poems expand Dunbar's canon and show us how to evaluate his achievements more clearly.

Editors' note: A few textual issues arose as widely scattered poems in various forms were collected. For example, Braxton's collection includes a four-stanza version of "Noddin' by de Fire" (1993, p. 201), a work which first appeared as six stanzas in *The Century Magazine* in 1901. The alternate version moves stanzas three and four to "The Suitor" (pp. 325–26), another poem published in the same edition of *The Century Magazine*. Stanzas three and four are here restored to "Noddin' by de Fire." Unless otherwise noted, we have arranged the poems chronologically—with undated works appearing at the end of our sequence.

POEMS

Sold—A C. H. S. Episode[1]

Sing, heavenly muse, in accents tender,
This bright romance of a local fruit-vender,
How fleeting are all earthly joys!
How badly did he soak the boys!
'Tis hard to dress the thing in rhymes
And narrate how they lost their dimes;
The vender pleaded, they heard, ah, well.
The fruit, you know, was intended to sell
But only the boys (not the fruit) were sold.
They gave their money, as you've been told,
All through the day they saw at hand
Their smooth-tongued friend and his welcome stand;
All Sunday night they dreamed the same
And longed for the fruit that never came,
And Sunday eve saw that vender slick
Aboarding the train, time doubled quick,
Lament, oh muse, the wiles of men!
Farewell, ye dimes, we'll ne'er see again.

Dayton, Ohio, *High School Times* 9 no. 6, February 1890.

[1]A Central High School Episode: Dunbar graduated from Central High School. In 1890, at age eighteen, he was president of the Philomathean Literary Society and editor of the *High School Times*.

Happy! Happy! Happy!

"Dear Julius" I've been cogitating,
    Long before expatiating,
On the hopeless alterations,
    In our mutual relations;
Having mounted in position,
    To a loftier condition,
And because I cannot flattah
    I must say you are *"non grata."*

Happy, happy, oh my best of queens,
Makes me feel as mealy as a pot of beans!
    Tell you what's the matter
I'm my lady's own *"non grata"*
An' I'm happy, happy, happy, cause I do not know what it means.

Dear Mandy I been readin'
    With a pleasure most exceedin'
All the pleasant bits of writin'
    Dat yo' han' has been inditin'
But you mo' dan fill my measure
    Wid de sugar—drip of pleasure,
When you say without a flattah,
    I's you' lovin' own *"non grata."*

Dayton, Ohio (ca. 1890–1891), Paul Laurence Dunbar Collection, Reel III, Box 10, OHS.

Oh, No

Why, once I met an Englishman,
        Rich both in gold and land;
He humbly kneels before my feet,
        And offered heart and hand.
If I would take him for his wealth,
        His title one mile long;
I smiled at that poor Englishman,
        And this was all my song:
Oh, no; oh, no; oh, no; oh, no.
I'm not so very bad at all,
        As some mean people say:
But then I'm young and all young folks,
        You know, will have their day.
I love the dukes I do confess:
        They're so much sport, you see:
But when they're smitten to the heart,
        And want to marry me.
It's oh, no; oh, no; oh, no.
You'd like to have me sing some more:
        My song is nice, 'tis true:
But then, too much of these nice things.
        Dear Friends, would never do.
So, bowing in the latest style,
        I'll bid you all good bye:
And don't you call me back again,
        Or I'll be sure to cry:
Oh, no; oh, no; oh, no; oh, no.

Dayton Tattler, December 13, 1890.

Lullaby (I)

Sing me, sweet, a soothing psalm,
Holy, tender, low, and calm,
Full of drowsy words and dreamy,
Sleep half seen where the sides are seamy;
Lay my head upon your breast;
Sing me to rest.

Oak and Ivy (1893), p. 23.

A Rondeau

'Twixt smile and tear so sways the world
Today on happy pinions whirled
      We tempt the blue and spirit-gay
      The neighbor with the stars today
We seek the heavens planet pearled

Tomorrow, ah, our wings are furled,
And heaven seems oh so far away
We lift our voices up to pray
      'Twixt smile and tear.

And then in eddies swiftly swirled
Poor straws upon the current twirled
We cling, and toss and sway the fray
Not where we will, but where we may
The lodger, on some far shore wave hurled
      'Twixt smile and tear.

Enclosed in a letter to James N. Matthews dated December 23, 1893. Paul Laurence Dunbar Collection, Reel I, Box 3, OHS.

The Farm House by the River

I know a little country place
    Where still my heart doth linger,
And o'er its fields is every grace
    Lined out by memory's finger.
Back from the lane where poplars grew
    And aspens quake and quiver,
There stands all bath'd in summer's glow
    A farm house by the river.

Its eaves are touched with golden light
    So sweetly, softly shining,
And morning glories full and bright
    About the doors are twining.
And there endowed with every grace
    That nature's hand could give her,
There lived the angel of the place
    In the farm house by the river.

Her eyes were blue, her hair was gold,
    Her face was bright and sunny;
The songs that from her bosom rolled
    Were sweet as summer's honey.
And I loved her well, that maid divine,
    And I prayed the Gracious Giver,
That I some day might call her mine
    In the farm house by the river.

Twas not to be—but God knows best.
    His will for aye be heeded!
Perhaps amid the angels' bliss,
    My little love was needed.
Her spirit from its thralldom torn
    Went singing o'er the river,

And that sweet life my heart shall mourn
            Forever and forever.

She dies one morn at early light
            When all the birds are singing,
And Heaven itself in pure delight
            Its bells of joy seemed ringing.
They laid her dust where soon and late
            The solemn grasses quiver,
And left alone and desolate
            The farm house by the river.

Dayton, Ohio (ca. 1892–95), Paul Laurence Dunbar Collection, Reel IV, Box 15, OHS.

Rondeau for a Lawyer

I love to lie the whole day thro'
Where skies outspread their tents of blue,
And canopy the waving trees
That whisper to the whispering breeze
Tales centuries old but ever new.

Where plaintive doves begin to sue
For that warm love which is their due,
And drown with moans the mock-birds glees,
            I love to lie.

In fact, while the aforesaid's true,
To lie is what I always do,
Whenever and where'er I please;
Not only at such times as these,
But any time, — I own to you,
            I love to lie.

The Green Bag 9 (1897), p. 294.

To Leila Ruth

Whither haste you maid, today
With your eyes a glistening?
Gentle sir, I take my way
Gladly to the christening
Of a dainty babe forsooth,
'Tis none else, than Leila Ruth.

Once when changing days were drear,
And the wind was blowing,
Angels sent our little dear,
Just to start us glowing,
This is, gentle sir, in truth
How we came by Leila Ruth.

So I may not longer stay
From the meeting, festal
For I have a prayer to pay
For this infant vestal
"Love of age and love of youth,
Be the lot of Leila Ruth."

Enclosed in a letter to Alice Ruth Moore dated May 14, 1897. Paul Laurence Dunbar
Collection, Reel V, Box 1, OHS.

We Crown Her Queen

Lines In Honor of the Christening of Leila Ruth Young[1]
May 30, 1897

I

Kind friends, perhaps if I should say
Aught of our doings here today
'Twere "new occasions teach new duty,"
And prove it by the earnest way
We laymen christened have a beauty.

2

It was our Lord's divine command
To Jesus' altar we should bring them,
Where touching children with his hand,
He gathered them unto his fold,
"Forbid them not," his servants told,
"For of such is the Heavenly Kingdom."

3

And if our Leila there had been
Amid those smiling children seen,
When Jesus those kind words had said;
We know the Master would have pressed her
Upon His bosom, and caressed her,
And with His gentle hand have blessed her,
Upon her sacred little head.

4

But Ruth was not when Christ was here;
'Twas in the nonage of this year

[1] Leila Ruth was the daughter of Alice Dunbar's sister M. Leila Young. Therefore she became Dunbar's niece by marriage.

That, with the birds and fragrant flowers,
With joyous spring ere Easter hours,
She came like sunshine's radiant powers,
Her home and parents' hearts to cheer.

5

And for the pleasure she has wrought,
Both friends and strangers here today,
We'll fold her gently in our arms,
Secure from danger's fierce alarms,
And with love's hopes and tokens brought,
We will crown her the queen of May.

6

We crown her queen but such she came
From mother nature who first crowned her;
The saintly presence of her face,
Her royal mien's angelic grace,
Her dimpled cheeks and gentle flame
Of eyes, now conjure all around her.

7

But when our Ruth 'mid stubbles bare
Goes forth in harvest fields a gleaning,
May she gain conquest in the fields
Of hearts the best that nature yields,
And then herself be garnered there
Encompassed by pert Cupid's snare,
Held subject to love's real meaning.

8

And after life's race here is ended,
And she has done the good intended
By Heaven who so kindly sent her;
May safe return to her be given
Back to her home within the Heaven,

Pure as the snow when it is driven,
Sweet angel that the Master lent her.

Enclosed in a letter to Alice Ruth Moore dated May 30, 1897, London, England. Paul
Laurence Dunbar Collection, Reel VI, Box 1–A, OHS.

The Song of the Gatherer

The plutocrat hoards up his treasures of gold,
    And smiles in his power and pride;
While he seals up his coffers, withholds his great store,
    From the paupers who wail at his side.
He has laid his foundation and built on it "Wealth,"—
    A tower that never will fall.
Then he scribbles a will and he passes away,
    And the lawyer he gathereth all.

The farmer he plants, and he tends, and he reaps,
    And he garners his grain with a will;
Then he finds a good market for all he would sell,
    And laughs at the winds growing chill.
For his pockets are full and his granaries, too,
    There's plenty for kitchen and stall;
But he places a mortgage—a small one of course,
    And the lawyer he gathereth all.

The miser goes ragged and lives on a crust,
    Then childless and will-less, he dies;
When, lo! from Obscurity's corners remote,
    How his heirs and relations arise!
And they quibble and fight about reason and right,
    And start up a terrible brawl;
But while they are spending their breath and their cash,
    The lawyer he gathereth all.

And so it goes on to the end of the tale,
　　That rich men and farmers and fools
Will bury their hands in the depths of the chest,
　　To play with the keen-edged tools.
But one jolly wight looks on at the sight,
　　And no tears for their follies lets fall.
And this song doth he sing as their tribute they bring:
　　"Oh, the lawyer he gathereth all."

The Green Bag 10 (1898), p. 355.

To a Golden Girl

Gold is thy hair, — a heart of golden is thine,
Golden thy voice whose strains last night I heard,
And in my veins, the sunshine and blood was stirred.

Sing on, raise into words your golden bass.
And men shall hear and bless you for your song.
And they shall write these words of you erelong.
This maiden's soul hath wings that mount the stars!

Dayton, Ohio, manuscript (ca. 1898), Paul Laurence Dunbar Collection, Reel II, Box 5, OHS.

The Lonely Hunter

Green branches, green branches, I see you beckon, I follow
Sweet is the place you guard, there in the [empty] tree hollow
There he lies in the darkness, under the frail white flowers
Heedless at last in the silence, of these sweet midsummer hours.

But sweeter, it may be, the moss whereon he is sleeping now
And sweeter the fragrant flowers that may crown his [calm] white brow.
And sweeter the shady place, deep in an Eden hollow
Wherein he dreams I am with him and dreaming of whispers "follow."

Green wrought from the green gold branches what's the song you bring?
What are all songs to me, now, who no more care to sing,
Deep in the heart of summer, sweet is life to me still,
But my heart is a lonely hunter that hunts on a lonely hill.

Green is that hill and lonely set far in a shadowy place;
White is the hunter's quarry. A lost-loved human face,
O hunting heart shall you find it with arrow of failing breath.
Led over a green hill lonely by the shadowy hound of death.

Green branches, green branches you sing of a sorrow older,
But now it is midsummer weather earth young surprise golden;
Here I stand, I wait here in the [tree] head hollow,
But never a green leaf whispers "Follow, oh follow, follow."

Oh never a green leaf whispers where the green gold branches swing
Oh never a song I hear now where one was wont to sing
Here in the heart of summer sweet is life to me still
But my heart is a lonely hunter that hunts on a lonely hill.

Dayton, Ohio, typescript (1898), Paul Laurence Dunbar Collection, Reel III, Box 10, OHS.

Dreams Only Dreams

Dreams only dreams herein are found
Count it not strange
If one turns out a nightmare.

Enclosed in a letter to Alice Ruth Moore dated 1898. Paul Laurence Dunbar Collection, Reel V, Box 1-A, OHS.

The Dreamer

To Leila

Temples he built and palaces of air,—
And with the artist's parent-pride aglow
He saw the fabrics of his fancy grow,
And to creation marvelously fair.

Enclosed in a letter to Alice Ruth Moore dated 1898. Paul Laurence Dunbar Collection, Reel VI, Box 1-A, OHS.

Remembered

Chant ye no dirges for the dead to-day;
    Upon these graves let not a teardrop fall;
Grief, 'mid these mounds, gives up her boasted sway,
    For Honor, pure and lofty, holdeth all.

Death may not bide where Glory walks the way
    In majesty of mien and peerless might;
Her Sun turns gloom into eternal day,
    And routes the sombre forces of the night.

Here lie our heroes in their peaceful sleep,
  Dreaming sweet dreams of vict'ries Nobly won.
The harvest of their labors now they reap
  While all the toils that wearied them are done.

Chant ye no dirges for the braves who sleep!
  They rest in Glory's laurel-mantled shrine.
Fresh as these blossoms shall their memories keep,
  With fragrance sweet, eternal and divine.

Sunday Journal, 1899, no by-line. Paul Laurence Dunbar Collection, Reel IV, Box 17, OHS.

Keeping in Touch

O keep me in touch with
      Thy spirit Divine
Lord Jesus, my heart would
      for ever be Thine
At home, or abroad, or
      wherever I be
Thy service I love when
      abiding in Thee.

If worldly in spirit what
      joy could I know,
For mourners in Zion what
      sympathy when
No mercy of mercy for sinners
      were mine
Unless keeping touch with
      Thy Spirit Divine!

A word for the weary
    a smile for the young
A song in my heart to be
    heartily sung.
Some witness, my savior,
    for Thou should be mine
If keeping in touch with
    Thy Spirit Divine.

How oft have I failed of the
    blessing they know
Who it saw of the Kingdom
    unworriedly some
Imparting to others some
    messages of Thine
While keeping in touch
    with Thy Spirit Divine!

More hearts by the word of
    Thy touch should be won
My feet on Thine errands
    more faithfully run,
More gladness in service
    should ever be mine
In keeping in touch with
    Thy Spirit Divine.

Faint hearts might be lifted
    from sorrow and care
My voice should be
    mighty for others in prayer.
My pen was lost, then used,
    and rich blessing be mine
If keeping in touch with
    Thy Spirit Divine.

O grant me dear Savior
    Thy witness to be
Nor Jonah-like ever
    Thy service to flee
That gladness around me
    may ceaselessly shimmer
Lord, keep me in touch with
    Thy Spirit Divine.

Original manuscript dated July 20, 1899. Paul Laurence Dunbar Collection, Reel III, Box 10, OHS.

Triolets

(After (a long way after) Dobson)

I've a notion to rhyme,
    Do you think't would be proper?
I've the skill and the time,
I've notion to rhyme,
It will certainly chime
    Out as clear as a copper,
I've a notion to rhyme,
    Do you think't would be proper?

Oh it's easy to do,
    I could go on forever,
The rhymes are so few,
Oh it's easy to do;
I think so, don't you?
    And it's really clever,
Oh it's easy to do,
    I could go on forever.

This is Dobson, you see?
    And he's grown quite "au fait," sir.

'T is a myst'ry to me
(This is Dobson, you see)
Where the merits can be
        In a bold triolet, sir;
This is Dobson, you see,
        And he's grown quite "au fait," sir.

The Transcript (1899), Paul Laurence Dunbar Collection, Reel IV, Box 17, OHS.

The Valse[1]

Life is for love and the night is for sweeting;
When to sweet music my lady is dancing
        My heart to mild frenzy her beauty inspires.
Into my face are her brown eyes a-glancing,
        And swift my whole frame thrills with tremulous fires.

Dance, lady, dance, for the moments are fleeting;
        Pause not to place your refractory curt;
        Dreamily, joyously, circle and whirl.

Oh, how those viols are throbbing and pleading
        A prayer is scarce needed in sound of their strain.
Surely and lightly as round you are speeding
        You turn to confusion my heart and my brain.

Dance, lady, dance to the viol's soft calling
        Skip it and trip it as light as the air;
Dance, for the moments, like rose leaves are falling.
        Strike, now the clock from its place on the stair.

[1] A variation of "The Valse" appears with a different ordering of the lines in Braxton 1993, p. 175.

Now sinks the melody lower and lower
     The weary musicians scarce seeming to play;
Ah, love, your steps now are slower and slower,
     The smile on your face is more sad and less gay.

Dance, lady, dance to the brink of our parting
     My heart and your step must not fail to be light
Dance! Just a turn—tho' the teardrop be starting.
     Ah—now it is done—so, my lady, good night!

The Telegram, February 8, 1900, Paul Laurence Dunbar Collection, Reel IV, Box 17, OHS.

After the Struggle

Out of the blood of a conflict fraternal,
     Out of the dust and the dimness of death,
Burst into blossoms of glory eternal
Flowers that sweeten the world with their breath.
Flowers of charity, peace and devotion
     Bloom in the hearts that are empty of strife;
Love that is boundless and broad as the ocean
     Leaps into beauty and fullness of life.
So, with the singing of paeans and chorals,
     And with the flag flashing high in the sun,
Place on the graves of our heroes the laurels
     Which their unfaltering valor has won!

Unnamed Henry Romeike newspaper service, May 24, 1900, Pittsburgh, Pennsylvania, Paul Laurence Dunbar Collection, Reel I, Box 2, OHS.

Noddin' by de Fire

Some folks t'inks hit's right an' p'opah,
      Soon ez bedtime come erroun',
Fu' to scramble to de kiver,
      Lak dey'd hyeahed de trumpet soun'.
But dese people dey all misses
      Whut I mos'ly does desiah;
Dat's de settin' roun' an' dozin',
      An' a-noddin' by de fiah.

W'en de ol' pine-knot 's a-blazin',
      An' de hick'ry's crackin' free,
Den's de happy time fu' snoozin',
      It 's de noddin' houah fu' me.
Den I gits my pipe a-goin',
      While I pokes de flames up highah,
An' I 'tends lak I's a-t'inkin',
      W'en I's noddin' by de fiah.

Mebbe some one comes to jine you;
      Well, dat's good, but not de bes',
Less'n dat you 's kind o' lonesome,
      Er ain't honin' fu' de res'.
Den you wants to tell a sto'y,
      Er you wants to hyeah de news
Kind o' half tol', while you 's stealin'
      Ev'y now an den a snooze.

W'en you 's tiahed out a-hoein',
      Er a-followin' de plow,
Whut 's de use of des a-fallin'
      On yo' pallet lak a cow?
W'y, de fun is all in waitin'
      In de face of all de tiah,

An' a-dozin' and a-drowsin'
          By a good ol' hick'ry fiah.

Oh, you grunts an' groans an' mumbles
          'Case yo' bones is full o' col',
Dough you feels de joy a-tricklin'
          Roun' de co'nahs of yo' soul.
An' you 'low anothah minute
          'S sho to git you wa'm an' dryah,
W'en you set up pas' yo' bedtime,
          'Ca'se you hates to leave de fiah.

Whut 's de use o' downright sleep'n?
          You can't feel it while it las',
An' you git up feelin' sorry
          W'en de time fu' it is pas'.
Seem to me dat time too precious,
          An' de houahs too short entiah,
Fu' to sleep, w'en you could spen' 'em
          Des a-noddin' by de fiah.

The Century Magazine 63, no. 22 (1901), pp. 22–23.

Darkie's Rainy Day

When I git up in de mo'nin' an' de clouds is big an' black,
Dey's a kin' o' wa'nin shivah goes a-scootin' down my back;
Den I says to my ol' ooman ez I watches down de lane,
"Don't you so't reckon, Lizy, dat we gwine to have some rain?"

"Go on, man," my Lizy answah, "you cain't fool me, not a bit,
I don't see no rain a-comin', ef you's wishin' fo' it, quit,
'Case de mo you think erbout it, an' de mo' you pray an' wish,
W'y de rain stay 'way de longah, spechul ef you wants to fish."

But I see huh pat de skillet, an' I see huh cas' huh eye
Wide a kin' o' anxious motion to'ds de da'kness in de sky;
An' I knows what she's a thinkin', 'dough she tries so ha'd to hide,
She's a sayin', "Wouldn't catfish now tas'e mon'trous bully, fried?"

Den de clouds git black an' blackah, an' de thundah 'mence to roll,
An' de rain hit 'mence a fallin', oh, I's happy, bless by soul!
Ez I look at dat ol' skillit, and I 'magine I kin see
Jes' a slew o' new-ketched catfish sizzin' daih fu' huh an' me.

'Tain't no use to go a-plowin' fu' de groun'll be too wet,
So I puts out fo' de big house a moughty pace, you bet,
An ol' mastah say, "Well, Lishy, ef you think hit's gwine to rain
Go on fishin', hit's de weathah, an' I 'low we cain't complain."

Wid my Pole erpon my shouldah an' my wo'm can in my han'
I kin feel de fish a-waitin' we'en I strikes de rivah's san',
Nevah min', you ho'ny scoun'els, need'n swim er-roun' an' grin,
I'll be grinnin' in a minute w'en I 'mence to haul yo' in.

W'en de fish begin to nibble, an' de co'k begin to jump,
I'se erfeared de'll quit bitin', case dey hyeah my hea't go "thump"
Twell de co'k go way down undah, an' I raise a awful shout,
Ez a big ol' yallah belly comes a gallivantin' out.

Spo't, dis fish'n'! Now yo' talkin', w'y dey ain't no kin' to beat;
I do' keer ef I is soakin', laigs, an' back, an' naik an' feet,
It's de spo't I's lookin' aftah. Hit's de pleasure an' de fun,
Dough I knows dat Lizy's waiting wid de skillet w'en I's done.

Current Literature 30 (1901), p. 673.

Ode

To John H. Patterson, Esq.[1]

The Builder

To hue a statue from the formless stone,
To lead a regiment when death is rife,
To walk the ways of sorrow all alone
        And laugh with life,
To write a paean that a nation sings
That art must own—
        All this is life.
What is it then, to sit beside the fire,
And dream of things and idly to aspire?
To live, to struggle, nobly to desire,
        And do is life.
It is not that one needs the world's acclaim,
Brief is the sweetness of the taste of fame,
But doing, building is the nobler thing,
By which men live, and which their poets sing.
Today a builder comes, one whom we know—
A dreamer say you, of the long ago—
But, ah, the dream's fulfillment is at hand,
And all in awe of the Creator's glow,
A city's people, glad and thankful stand
To welcome one who found it good to know
And better yet to do
The things that prove man nobly great and true.

Dayton Daily Journal, July 4, 1905, Paul Laurence Dunbar Collection, Reel III, Box 10, OHS.

[1] John H. Patterson (1844–1922) was a salesman and manufacturer. In 1884 he purchased a small failing company in Dayton, Ohio, and built it into the highly successful National Cash Register Co. Dunbar's "Ode" was written to him. The company for many years had a signed copy which hung in the executive dining room. It is now kept in the company's archives.

John Hay[1]

Why droops the flag so sadly from the mast?
    Is it because the mariner is past?
Why rolls the drums so dully in the field?
    Is it because a state bereft must yield
One of its greatest to the great unknown?

And yet it is not that we make our moan
    For him, ah no, strong faced he sees the throne
But pities us who weep for him here alone.
    He was the master of a mighty day,
Made as all humans but of finer clay.

Let fly the flags, let beat the drums,
    The day of glory to our hero comes,
Dry up the tears, the wound that sears,
    But blossoms in the teeming years.

Great is the man of great intent,
    And greater he whose life is spent
In the wise conduct of the state
    Whose note of empire comes not late
But lags on the heels of fate.
    To weep for him were coward shame,
He has his glory and his fame
    He waves the world, farewell, farewell,
A master mind and spirit without blame.

Dayton, Ohio, undated typescript, Paul Laurence Dunbar Collection, Reel III, Box 10, OHS.

[1] John Hay (1838–1905) was the American ambassador to Great Britain. He was instrumental in arranging a reading for Dunbar, before a distinguished group of royalty and other important dignitaries, while Dunbar was in London in 1897. In 1898 Hay returned to Washington to become U.S. Secretary of State. Hay was a successful author of fiction, non-fiction, and some poetry written in dialect.

Kindness

Was he not kind to you, this dead old Year?
Did he not give enough of earthly store?
Enough of laughter and good cheer?
It is not well to hate him for the pain
He brought you, and the sorrows manifold.

To pardon him these hurts still I am fain,
For in the panting period of his reign,
He brought me new wounds,
But he healed the old.

The Journal of Education 80 (December 31, 1914), p. 652.

A Toast to Dayton

Love of home, sublimest passion
        That the human heart can know!
Changeless still, though fate and fashion
        Rise and fall and ebb and flow,
To the glory of our nation,
        To the welfare of our state,
Let us all with veneration
        Every effort consecrate.

And our city, shall we fail her?
        Or desert her gracious cause?
Nay—with loyalty we hail her
        And revere her righteous laws.
She shall ever claim our duty,
For she shines—the brightest gem

That has ever decked with beauty
Dear Ohio's diadem.

For Memory's Garden (1917), Lucia May Wiant, ed., p. 55.

(For the Palladium[1])

To: Mrs. D. M. Jordan

1

Take heart, and hope and pray
The darkness cannot stay;
Fill thou thy soul with cheer,
The light is here.
Christ died for thee and me,
And so eternity
Our span of life shall be.

2

Bear well and rise again,
Deny the pow'r of pain—
Its grasp is not for you!
All things are new.
Rise up, sweet child of song,
And strew thy pearls along
Where needy thousands throng.

3

Walk not amid the shades
Where mortal beauty fades;
Good is not meant to die,
But live forever.

[1] The *Daily Palladium* was a nineteenth-century journal.

Live then, like love and light,
Put spirits dark to flight,
The new age dawneth bright!

Undated clipping, *Daily Palladium,* Paul Laurence Dunbar Collection, Reel IV, Box 15, OHS.

New York

There is a town that's New York.
The swiftest that a town may be.
    It's always gay
    And there's only one Broadway.
So it's the only place for me.
When on its broad Rialto, I
With others if my set go by,
    I may not have a cent
    But I'm thoroughly content
For on Broadway I'm within the public eye.

Now that's New York, that's New York,
In your best or worst condition,
It's a sporty proposition
And that's New York, that's New York.

If some time walking down the street,
A pretty girl you chance to meet
    Of course she's modest quite;
    And should not be out at night;
But then her trust in you is complete,
So then you take her out to dine,
And freely blow her off to wine.
    She's just a little shy,

But you find out by and by,
That to feed her you would have to own a mine.

Chorus:

Now when you pay five cents to ride,
And somehow chance to go inside,
You get a little strap
In a girl's reluctant lap,
The company says "Be satisfied"
If some sad night you lose your head,
And one cold copper cops you dead,
Just show that you are alive;
Spring a crisp inviting five,
And I warrant you that nothing will be said.

Undated typescript, Paul Laurence Dunbar Collection, Reel IV, Box 13, OHS.

Kitty

Oh Kitty and I went out strollin' one evenin',
Kitty was dressed in a mantle of white;
Ah, but her brown eyes were worth your believin' in,
An' said I, "Won't you give a sigh for my plight?
Then did the dimples come sparklin' and revellin',
"That will I do," said the maiden for sure.
(How could I guess she'd be teasin' an devillin'?)
"If it's the croup, I've a tea for your cure."

Oh Kitty is pretty,
And Kitty is pretty,
But, oh, what a pity,
She laughs at my pain.
For tho' I love Kitty

The best in the city,
An' grief of my ditty,
    I love her in vain.

Now pity me darlin', an' leave off your chatterin',
    Tell me this minute now, will you be wed?
So softly an' sweetly the dear feet came patterin',
    Low was her accent, an' low was her head;
"Now will I answer you since you are taskin' me,
    That will I do, Jack, some bright summer's day,
Thank you, oh thank you, my darlin' for askin' me,
    But I'll be wed to my Shamus O'Bray."

Undated manuscript, Paul Laurence Dunbar Collection, Reel IV, Box 13, OHS.

A Girl

You meet with a girl who is sweet and demure
Ad zooks!—you are a beau, you will win her for sure.
She is only just sixteen or eighteen or so,
They never get quite [honest] and that you know.
So here's to deceive her, you mighty wise guy,
And to bring the love light to her little blue eye;
Oh it's really too wicked, you've got to confess
She will fall in your arms with the first caress.
Maybe she will, and maybe she won't,
For a woman's will and a woman's won't
Are difficult things you know.

   Chorus:

The girl of the day
Is knowing they say,
And takes a delight in her own sweet way;

So gentlemen dear, there's just this to fear
She may not take heed to the words in her ear.
Maybe she will, and maybe she won't,
For a woman's will and a woman's won't,
Are difficult things you know

And then, at a gay little supper for two,
You will ask for a kiss; now, don't tell me,—
And then later on in the after-glow,
In accents sweet, with the lights turned low,
You will murmur something into her ear
Which will end with a tender "Now, won't you dear?"

And you'll get a bit closer, and breathe and sigh;
Will she giggle and wink the other eye?
Maybe she will and maybe she won't,
For a woman's will and a woman's won't
Are difficult things you know.

Chorus:

Undated manuscript, Paul Laurence Dunbar Collection, Reel IV, Box 13, OHS.

Rocking in the Old Canoe

Oh a dear and tender memory
        Draws the curtain of my mind,
And with soft and holy footsteps
        Comes creeping from behind.
'Tis a memory of my childhood,
        Sweet as flowers touched with dew,
When I sat an idle youngster
        Rocking in the old canoe.

Rocking, gently rocking,
Till the shadows gathered low
Rocking, gently rocking
With the mill-stream sluggish flow.
Rocking, gently rocking
Till the night was in the skies,
And the stars looked down upon me
Like a spirit mother's eyes.

In the days of early manhood,
    When my cheek was in the flush,
And my heart went gaily singing
    Like the singing of the thrush.

Undated typescript, Paul Laurence Dunbar Collection, Reel, IV, Box 13, OHS.

Tim

Well, mebbe ya don't remember Tim
Little feller, lank an' slim
Jest about as big as a minute
With an eye like coal, with a sparkle in it
Newsboys ust to carry *The Press*
Littlest one on the force I guess
But he wasn't afeared to run and holler
Spry as a cricket an' bright as a dollar
Wall, like a book I knowed this Tim
Ust to work along a' him
When the Press was a little measley sheet,
An' I reckon this team was hard to beat,
Sell papers, well know you're a talkin' sin;
When we got out we made a din

All up and down the busy street
Till every blessed printed sheet
We had was gone, then me and Tim
We'd hurry home in the twilight dim
Down to our cellar an' while away
The darkenin' hours in quiet play
Fur we wuz only kids, us two
And played like other youngsters do.
Orphans, we wuz without friend
His aid er helpin' hand to lend
Yes we wuz poor as poor could be
But we wuz happy—Tim and me
And the days went by like a song of joy
You know what it is to be a boy
I reckon you'll laugh when you hear me say
That we fell in love in a boyish way.

Undated manuscript, Paul Laurence Dunbar Collection, Reel III, Box 10, OHS.

The Making Up

Little Miss Margaret sits in a pout,
She and her Dolly have just fallen out.

Dolly is gazing with sorest stare,
Fitted dejectedly back in her chair.

Angry at Margaret, tearful and grieved,
Sore at the spanking so lately received.

Pursed are the maiden's lips close as can be,
They are not speaking, Miss Dolly and she.

Five minutes passes in silence and then,
Margaret's ready for playing again.

Dolly unbendingly sits in her place,
Never a change coming over her face.

Up mad goes, Margaret dropping her pout,
Clasping her playmate she whispers in doubt.

Let's don't play and cry, it's too much like true,
Let's make up Dolly I ain't mad is you?

Undated manuscript, Paul Laurence Dunbar Collection, Reel III, Box 10, OHS.

Our Hopes and Home

Oh the day has come at last, when oppression's fiery blast,
    Has been quenched in Freedom's waters, calm and cool,
And our children no more wild, rake or hoe on lawn or field,
    But are learning Wisdom's way within the school.

   Chorus:

Tramp, tramp, tramp, the Negro's marching,
    Onward, onward, to the goal,
So then foemen, clear the track, for you cannot keep him back,
    He has got the fire of freedom in his soul.

You may argue all you please, of our going o'er the seas,
    But you cannot turn our loyal steps away,
For this country is our home, and from it we will not roam,
    You have brought us over, and we'll stay.

Oh America the free, since our lot is cast with thee,
    We will never see thy glorious flag in shame,
Not a blot shall e'er appear, on the folds to us so dear,
    For thy dark sons shall protect thy honored name.

Undated manuscript, Paul Laurence Dunbar Collection, Reel III, Box 10, OHS.

The Drowsy God

The Drowsy God is wroth with me tonight
And hides himself disdainfully aloof
His stubborn will is tried and tested proof
Gainst all my pleas, he tickles at my nose
Then floats away and mocks my doleful plight
And with him beams the blessing of repose.

So must I lie while Night moves on apace
And beckons to the stars to follow him
My mind and all the world is strong and . . .
I toss about and beat my burning brow
Afraid to look my own soul in the face
To probe the past, the future or the now.

I bear the burden of the Universe
All self imposed upon my heavy soul
No mortal helps the prom'sing slime to mould
My fate belongs to none, but all are mine
No mortal helps me bear the crushing curse
I bear alone the secret and the sign.

And all the creatures of the world to me
Are not; they live in mind but are not men
I, I alone must live and die and — then?

And all the worlds' distressing I own it all
A monarch of majestic misery
With none to bail me for my cup of gold.

Eternal dissolution,—that avails
Ah yes, if it were true, 'twere more than joy
But spirit alone, that I can't destroy
Will live forever and maintain the thought
Thro' all the ages where I chase the fates
Eternal dissolution meaneth naught.

So thought drags on and all in vain
I try to drown it in forced respose
But hark, what sound, a cock awaking crows
The light comes up the sounds of labor start.
I am one among the millions once again
And what I hear, hears every other heart.

Undated manuscript, Paul Laurence Dunbar Collection, Reel III, Box 10, OHS.

Incantation/Invocation

Lightly, lightly, spew-some spell,
Veil, O veil, vile evil smell
Devil, evil, vile, and ill
So naught is wrought, all still is nil!

Hail! All hail! Allah
Hail! All hail! Jaweh
    Hail! Allah! Jaweh!
     Hallelujah
      Hail!

Undated manuscript, Paul Laurence Dunbar Collection, Reel III, Box 10, OHS.

A Letter

Deah Mammy I's a-writin'
      Dis hyeah lettah full o' glee,
An' I guess you'll be a-wondrin'
      What on earf's a-ticklin' me.
But you needn't try to guess it,
      An' you needn't spread yo' eyes,
Fu' I sholy gwine to hit you
      Wid a moughty big su'prise.

W'en I lef' de souf, you tol' me
      Dey was lots o' tings I knowed
Dat was common, but I wouldn't
      Fin' erlong de no'thun road,
An' you said de day was comin'
      W'en my heaht 'u'd to long
Fu' my cheer erside de table
      An' de hangin' kittle's song.

Well, hit's all come true, an' mammy,
      Dey was lots o' times, I know
W'en I'd give de whole creation
      Fu' to hit yo' cabin do',
An' to see de smoke a-risin'
      An' to smell dat bacon smell;
An' hit made me kin' o' homesick,
      But dat's ovah now, fu'—well—
I was feelin' kin' o' lonesome
      W'en I went to wo'k today,
T'inkin' 'bout de ol' plantation
      An' de good ol'fashioned way
Dat we ust to hunt de possum
      W'en de snow had kep' his trace,

An' I seemed to see de vision
       Of de woods behind de place.

An' my mouf des sot fu' possum,
       But I say, "Now what's de use?
Ain't I no'f? Dey ain't no possums
       In dis lan' a-runnin' loose."
Den I mos' night drap wid trimblin'
       At a somep'n' dat I see,
'Twere a possum, froze an' hangin'
       In a winder des by me!

Well, I buyed de critter, mammy,
       Dough de buyin' seemed a sin,
An' I had 'em scrape de gent'man,
       An' I's called my neighbohs in.
You was right erbout me wantin'
       Some t'ings dat de cabin had;
Bit hit's des one houah 'fo' dinnah,
       An' de no'f, hit ain't so bad!

Undated manuscript, Paul Laurence Dunbar Collection, Reel III, Box 10, OHS.

A Lament

Oh why am I dead when the sun is aloft
And the day is aflush like a freshly blown rose
When the haze o'er the meadows is fragrant and soft
And the pulse of the brook crows low of repose
Oh the sun cannot warm me the breeze cannot cheer
I am dead to the breath and blooms of the day
I meet the sun's smile with the shine of a tear
For my love is away, my love is away.

He went o'er the mountains at the break of dawn
With a smile on his lips and a cheery goodbye
And I long stroved to listen, the wind of his horn
While the voice of my heart was swung in reply
But the days have worn on and the seasons have changed
And the looks that were [green] are sprinkled with gray
Since the morning when over the mountain he strayed
And wandered away and wandered away.

The sound of the water falls soft on my ear
And the glint of the stream meets the glance of my eye
The song of the violin soars gleeful and clear
And a joy-drunken blue-bird goes rollicking by
But I wander distraught in the woodland alone
Mid the beauty and sparkle and spirit in gray
And the grief in my heart welleth out in a moan
For my love is away, my love is away.

Undated manuscript, Paul Laurence Dunbar Collection, Reel III, Box 10, OHS.

To Miss Mamie Emerson[1]

Your spoken words are roses fine and sweet
The songs you sing are perfect pearls of sound
How lavish nature is about your feet
To scatter flowers and jewels both around
Oh speak to me my love, I crave a rose
Sing me a song, for I would pearls were mine
Blushing, the stream of petaled beauty flows
Softly, the white strings trickle down and shine.

Undated manuscript, Paul Laurence Dunbar Collection, Reel III, Box 10, OHS.

[1] Miss Mamie Emerson remains unidentifiable.

A Brown Hair

A brown hair here, on my coat sleeve,
      Say what may the mystery mean?
And why comes a mist of surging tears,
      Me and my page between?
Brown hair has many a woman,
      And strange must seem the sight,
That I should tremble and flush and weep
      At anything so slight.
In sooth, this strand so silken
      Is only the secret's door;
I look at it, and my loving eyes
      Look further, and see more.

I see a form like a fairy's,
      As lithe and graceful and light;
And I see the sheen of a dear, brown head
      That lay on my arm last night.
I hear a voice like the cooing
      Of some soft-throated dove.
And my heart is held by a joy that weeps
      At the dream of the wife I love.
A brown hair here on my coat sleeve,
      Where the little head has lain,
And it holds my heart with a greater strength
      Than bides in an iron chain.

Undated manuscript, The Papers of Carter G. Woodson, Reel 6, Box 10, Library of Congress.

Lullaby (II)

A little brook runs where the shadows creep,
    And the whispering rushes grow,
And over the brook is the Land of Sleep,
    Where the tired children go,
And down to the water the white sheep come,
    And they nibble the tender clover,
And the children must wait in the shadows dim,
    Till all of the sheep go over.
        So it's one, two, three, and it's one, two, three,
        Counting the snow-white sheep.
        And fly away, little one, fly away, pretty one,
        Fly away to the Land of Sleep.
The little brook laughs in the moonlight fair,
    With the dancing shadows playing,
And over the bank where the daisies grow
    The wayward lambs are straying.
And the children wait while the night-birds call
    From their nest in the hazel-cover,
And they count the sheep—for they must not sleep
    Till the last little lamb goes over.
The little brook hushes its rippling song
    To a tender lullaby,
And the shadows grow heavy, and deep, and long,
    And the clouds are white in the sky.
But the children have gone to the Land of Sleep,
    And sweet is the breath of the clover.
And the world lies dreaming beneath the stars,
    For the sheep have all gone over.

Undated manuscript, The Papers of Carter G. Woodson, Reel 6, Box 9, Library of Congress.

I Been Kissin' Yo' Picture

A lady an' huh lovah had a quarrel,
    De gal got in a huff.
An' she played huh pa't almighty independent,
    But de dark, he raised huh bluff.
So he packed his little grip an' went to Georgy,
    But de lady laffed an' said
"Yain't no use to try no foolin' Mistah Dahky,
    Fu' you same ez you was dead."
But huh days commence a-gittin' lonesome,
    An' she couldn't rest at night;
So she took some lettah papah an' a pencil,
    An' set huhse'f to write:

   Chorus:

I bin kissin' yo' picture, honey,
I bin thinkin' o' you.
Ef you'll come, I'll send you de money,
Come back, da'lin', do.
Yes I knows dat I's been scan'lous
But I'll ever be true,
But don't you know it might-a been wusser,
Come back da'lin', do.

The darky down in Georgy got the lettah
    At a mos' onhappy time,
He had spo'ted till his pocket-book was empty,
    An' he didn't have a dime.
His heart, it jumped with pleasure at the message,
    An' he laffed in happy glee;
"I'm a hot one, I'm a lulu, I'm baby,
    An' she's jes' dead stuck on me.
Tho' she'll nevah know I was a starvin'

I'll jest let huh do kin' o' light."
So he begged the regular equipments,
    An' set hisse'f to write:

Chorus:

I been kissin' yo' picture, honey,
I been thinkin' o' you.
Yes, I'll come home, ef you'll send de money,
I'll come back to you.
Yes, I know dat I's been scan'lous,
But I'll evah be true,
But don't you know it might-a been wusser,
I'll come back to you.

Undated manuscript, Paul Laurence Dunbar Collection, Reel IV, Box 13, OHS.

Bibliography

Selected Books by Paul Laurence Dunbar

Poetry:

1893. *Oak and Ivy*. Dayton: United Brethren Publishing House.
1895. *Majors and Minors*. Toledo: Hadley and Hadley.
1896. *Lyrics of Lowly Life*. New York: Dodd, Mead and Co.
1899. *Lyrics of the Hearthside*. New York: Dodd, Mead and Co.
1899. *Poems of Cabin and Field*. New York: Dodd, Mead and Co.
1901. *Candle Lightin' Time*. New York: Dodd, Mead and Co.
1903. *Lyrics of Love and Laughter*. New York: Dodd, Mead and Co.
1903. *When Malindy Sings*. New York: Dodd, Mead and Co.
1904. *Li'l' Gal*. New York: Dodd, Mead and Co.
1904. *Lyrics of Sunshine and Shadow*. New York: Dodd, Mead and Co.
1905. *Howdy, Honey, Howdy*. Toronto: The Musson Book Company.
1906. *Joggin' Erlong*. New York: Dodd, Mead and Co.
1913. *The Complete Poems*. New York: Dodd, Mead and Co.

Lyrics and Texts for Musicals and Operas:

1897. *African Romances*. Music: Samuel Coleridge Taylor. London: Auginer and Co.
1898. *Clorindy, or the Origin of the Cakewalk*. Music: Will Marion Cook. New York: Witmark Music Publishers.
1898. *Dream Lovers*. Music: Samuel Coleridge Taylor. London and New York: Boosey and Co.
1902. *In Dahomey*. Music: Will Marion Cook. Witmark Music Publishers.

Short Stories:

1898. *Folks from Dixie*. New York: Dodd, Mead and Co.

1900. *The Strength of Gideon and Other Stories*. New York: Dodd, Mead and Co.
1903. *In Old Plantation Days*. New York: Dodd, Mead and Co.
1904. *The Heart of Happy Hollow*. New York: Dodd, Mead and Co.

Novels:

1898. *The Uncalled*. New York: Dodd, Mead and Co.
1900. *The Love of Landry*. New York: Dodd, Mead and Co.
1901. *The Fanatics*. New York: Dodd, Mead and Co.
1902. *The Sport of the Gods*. New York: Dodd, Mead and Co.

References Consulted

Adoff, Arnold ed. 1973. *The Poetry of Black America*. New York: Harper and Row.

Andrews, William L., Frances Smith Foster, and Trudier Harris, eds. 1997. *The Oxford Companion to African American Literature*. New York: Oxford Univ. Press.

Bender, Bert. 1975. The Lyrical Short Fiction of Dunbar and Chestnutt. In *A Singer in the Dawn*, ed. Jay Martin, pp. 208–222. New York: Dodd, Mead.

Blount, Marcellus. Caged Birds: Race and Gender in The Sonnet. In *Engendering Men: The Question of Male Feminist Criticism*, ed. Joseph A. Boone and Michael Cadden, pp. 225–38. New York and London: Routledge, 1990.

Brawley, Benjamin. 1936. *Paul Laurence Dunbar, Poet of His People*. Chapel Hill: Univ. of North Carolina Press.

Braxton, Joanne, ed. 1993. *The Collected Poetry of Paul Laurence Dunbar*. Charlottesville: The Univ. Press of Virginia.

Conover, Charlotte Reeve. 1907. *Some Dayton Saints and Prophets*. Dayton: United Brethren Publishing House.

Cunningham, Virginia. 1947. *Paul Laurence Dunbar and His Song*. New York: Dodd, Mead and Co.

DuBois, W. E. B. 1903. *The Souls of Black Folk: Essays and Sketches*. Chicago: A.C. McClurg and Co.

Engle, Gary D. 1978. *This Grotesque Essence: Plays From the American Minstrel Stage*. Baton Rouge: Louisiana State Univ. Press.

Fiske, John. 1989a. *Reading the Popular*. London and New York: Routledge.

———. 1989b. *Understanding Popular Culture*. Boston: Unwin Hyman.

Gaines, Andrea M. 1997. The Poem Maker. *The Dayton Voice*, July 28.

Gates, Henry Louis Jr. 1988. *The Signifying Monkey: A Theory of Afro-American Literary Criticism*. New York: Oxford Univ. Press.

————. 1989. Canon-Formation, Literary History, and the Afro-American Tradition: From the Seen to the Told. In *Afro-American Literary Study in the 1990s*, ed. Houston A. Baker, Jr. and Patricia Redmond, pp. 14–50. Chicago: Univ. of Chicago Press.

Gayle, Addison Jr. 1971. *Oak and Ivy: A Biography of Paul Laurence Dunbar*. Garden City, N.J.: Anchor.

Gentry, Tony. 1989. *Paul Laurence Dunbar*. New York: Chelsea House Publishers.

Gould, Jean. 1958. *That Dunbar Boy*. New York: Dodd, Mead and Co.

Hayden, Robert. 1978. Paul Laurence Dunbar. In *American Journal*. Taunton, Mass.: Effendi Press.

Hayden, Robert, David J. Burrows, and Frederick Lapides, eds. 1971. *Afro-American Literature: An Introduction*. New York: Harcourt Brace Jovanovich.

Howells, William Dean. 1896a. Introduction to *Lyrics of Lowly Life* by Paul Laurence Dunbar. New York: Dodd, Mead and Co.

————. 1896b. Review of *Majors and Minors* by Paul Laurence Dunbar. *Harper's Weekly* (June 27): 630.

Hughes, Langston. 1926. The Negro Artist and the Racial Mountain. *The Nation* 122 (June 28): 692–94.

————. 1954. Paul Laurence Dunbar, the Robert Burns of Negro Poetry. In *Famous American Negroes*, pp. 85–91. New York: Dodd, Mead and Co.

Inge, M. Thomas, Maurice Duke, and Jackson R. Bryer, eds. 1978. *Black American Writers: Bibliographical Essays*. Vol. 1. New York: St. Martin's.

Johnson, James Weldon. 1922. *The Book of American Negro Poetry*. New York: Harcourt, Brace (rev. ed. 1931).

————. 1928. The Dilemma of the Negro Author. *American Mercury* 15: 477.

————. 1933. *Along This Way*. New York: Viking Press.

Kindilien, Carlin T. 1956. *American Poetry in the Eighteen Nineties*. Providence: Brown Univ. Press.

Kinnamon, Keneth. 1994. Three Black Writers and the Anthologized Canon. In *American Realism and the Canon*, ed. Tom Quirk and Gary Scharnhorst, 143–153. Newark: Univ. of Delaware Press.

Lawson, Victor. 1941. *Dunbar Critically Examined*. Washington: The Associated Press.

Lorde, Audre. 1984. *Sister Outsider*. Tremansburg, N.Y.: Crossing Press.

Martin, Herbert Woodward. 1979. *Paul Laurence Dunbar: A Singer of Songs*. Columbus: The State Library of Ohio.

————. 1992. *Paul Laurence Dunbar: The Eyes of the Poet*. Videorecording. Produced by Herbert Woodward Martin. Directed by Thomas Skill. Written and performed by Herbert Woodward Martin. Available from the Department of English, University of Dayton.

―――. 1995. Program notes for the opera *Paul Laurence Dunbar: Common Ground* by Adolphus Hailstork. Produced by Dayton Opera Co. at the Victoria Theatre, Dayton, Ohio (February 19). .

Martin, Jay, ed. 1975. *A Singer in the Dawn: Reinterpretations of Paul Laurence Dunbar*. New York: Dodd, Mead.

Martin, Jay, and Gossie H. Hudson, eds. 1975. *The Paul Laurence Dunbar Reader: A Selection of the Best of Paul Laurence Dunbar's Poetry and Prose, Including Writings Never Before Available in Book Form*. New York: Dodd, Mead.

Metcalf, E. W. 1975. *Paul Laurence Dunbar: A Bibliography*. Metuchen, N.J.: Scarecrow Press.

Morris, Terry. 1993. UD Professor finds Dunbar Original. *Dayton Daily News* (August 18): IA.

Nettles, Elsa. 1987. *Language, Race, and Social Class in Howells's America*. Lexington: Univ. Press of Kentucky.

Pawley, Thomas D. 1975. Dunbar as Playwright. *Black World* 24 (April): 71–79.

Ramsey, William M. 1999. Dunbar's Dixie. *The Southern Literary Journal* 32 (Fall): 30–45.

Randall, Dudley. 1971. *The Black Poets*. New York: Bantam.

Redding, J. Saunders, and Arthur P. Davis, eds. 1971. *Cavalcade: Negro American Writers from 1760 to the Present*. Boston: Houghton Mifflin.

Revell, Peter. 1979. *Paul Laurence Dunbar*. Boston: Twaye Publishers.

Ring, Cassie, and John Fleischman. 1992. Star Professors. *Ohio Magazine*, April.

Rodgers, Lawrence R. 1992. Paul Laurence Dunbar's *The Sport of the Gods:* The Doubly Conscious World of Plantation Fiction, Migration, and Ascent. *American Literary Realism* 24 (Spring): 42–57.

Schultz, Pearle H. 1974. *Paul Laurence Dunbar: Black Poet Laureate*. Champaign, Ill.: Garrad Publishing Company.

Turner, Darwin T. 1967. Paul Laurence Dunbar: The Rejected Symbol. *Journal of Negro History* 52 (January): 1–13.

―――. 1975. Paul Laurence Dunbar: The Poet and the Myths. In *A Singer in the Dawn*, ed. Jay Martin, pp. 59–74. New York: Dodd, Mead.

UD Sponsors Dunbar Memorial. 1972. *Wright State Univ. Guardian*, October 30.

University Marks Dunbar Centennial. 1972. *Univ. of Dayton Alumnus*, December.

Unpublished Dunbar Play Discovered. 1993. *Columbus Dispatch*, August 27.

Wagner, Jean. 1973. *Black Poets of the United States: from Dunbar To Langston Hughes*. Urbana: Univ. of Illinois Press.

Wakefield, John. 1977. Paul Laurence Dunbar: The Scapegoat (1904). In *The Black American Short Story in the Twentieth Century*, ed. Peter Bruck, pp. 39–50. Amsterdam: Grüner.

Wiant, Lucia May. 1917. *For Memory's Garden*. Dayton, Ohio: Christian Publishing Association.

Wiggins, Lida Keck. 1907. *The Life and Works of Paul Laurence Dunbar*. Naperville, Ill.: J. L. Nichols and Company.

Williams, Kenny J. 1975. The Masking of the Novelist. In *A Singer in the Dawn*, ed. Jay Martin, pp. 152–207. New York: Dodd, Mead.

Index of Titles

Index to the First Lines of Poems